FIFTY SHADES OF TARMAC

FIFTY SHADES OF TARMAC

Adventures with a Mack R600 in 1970s Europe

A Novel by

Andy MacLean

First published 2015

Published by
5M Publishing Ltd,
Benchmark House,
8 Smithy Wood Drive,
Sheffield, S35 1QN, UK
Tel: +44 (0) 1234 81 81 80
www.5mpublishing.com

A Catalogue record for this book is available from the British Library

ISBN 978-1-910456-03-3

Book layout by
Servis Filmsetting Ltd, Stockport, Cheshire
Printed by Berforts
Photos by Andy MacLean

Contents

Dedication

To Janet, my long-suffering other half, without whom I would not be here to tell these tales.

Acknowledgements

For help with clarification of certain events in the story: ICC drivers Steve Trybowski, Mike Phillips and George Fardell.

1

On the Road Again

IT was 1972. It was summer – and the living was easy! I was earning reasonably good money, had a share in a flat on the Cromwell Road, was not tied down and had no responsibilities. An enviable position you might think, but for many months I'd been seriously looking for a continental driving job. At that time foreign lorries were eyed more with curiosity than envy. However, my ambition was to drive the biggest, the best and the furthest! Even then that meant the Middle East and I saw a European driving position as the springboard to that end.

In those days I was driving a car transporter for Capel Drivers, a Dodge K1010 equipped with an unusually reliable Cummins V8 engine and an Eaton 2 speed rear axle. Cars were a light load for such a powerful unit and I was up and down the length and breadth of the country every week as regular and fast as the proverbial dose of salts!

But the continent was still the plum in the pudding as far as I was concerned and I was determined to get over there. I contacted countless companies – Union Transport, SCA, Air Products, MAT, even several European ones: Atramef Ghent, Betz Reutlingen, Asian Transport Denmark and even some of the "dodgies" like U.K.–Europe Express and Freightlanes. However, I was always being asked the same question: "What experience do you have?" At that time I was young and honest and therefore was never offered employment except with one or two of the fly-by-nighters whose drivers were punching the hell out of cranked out Seddons, Bedford TKs and Guy Warriors, risking their lives every trip for £40 a week and all the rice they could eat! I was certainly not prepared to make that sacrifice just for a trip over the water.

Then one day I bumped into Wally. It was in the Old Gate cafe on the A2 between Canterbury and the start of the M2. I was sitting there aching from head to back to sides to toes after a night in Dover's Wellington Dock spent stretched out across the seats of the Dodge. Devouring my bacon, egg, tomatoes and fried slice, I was worrying about what was going to happen to Garth now that Lumiere had been imprisoned by the Androids (I hadn't read that day's copy of the *Mirror* yet) when "Mind if I sit here?" a hearty voice thundered in my ear.

"No, please do," I mumbled through my early morning fug and Wally sat down opposite me. I immediately recognised him as the guy who'd just swept into the parking lot with a Scania 110 sleeper cab and 12 metres of aluminium Crane Fruehauf boxvan. Would he deign to engage me, a mere Dodge driver, in conversation? What would I have to say which would interest him, this god who had descended from on high (well the Scani was high compared to other trucks at the time) and sat at my table? I could start with "What sort of engine have you got in there?" No, I couldn't stoop to that. "Just come from the continent have you?" Even more stupid. "They tell me Scani and Volvo drivers are a load of poofters, is that true?" Definitely not. I couldn't decide, so in the end I plumped for the imaginative, "That your Scani ton ten out there?"

"Yes, it is," came the reply. "That your Dodge with the Toyotas?" I had the company's name tattooed across my overalls so I couldn't lie.

"'Fraid so," I confirmed.

"Nice powerful motor for your job," he said. "I used to drive one on Readymix but that was only a six wheel rigid with a straight six Perkins." Wow, I had a conversation going. "Never actually driven one of those," he gestured towards my rig, "but they're always passing me on the M1 so they can't be bad tools."

"It's pretty nippy," I agreed, "but I'd sooner have your Scani with its sleeper cab."

"Not much good for your kind of work though," he said between mouthfuls of the Gate's stewed tea. "Never get it under your trailer!"

"I'm not talking about my job, I'd like to drive on the continent," I interrupted.

"Just the same as me a year ago," he laughed. "What's your name by the way?"

"Arthur," I replied.

"Mine's Wally, pleased to meet you," he smiled, extending his hand.

"Hm, very continental," I thought. But what a nice guy and here I was feeling very honoured to be conversing with a man of such obvious knowledge of international trucking.

"Trouble is," I ventured, "I've tried every firm I know but they're only interested if I already have experience or they want me to drive some old death-trap to Italy without permits which I'm not willing to do."

"You're quite right I'm afraid, mate," said Wally, "good continental jobs is hard to come by. What you'll have to do is employ a little cunning." He paused to take a bite out of his cheese and tomato

3

sandwich. I looked out of the misted windows to see two of Husk of Dover's Guy Big J's with flatbed trailers loaded with what looked like crates of fruit and one of George Hammond's Atkinson Borderers negotiating their way out of the parking and onto the A2 heading north.

"What do you mean?" I asked. Wally looked straight at me, his brown eyes twinkling mischievously.

"Have you ever been abroad?" he continued.

"Well, I did have a two week holiday in Austria when I was at school," I answered.

"Great, so you know the route," Wally pointed out.

"I flew," I confessed.

"Don't worry. As long as you can say that you've been to Austria and add a bit of authenticity, study the maps, the route you'd take for instance – Zeebrugge, Brussels, Aachen (nasty customs post that), Cologne, Frankfurt, Munich (say Munchen, sounds more impressive), Salzburg." He stopped to finish the rest of his breakfast.

I looked around the large prefabricated build-ing which housed the cafe. On my left was the long white self-service counter and behind it the grill cur-rently sizzling away with preparations for the countless fry-ups they were about to serve to the trucking frater-nity. At my end was a fishing tackle counter catering for anglers on their way to the coast. At the other end was a Wurlitzer jukebox, quiet now thank goodness. Behind that, through the misted windows, I could see my red Dodge parked next to Wally's Scania, both illuminated by the eerie green fluorescent floodlights which were the Gate's night-time trademark. It was that moment just before dawn when the birds all start to sing and you know that the business of the day is about to start. I was becoming determined more than ever to get that continental job.

Wally was human and ordinary, two facts which surprised me. About my height at five foot eight or thereabouts, crewcut, and clean shaven wearing a black donkey jacket over a blue checked shirt and black jeans, he must have been about 35 years old whereas I was still only 27, but he did seem to think that I could make the grade otherwise why was he giving me these tips?

His meal over, he pulled a packet of Gauloises out of his top pocket and, after offering me one, which I declined, he lit up and spoke again.

"One thing though, they're bound to ask you some questions – customs formalities, names of borders, that kind of thing – oh, maybe customs agents as well. Your best bet would be to tell them that you've only travelled on T.I.R. carnets, then you'd only need an agent at your point of offloading. Don't forget that you need road permits and you have to pay road tax in Germany based on so much per tonne load per kilometre; normally around 40 Deutschmarks when you're transiting through to Austria. If they want the name of your agent in Austria tell them Franz Welz, they're a big enough outfit."

"What about the company I'm supposed to have worked for?" I asked.

"Oh, just tell them it was a cowboy firm you've left because you didn't like their way of working. Companies rarely check on references anyway," he said rising from his seat. "I've got to get up the road now," he continued. "Tipping at Stratford L.I.F.T. today I hope. Good luck, Arthur. Maybe I'll see you over the other side before long!"

"Thanks a lot for the info, Wally," I said, "I really hope I will." Heads turned in admiration as Wally manoeuvred his ton ten out of the parking following a G.L. Baker Guy with a Marks and Spencer fridge trailer out onto the A2.

For some time after that I was still unable to find a continental job. They all reckoned either that they had no jobs available or that they had a large waiting list for drivers' positions. I was beginning to despair when one day, quite by accident, I picked up a copy of the *Evening Standard* left on a table in the driver's restaurant at Newport-Pagnell services. More out of boredom than the hope of finding employment, I started scanning the sits vac. As usual under Drivers Wanted there was not much there. Most of the ads which caught my eye continued "own cars". There were one or two from the agencies and a couple for rigid drivers for London Deliveries – Top Rates Paid but nothing for me. I finished my mug of coffee and picked up the paper again and there in the display ads section, neatly blocked in, was *Drivers required – Continental work – Must be experienced – Phone* ... So I did, that very minute, from the kiosk outside the restaurant.

"Pars Container Services," came the reply when the ringing finally ceased.

"Oh?" I said, rather taken aback. This was a Middle East job? I wasn't really ready to make that quantum leap! "Er, I'm calling about your ad in the Standard. Do you still need drivers?"

"Would you hold for a second please?" said the secretary.

Then a man's voice, "Good afternoon" – definitely a foreigner. "Do you have continental experience?" he continued.

"Yes," I replied, "I've been driving in Europe but I'm not happy with my present company."

"Very good. Why don't you come and discuss the matter with me. My name is Achemian and our address is 3 Wolf Street, London W1, just behind Oxford Street, close to the Marks and Spencers shop. When will you be coming?" he finished.

"I have a day off tomorrow," I said trying not to sound too anxious. "I think I should be able to make it up there by 10 o'clock."

"That will be fine," Mr Achemian replied, "Ten o'clock then. Your name please?"

"Jackson, Arthur Jackson," I said pressing another two shilling piece into the phone box as the pips started to sound.

"Goodbye, Mr Jackson. We will see you tomorrow," he finished.

"Goodbye," I said and replaced the black receiver on its rack hoping, fruitlessly as it turned out, to reclaim my two shilling piece.

I have to admit that I was somewhat stunned. This was the closest I'd yet come to that coveted continental job and the guy at the other end of the line had sounded like a real gentleman. That meant, with luck, that he'd know very little about road transport operations. I flew down the remainder of the M1, skirted the West End and went out further west via the Cromwell Road to the truck park at Olympia. As it is my wont to celebrate before final achievement, I did, in style – in the Kings Head, Earls Court that night with James and Auberon my two Aussie flatmates, mere temporary drivers they, working for the Industrial Overload agency mainly on London delivery work which involved lots of stop-starting and humping and bumping.

Next morning, definitely the worse for wear, I slept until 9:05. "Oh, my God!" I panicked, jumping out of bed. "I've got to be at Pars for 10 o'clock!" With a nagging, dull ache in my brain and a nasty, queasy feeling in my stomach, I dressed, caught the District line from Earls Court to Notting Hill Gate and then the Central line, arriving at Marble Arch by about 9:55. It was only as I climbed the stairs to the offices Pars Container Services – Import Export – 3rd Floor, that I realised with a depressingly sinking feeling that I hadn't done my homework. I had meant to do it the previous evening but my agency Aussie flatmates had put paid to that plan. In the pub I had promised myself to wake up early and study the maps and memorise some place names but I'd seriously overslept. Hell! I'd never get through this interview.

2

Wolf Street

CLIMBING the narrow stairs at Number 3, Wolf Street, I couldn't help noticing a number of young women descending and another behind me on the way up. Luckily I kept my thoughts to myself because as I reached the second floor, there was a door marked "Robin Nursing Bureau"! The stairs were somewhat dingy and I was wondering what kind of company this could be as I laboured up the final flight to the third floor. At the head of the stairs there was a glass door with the Pars International Containers logo emblazoned across it, seemingly the outline of a map of Iran containing the Iranian flag next to the company name. Opening the door, I entered the office smack on 10 o'clock, congratulating myself on that achievement at least.

"Can I help you?" the receptionist asked helpfully, her smile lost on me as I was desperately trying to recall customs borders, routes, taxes and agents through a blurry haze separating my brain from my thoughts.

"I have an appointment with Mr Achemian," I ventured.

"Ah, you'll be Mr Jackson," she replied. I nodded, noting for the first time a trim figure and a not unattractive face behind horn-rimmed spectacles worn slightly low so that her grey-green eyes were rather fetchingly peering at me over the top of them. "Please sit down," she gestured to a generously upholstered executive type swivel chair in front of a window so begrimed that its only purpose in life was to let an absolute minimum of light in. There certainly was no view out of it. The receptionist's pert behind disappeared through the door to an adjoining room and I had to remind myself to concentrate on the routes to Austria and not the insanely vague chance of asking her out for a lunchtime drink. Unfortunately, the thought of the pending interview brought on a terrible feeling of a battalion of butterflies fighting each other in my empty, alcoholic stomach. The omens were indeed not good.

A couple of infinitely long minutes later she reappeared. She threw another winning smile in my direction. "Please go through to Mr Achemian's office," she said. I stumbled through the doorway into a spotless grey pile carpeted office. White walls were brilliantly lit by concealed neon lighting making me wince blearily. On my right, at the other end of the room behind a shiny mahogany desk and in front of a wall festooned with bookcases full of tomes of various sizes and thicknesses sat Mr Achemian. He was of slight build, with a thin sallow face topped with a shock of well-combed black hair.

"Good morning Mr Jackson," he said, "How nice to see you and right on time too. Please take a seat." I cautiously sat down on one of four chairs arranged in front of his desk on either side of a small coffee table which had a photo album sitting in the middle. I certainly did not want to miss the chair and fall over, making a complete fool of myself, which had been known to happen in the past. I made a mental note of his courtesy, his immaculate English (Savile Row?) suit, and his intelligent lively demeanour.

"Now let me see," he continued, shuffling through a small pile of filed paperwork. "You informed me yesterday on the telephone that you have some experience in Europe. To which countries have you been?" I decided to be semi-truthful.

"I'm afraid that I've only been as far as Austria," I answered.

"Which route do you normally take?" he asked. Oh no! Which route, which route? I racked my brain. Should I mention British European Airways? Er, no! I decided to lie.

"Umm, Belgium and Germany?" I ventured.

"Oh, that's a pity. We use Holland but I don't think it will make a great deal of difference," he smiled, "Now I want to ask you just a few questions to establish whether or not you will suit our requirements." Here it comes I thought – the grilling!

"First, have you ever driven a Mack?" he asked.

Drive one? I'd hardly even heard of one! I had to shift my brain into high range quickly or I was lost. "No," I replied, "but I have seen one or two around on the continent."

"Oh dear, that is a problem," he said. "You see, all of our vehicles are Macks and they have crash gearboxes controlled by two gear levers."

What luck! I'd heard about this arrangement on old wartime army Diamond Ts. "I have driven a gate crash Scammell," I replied. I had, about three hundred yards round a truck park. "And that had a main and auxiliary box setup."

That seemed to impress him. Come to think of it, it impressed me. I had seen the phrase in a Motor Transport issue some weeks before, referring to a cross country fire engine.

"Well," Mr Achemian continued, "we do give all of our new drivers a short training course on our vehicles in England before we send them over to Europoort. Now," he looked suddenly more serious,

11

"please could you tell me what is the important thing to remember when you arrive at the German frontier?"

Oh dear! I just could not think of the answer to this one.

To learn German?

To wait until the gate opens?

To cut my hair and shave before entering the country?

I nervously fingered the stubbly two days growth on my chin.

What the hell had Wally said? Then I had a sudden flash of inspiration.

"Tax!" I asserted triumphantly.

"Could you be more precise?" he pressed on.

"Oh yes, you have to pay road tax for each day in Germany," I gushed.

"That is correct," he agreed. "But I was really thinking of something more important concerning your fuel."

My high range brain jumped into action. "Fuel tax," I said, somewhat too smugly.

"Ah, good, you know about that then," he smiled.

Well, no, actually. All I'd done was put two and two together.

"Last week," he leaned towards me with an air of confidentiality, "two of our most experienced drivers were fined most heavily for not making their *tankshein* declarations."

I smiled knowingly. "Ah, the *tankshein* – a lot of drivers make that mistake," I said even more smugly. "Stop the smugness," I told myself, "or you'll lose it big time." I changed my look to one of concern empathising with the tribulations of management faced with the terminal stupidity of the driving race.

Mr Achemian narrowed his dark brown eyes and

looked straight into mine. "Which agent did your company employ at the Austrian border, Mr Jackson?" he demanded.

He might just as well have said, "Ah, Mr Jackson, we have been waiting for you. Please step into this fish tank full of harmless-looking piranhas."

A bombshell! Frankly I did not have the answer. Oh Wally, what did you say? I had to make a split second decision to lie like a pig with its snout in the trough.

"I'm afraid I don't know," I said. "We were delivering direct to the Ford plant in Vienna and they handled all the paperwork at that end."

Mr Achemian's face narrowed into a frown. Oh no – I'd blown it!

"That surprises me," he said at length. "It was my understanding that all drivers needed to use an agent at the Salzburg border. Our agent there is Franz Welz."

Oh damn, damn, damn! That was the name Wally gave me. However, I was up to my neck in it now so I had no option but to blunder still further.

"Not if you're running on a T.I.R. carnet," I asserted.

"Ah, yes. That would be so," he agreed, nodding wisely as though I had come up with a formula to cure an as yet incurable disease.

I almost audibly heaved a sigh of relief. I looked directly at Mr Achemian, my eyes aching, my head a dull heavy lump, my mouth tasting like a chicken run.

"Our vehicles all run on European T forms," he explained, "because at this moment we cannot use T.I.R. carnets through Turkey."

Leaping Leylands, I'd cracked it!

"Now, just one more question, Mr Jackson," he persevered, leafing again through some of his papers as if he were searching for the standard form of inter-rogation to thwart all drivers' ambitions.

Just what was he going to ask me? I couldn't take much more. I silently swore never again to go on a binge the night before an interview.

"Do you have a clean driving licence and have you been involved in any accidents during the past three years?"

3

Last Days on the Tranny

I looked Mr Achemian straight in the eye for the first time and answered, "I've got one endorsement for speeding two years ago but so far I've been lucky and steered clear of accidents." I handed my licences to him.

"Thank you," he said closely perusing my car driving licence and my Heavy Goods Vehicle licence. "Did you pass a test for this?" he asked, flourishing the black covered HGV licence.

"No, I was already driving trucks when these came into force so I was given one automatically," I said. There was a short pause while he noted my comments and copied down licence numbers.

He turned to me and smiled. "I think we would like you to join our company if you wish, subject to your application form being acceptable to our insurers. But before you make a decision I will explain our operation to you." I settled back in my chair, waves of relief wafting over me. I was so thrilled that he could have offered me a job driving sewage tankers and, so long as it was abroad, I would have accepted. "We are an Iranian company," he continued, "operating a large fleet of Mack R600 trucks carrying containers between Europe and Iran, though most of our eastbound cargo comes from England as we have the contract to carry the Hillman Hunter parts for assembly in Tehran."

"I'm afraid I don't have any Middle East experience," I interjected.

"That won't matter," he replied. "because our system is that our English drivers remain in Europe, based in Salzburg actually, while our Iranian drivers make the rest of the journey. Our depot transfers the containers from one truck to the other and it works very well. Your job would be to take the loaded containers from Salzburg. We bring westbound things like cotton and mohair, unload them all over Europe, reload them with export goods for Iran and return them to Salzburg. If you open that book," he pointed to the photograph album I had noticed on the coffee table by my side, "you will see some photographs of our vehicles."

I opened the album and inside on the first page was a blown up photograph of a dark blue Mack R600 tractor unit, the "plastic Mack" as all the drivers called them owing to their fibreglass bonnets. It certainly looked a glamorous motor with its oversize five spoke wheels, its massive bonnet, its exhaust stack extending above the rear of the cab and its huge air cleaner sticking out from the engine housing immediately in front of the passenger door. The next page showed a picture of about fifty of them lined up alongside each other with their trailers and containers. My mind boggled!

"We brought the first batch over from America to Southampton on pallets without the wheels and we built them up on the dockside," Mr Achemian explained. "Then they collected their trailers from Crane Fruehauf in Dereham, Norfolk and their containers from Central Containers in Walsall. All of them travelled in convoy. It was quite a sight. One of our drivers who is now our road foreman – you will meet him in Europoort – led the way with the rest of the trucks all driven by Iranian drivers we had flown in from Tehran. They loaded at the Hillman plant in Coventry and then off they went. That was two years ago," he sighed. "Since that time we have gradually added to the fleet and we now have 125 of these units operating from Tehran. Now we have bought 30 new units, slightly more modern than those ones, to base in Salzburg and we want to put mainly European drivers in them as they seem to find their way around Europe a lot more easily than our Iranians. Also we bought more trailers but this time from Pitt as they were a better price and they are all waiting in Europoort with our road foreman. Normally, we don't bring the Macks to England anymore because they contravene the weight limit, but we do have one over here at the moment shuttling containers from Coventry to Felixstowe while we wait for delivery of two Guy Big J tractor units. Do you have any questions you would like to ask me?"

I was still somewhat dumbfounded. Would I be able to drive one of these brutes? Even worse, I'd never driven a left hand drive tractor (hooker) before. "You said that you gave new drivers some training. Is that in England or in Holland?" I asked.

"Well since we have one Mack in England with our shunter driver, Mr Ray Fagan, you could make a trip with him and try your hand and if all goes well he could drop you off in Felixstowe to catch the ferry to Holland. How would that be?" He looked at me enquiringly. I hesitated and must have looked a little startled. "Don't worry too much," Mr Achemian laughed, "you will still get full training from Mr Ron Daly, our foreman in Europoort. He's been with us from the start and what he doesn't know about our trucks is not worth knowing. He will go out with you in your truck to make sure you know how to drive it." He became suddenly more serious. "Of course if

17

you cannot master it I'm afraid that we shall not be able to employ you but we will pay your fare back to England. But," he continued, "Mr Daly is very fair. He's a first class driver as well as a mechanic, an extraordinary man – very calm – never worries too much. I think that you will get on well with him," he finished, chuckling to himself at some recollection of Ron's calmness in adversity, no doubt. Oh dear, a boss with a sense of humour! I looked back at the photograph album.

"One thing," I said. "I notice that these trucks don't have sleeper cabs."

"That is correct," Mr Achemian replied. "We do have forward control Mack F700s on order for next year. These will have sleeper cabs but, in the meantime, I'm afraid that you will have to put up with the R600s. However we do pay your expenses to stay in guesthouses overnight if you wish. Now when would you be able to start with us?"

Immediately? No, better not sound too keen. "I have to work a week's notice for my present company," I said, "so I'll be free at the end of next week if that's OK?"

"Oh, that's very good." He smiled again. "I am always pleased when a driver shows a sense of responsibility to his employer. Please complete the forms which my secretary will hand to you, then give me a call in the morning and I hope to be able to confirm your employment with us."

I stood up, still a little dazed, but feeling a lot better than when I'd arrived. Mr Achemian extended his hand and shook mine saying, "Goodbye, Mr Jackson, we do hope to be seeing you next week." In the outer office the secretary handed me a form which I completed. Name, address, telephone number, previous employers. Next to "P & W European Transit

Company" I wrote "Bankrupt" just to make sure they wouldn't check! Then, with what I hoped would be seen as an inviting smile to the secretary, I was out on the street again. I looked at my watch. It showed 10:45. Such a short time had elapsed since I had entered that office and I was already feeling elevated to the hallowed ranks of continental driver.

The following twenty four hours dragged by. Next day I drove my Dodge with its Carmichael car transporter trailer from Olympia down to Dover ready to load. I noticed as I entered the Portakabin that passed for an office in the corner of the Wellington Dock that I'd been rostered for the Aberdeen, Inverness and reload Hillman Imps at Bathgate run, a good five-day tramp.

"Can I use the phone, Dave?" I asked the despatch manager dead casually as 10:30 came around on the office clock.

"Local call is it, mate?" he asked, grumpily looking at me through half-rimmed spectacles perched halfway down his burgundy nose, too many drinks each lunchtime in the 'Albion' over the road, I thought.

"Yeah, just a London number if that's OK," I replied.

"Alright, but don't make a meal of it. I want you up in Aberdeen for the morning." I smiled. Up till now I hadn't realised that Dave had a humorous side. Anyway, with luck I was just about to tell him what to do with his slave-driven job.

I dialled the number with shaking fingers and an empty pit in my stomach. The call connected.

"Pars Container Company," came the secretary's honeyed tones.

"Er, Arthur Jackson here," I spoke softly and slowly desperately trying not to sound nervous.

"Oh yes, Mr Jackson" she replied sweetly, "you were here yesterday, I think. I'll put you through to Mr Achemian."

I waited several long seconds, scanning the nicotine stained walls of the Capel Drivers office and looked down at Dave's careworn face as he fumbled through a pile of logsheets. I was almost feeling sorry for him when Mr Achemian came onto the line.

"Good morning, Mr Jackson," he said. "Thank you for calling so promptly. I have examined your application and after our interview yesterday I checked with our insurers and all appears to be in order." There was a pause. Dave looked up, his eyebrows arched, possibly he smelt a rat. "If you would like to join our company, we would be pleased for you to start," he concluded.

I almost threw the phone in the air, jumped up and down and kicked Dave Ashton, the sour-faced bastard, but I remained calm. Dave on the other hand was looking decidedly quizzical. "Thanks," I said. "What happens next please?" Dave looked up again and frowned. He was smelling trouble and the resulting problems that they might bring for him.

"Please come to the office next Friday morning," Mr Achemian continued, "bringing all you need to travel to the continent and you will meet Mr Fagan and we will give you your ferry ticket and all necessary instructions. Oh, and don't forget your passport!" he finished.

"OK," I excitedly replied. "I'll see you next Friday." I handed the phone back to Dave.

"See who next Friday?" he demanded, slightly menacingly I thought.

"My new employer," I explained somewhat cockily I must admit. "I'm giving you a week's notice. I'm off to the continent next week."

"You cheeky young monkey," Dave spluttered. "Using my phone as well. That'll be a shilling off your wages!"

Do you know, that miserable sod wasn't joking either? He deducted the shilling from my final wage packet, but I didn't care. No more loading, chaining or offloading, often in the wet. No more roping and sheeting. No more dirty tranny caffs. No more pitiful wage packets. Now I was indeed, or so I thought, a continental driver, one of the new kings of the road.

How little I knew!

4

Ferry Across the Humber

AS it turned out, my Scottish load was a one drop at the Toyota dealership in Aberdeen with no onward journey up to Inverness. Once tipped of my load in the Granite City, I rang Dave from the Toyota dealer's phone only to discover that there was nothing to pick up in Bathgate either. There were no Hillman Imps and no mini tractors as had usually been the case.

"Come back empty and we'll have your wage packet ready," he said in a sort of resigned voice. He was treating my leaving and move to better things as a personal slight. He'd been the one to take me on and he felt I'd let him down by only working for the company for nine months.

To be honest, I didn't care a bit. I'd seen the way that they treated drivers who tried to assert their rights. They'd built their business up by undercutting the big boys and underpaying the drivers. Car transporter drivers were generally at the top end of the wage bracket but not at this firm. We were still paid the basic wage plus copious overtime at way below union rates which we either did or found ourselves out on the street. Then they became too big for their boots and circumstances forced them to insist that all drivers joined the Transport and General Workers Union otherwise the company couldn't take advantage of backloads out of unionised plants. We joined but then wondered why we weren't being paid the union rates which were quite specifically laid down. Matters came to a head when a RoRo vessel load of cars arrived at Dover and we were all asked, as usual after returning from trunking, to shunt loads up to the storage depot at Lydden from the docks for which, once again, there was a specific union rate which we were not being offered. We had no shop steward but one of our number volunteered to represent us all and he had the onerous task of informing Dave that we would only do the extra shunting if the firm agreed to pay the union rates of pay. They were furious but had no option but to back down and agree or they would have lost lucrative contracts. Within a fortnight the poor sod who had agreed to represent us was out on his ear. The union were called in to a meeting but management presented the union representative with dockets showing that our spokesman had seriously damaged a whole load of cars and they refused to take the matter any further. I learned later while in the depot that the dockets had been forged. So much for unions and so much for cowboy operators!

So, as I cruised back down the M6, the M1 and the circuitous route around north London to the Dartford Tunnel, I felt no remorse as far as Dave was concerned but little did I know that the sod was cooking up a nice little leaving present for me.

"Hi Arthur, would you do us a last favour?" he smiled his crooked smile at me, "I've got an urgent load of BMWs for Grimsby and Hull ready loaded at Lydden depot and Frank's just gone sick. If you leave now you'll be tipped out by tomorrow night and back here for Thursday."

I started to protest. These quickie loads often went wrong and I had to be at Pars Containers office in London on Friday morning. Dave suddenly looked a bit serious.

"Let's put it this way," I detected a definite under-
tone of a sneer in his voice, "your money's not
ready and technically you're still working for us till
Thursday." There was no arguing and so it was that
that Tuesday night I was back up the road and out of
hours by the time I reached South Mimms. There was
not enough time to bother with finding a B&B so I
cabbed it across the Dodge's seats in the Shangri La
transport cafe car park.

Next morning dawned cold and grey and I awoke
to the sound of diesels coughing and spluttering into
life all around me. There was a knock on the cab
door. I blearily lowered the window and peered out
into the gloom. There was Alan, one of the longest
serving drivers on the company.

"Hi mate, I thought you were leaving and off to
better things," he said.

"I'm just doing one final trip for bloody Dave," I
replied.

"Where you off to?" he asked.

"Just Grimsby and Hull then empty back to Dover
on Thursday," I said.

"You'll be bloody lucky," Alan laughed. "You'll
get tipped in Grimsby today but have you any idea
how long it takes from there to Hull?" I pulled out
my road map.

"They're right next to each other aren't they?" I
asked somewhat hesitantly as I opened the maps.

"Oh yes they are," Alan agreed, "But there's a
thing called the Humber Estuary in between. You've
to come all the way back up the A18 as far as Goole,
then over the river and down the 63 to Hull. That'll
take you all of three hours. I've done that run before.
It's a sod. Good luck with your new job mate!" Alan
laughed again as he turned on his heel and disappeared
off to his truck.

Bloody Dave had stitched me up good and proper. He must have known I couldn't do both tips in one day and would have to overnight in which case I couldn't get back to Dover within legal running hours by Thursday evening.

I didn't bother with breakfast but cranked the motor into life and set out up the A1 determined to find a way to thwart Dave's crooked little machinations. I stopped for a quick lunch just before Stamford, having made quite good time. Over lunch I had a good hard look at the map to see if there was any way I could save time on the leg between Grimsby and Hull but there seemed to be no option. Out in the truck park there was an Edwards of Hull truck so I thought I'd have a quick word with the driver.

"No mate, you've no chance of any way that'll save you time," he said. "But," he added, "there's a ferry from New Holland into Hull. Old steam paddlers but they do take cars. Think on," he finished.

I pulled into BMW Grimsby at 3:30 and had offloaded their five cars by 4 o'clock.

"Mind if I use your phone?" I asked.

"No problem, driver," said the sales manager. I explained my problem to him. I had three cars to deliver to Hull and I would shortly be out of hours and had to get back to Dover for Thursday night. I asked him about the ferry.

"It's at the end of a long jetty at New Holland, you'd have to drive the cars down to it," he said. "But it does go virtually into Hull town centre. Eh, lad, I'll give Tom over in Hull a ring for you!" He dialled the number. "Tom old lad," he said. "We've got a little problem." He explained everything to Tom and after a further conversation he put the phone down. "Tom's agreed to meet the ferry in Hull with trade plates for the cars so if you can get over there and load the cars onto the boat, they'll be there to meet you and sign for them." I couldn't thank him enough.

"Don't worry," he laughed, "that's my gratuitous good deed for the day. I'll also call British Rail and book the cars on for you. The *Lincoln Castle*'s on the run at the moment and she only carries seven vehicles maximum."

I was at the end of the quay at New Holland for 5 o'clock and noted the next ferry due at 5:30. I offloaded the BMWs and then drove each one the length of a very long and rickety wooden pier at the end of which there was a steep drop down to a landing stage. By the time I'd driven each car on and run back to get the next three times, I was knackered. Luckily my friend at BMW Grimsby had booked the cars on and all I had to do was pay the ferry fares and by 5:25 I was ready. I love old paddle steamers and was over-joyed in more ways than one when the PS *Lincoln Castle* hove into view through the mist, black smoke belching from her funnel and her paddles thrashing through the dirty Humber water as she spun on her axis and was expertly aligned with the landing stage and the paddles stopped and she was moored alongside by heavy hawsers pulled around steam capstans. What a wonderful sight! I loaded each car on board much to the amusement of the crew. "Technically," the mate pointed out, "we're supposed to have a driver with each car. And, by the way, they should be on trade plates," he added, "but I'll take the Nelson stance this time." He winked and left for the bridge.

We cast off and I had a feeling of elation that this was to be my last car delivery. I'd be heading back south tonight and I'd pulled one on Dave! I walked forward from the car area on the deck to have a look at the engines. Through an open hatch you could see the massive pistons beautifully greased and oiled, thrusting back and forth as they drove the paddles forward. I looked down through the next hatch and there was something even more unbelievable than loading 1970s BMWs onto a 1930s paddler. There was some poor creature down there actually shovelling coal into the furnace! That really made my day and I watched him until he looked up at me with his heavily begrimed face and grinned. He must have realised the absurdity of the situation too!

Soon the Hull waterfront skyline loomed in at us through the autumn mirk and the streetlamps were throwing weird fuzzy shafts of amber sodium light beaming at us across the water as we came alongside Hull pier. As the gangway came down onto the little ferry I could see three men armed with trade-plates making their way along the quay and I called over to them, "You from BMW?"

"Yes that's us," they shouted back. We offloaded the cars which they then examined and signed all my paperwork for clean delivery.

"Is one of you called Tom?" I asked.

"Yes that's me, I'm the boss," admitted a tall slim man dressed in an immaculate grey suit.

"Thanks so much for this, I really appreciate it," I said. "You've got me out of a real jam."

"Oh, don't mention it," said Tom. "We were desperate for these cars and didn't really want to pay for a full transporter to get them delivered quickly so you've actually done us a favour! Here's your ferry fare," he said, handing me the £15 it had cost me.

"Oh thanks, that's really nice of you," I said. "Would you do me one big favour too? Please don't tell my boss we did this. He's never going to understand why I got back so quickly."

"Don't worry, the secret's safe with us," Tom

chuckled as I darted back on to the ferry just as the gangway started to lift. I waved goodbye and the steamer left the pier, paddles revolving furiously churning up the Humber and leaving a wide creamy wake as the shafts of orange light from the streetlamps rapidly faded into the night and then disappeared altogether.

I glanced down through the open hatch at the coal streaked stoker shovelling coal for all he was worth, his sweating features highlighted by the fireglow from the furnace and within minutes we were already approaching the New Holland landing stage.

"Did that well, didn't you, young 'un?" said the mate as I waited for the gangplank to lower.

"Those guys helped me out no end," I said.

"Oh, they do it all the time, cars going back and forth," he declared as I gingerly walked down the lowering ramp.

Regaining the Dodge, I took the A15 down through Lincoln and then the A46 to Newark where I joined the A1 and parked up for the night just north of Stamford where there was a lorry B&B I'd used before; very clean, a decent evening meal and only one person per room!

Next morning I set off early and was skirting London by 10 o'clock and reached the Dartford tunnel round about noon unfortunately to join a queue and it took me a good hour to get through into Kent. I soared down the A2 and M2 like a thing possessed and luckily Old Bill was nowhere to be seen. Running down south of Canterbury through Bridge I smiled as I passed the bakery demolished by a European who'd lost his brakes a year or so earlier and brought his truck to a halt with the cab at the serving counter. Then it was out across Barham Downs, through Lydden and the S bend under the railway arch where an unfortunate Romanian had piled it and himself and his co-driver a couple of years back. Then it was an easy ride through Temple Ewell, Buckland, into Maison Dieu Road and Townwall Street and I turned the rig majestically, or so I thought, into Wellington Docks bang on 3 o'clock.

You should have seen Dave's face as I handed him the signed paperwork.

"How the hell?" he started.

"Oh," I said, "so you knew I had little hope of getting back here in time to take my new job when you sent me up the road?"

Dave spluttered but failed to notice that I had seen my pay packet on his desk. I grabbed it.

"What do you think you're doing?" he exploded. "I need proof you've actually delivered these cars undamaged. If you walk out of here now I'm calling the police and then there's no way you'll make your new job tomorrow."

"OK," I said, cool as a cool customer could be. "Phone BMW Hull and check it out."

He phoned and placed the receiver into his loudspeaker.

"BMW Hull," the secretary answered.

"I'd like to speak to Tom Hardman," Dave said curtly. A few seconds silence.

"Hardman," Tom answered.

"Dave here, Capel Drivers. Just wanted to check on that last load of three cars we sent up on Tuesday," he explained.

"Oh yes," said Tom. "Bang on time, excellent service and driver a credit to your company. Wish they were all like that."

"Any damage at all?" asked Dave somewhat desperately clawing for a reason to discredit me.

"No, we signed for them all absolutely clean. I'll be

recommending you to BMW head office to help me out with the new contract coming up," Tom finished. Dave was furious, veins standing out on his forehead.

"There's something wrong here," he loured at me. "I'm going to get to the bottom of this." He reached for my pay packet and papers but I calmly put them in the inside pocket of my black reefer jacket.

By this time a couple of the regular shunter drivers had entered the Portakabin and I decided to go out on a high.

"Dave," I said, "as far as I'm concerned you can piss off! You deliberately tried to sabotage me after I gave you due notice in good faith. You can phone the police, kick up trouble with BMW or do anything you like but I'm out of here. I hope the rest of the drivers start to stand up for themselves," I added, casting a meaningful glance across the cabin to the shunters, both of whom were staring incredulously at the scene in front of their eyes. I sauntered deliberately slowly out of the office and onto the quay and could feel Dave's eyes stabbing me in the back but boy did I feel good!

I caught the East Kent Road Car 007 service from Dover to London and spent the evening with my Aussie mates in the Kings Head.

Next morning, prompt at 10 o'clock, I was climbing the stairs in Wolf Street with my suitcase full of t-shirts, spare underwear, jeans and toiletries. The luscious secretary with the pert bottom welcomed me and asked me to sit down opposite her desk which I was more than willing to do. I tend to fall in love quite easily; "Rainbows I'm inclined to pursue," as the song says, but just as I was about to indulge in some small talk, Mr Achemian stuck his head around the door to his office. "Ah, Mr Jackson, please come in. We have a slight change of plan."

"Oh dear," I thought, as I entered his office and he motioned me to sit down. "Please don't tell me he's going to ask me to shunt trailers in the U.K."

"We have a top urgent load," he started to explain, "which must be in Salzburg by Monday, so Ray Fagan is picking it up from Coventry at the moment and will take it through to Austria. That means that you ('Oh no, U.K. shunting – I could see it coming!') will have to meet him somewhere east of London, Upminster or near some other Underground station, this afternoon and you can both be on tonight's Transport Ferry Service from Felixstowe. You look a little concerned, Mr Jackson!" he looked at me quizzically.

"I thought you might be about to ask me to shuttle containers in England," I said, kicking myself for making such a stupid suggestion.

"Oh no," Mr Achemian smiled. "Mr Bernie Fletcher has just collected our first Guy Big J so once Mr Fagan delivers his load to Salzburg he will fly back and take delivery of our second Big J. We are more than adequately covered over here."

I allowed myself a sigh of relief as Mr Achemian continued, "Here are the tickets for the truck, Mr Fagan and yourself." He handed me a small wallet just as the phone rang. "Good morning, Mr Fagan," he said. I was becoming quite impressed with this company. They actually treated drivers with a degree of respect.

"Yes, you're loaded and ready to leave? Good, good. Where would be the best place for you to meet Mr Jackson? That's a good plan, Mr Fagan. Please call me when you have met him." He put the phone down. "As I thought, Mr Jackson. You'll meet Mr Ray Fagan at Upminster tube station. It's on the District Line so you'll need to change trains but I'm sure that you know the Underground system better than I do," he laughed. "Now just one more thing, I need you to sign for this money." He handed me an envelope containing 500 Deutschmarks. "This will tide you over until you reach Salzburg and you can put your expenses against it. Please keep all receipts as Mr Rahimi in our Salzburg office refuses to pay any expenses without them. Now when you reach Europoort tomorrow morning, Mr Ron Daly will be there to meet you and show you the ropes." He rose from his chair and extended his hand. "Good luck and welcome to our company, Mr Jackson" he said, ushering me to the door. I just had time to smile meaningfully at "luscious secretary" and I was descending the stairs, obstructing the passage of several agency nurses, and then I was out on the street in the weak autumnal sun and walking on air.

Oh wow! I was on the way to the continent at last. I had loads of time before my rendezvous at Upminster so I blissfully strolled along Oxford Street to Oxford Circus stopping for a coffee in one of the Wimpy bars. Then it was down into the Underground, Central Line to Bank, travolator to Monument and then a nice long rattly ride on the District out to Upminster.

I had no idea how long Ray would be so I crossed the road outside Upminster Underground and sat down in a small coffee shop where I had another coffee and a couple of cheese rolls while nervously awaiting the arrival of the Mack. Upminster was on one of the London rat runs which existed before the creation of the M25 and linked the A12, A13 and the Dartford Tunnel so it was quite heavily trafficked with lorries of all kinds and I idly watched a succession of Chris Hudsons, Ferrymasters and MATs passing by in both directions.

Eventually, as I was on my third coffee, I heard a different deeper throatier diesel roar and with a hissing of air brakes there she was, stopped immediately outside Upminster station, a gorgeously huge blue cabbed Mack R600 suddenly quiet as the engine died. Without finishing my coffee I grabbed my case and raced over the road.

"Ray Fagan?" I shouted up at its driver.

"Yup, that's me," Ray said opening his door and jumping down to the pavement. He shook my hand. "Latest recruit eh?" he said. "Jump in. Can't stop here, we're boxing cars in. You'll have to put your case in the footwell." I walked gingerly round to the offside passenger door looking admiringly up, but with some degree of trepidation, at this wonder of American engineering. Opening the door I just managed to wedge my case in the footwell before squeezing myself onto the passenger seat, the only place now for my legs being up against the split windscreen. I noted that Ray's case was wedged between the seats. Otherwise there was no storage space whatsoever: such a small cab for such a big truck!

Ray swung himself into the driver's seat, started the engine with that delightful roar once again, selected gears on the two sticks, pulled the indicator stalk back, pushed the parking brake button and with a hiss of air entering the brake cylinders we were off. The ride was not too bad. Even though the seats were not air- suspended, the huge tyres must have cushioned us from road-shock and soon we had turned on to the A127 and back up to the A12 where we turned east. I was already feeling quite proud riding this noble beast and had noticed that heads turned as we approached. Macks were a very rare sight indeed in those days.

Once out on the A12 Ray turned to me. "I'm supposed to test you out on this thing before we reach Felixstowe," he shouted, "but we're pushed for time and we've got to get on this evening's ferry or I've no hope of reaching Salzburg in time. Besides Ron'll show you the ropes in Europoort. They look a lot worse than they are." I sat back watching Ray's expert handling of the gears as we paced ourselves through the heavy A12 traffic approaching another wet dreary rush hour with the light already starting to fade. The wipers were now tracing fast across the two wind-screens and gusts of rain were noisily splashing on the bonnet and ricocheting up onto the screens. Ray saw me investigating the sticks.

"Don't worry about them," he shouted. "Basically we've got a main box with six forward speeds and one reverse and a 'splitter' box if you like, with four splits. You select each gear on the main box and then split it four times up or down. It's a crash box so you need to double declutch on every gearshift. The secret," he confided, "is to get the revs right. Once you get used to that you really don't need the clutch apart from starting and stopping."

Most of this information was going over my head. It was too much to take on board in one go but I watched Ray all the way through to Felixstowe espe-cially as we approached and negotiated the ridiculous number of roundabouts on the bypass and was starting to get the feel for the machine by the time we turned through Felixstowe dock gates.

Once in the port offices, Ray took charge of all the paperwork and by 8 o'clock we were in the queue for the ferry. The rain was lashing down, but luckily the wind appeared to be light as we were called forward and nosed our way to the head of the ramp. *Celtic Ferry* I saw in bold black lettering across the stern of the vessel starkly lit by the neon floodlighting from the quayside.

"Now's the interesting bit," Ray said, as he swung the rig around to face away from the boat and commenced to reverse down the ramp. Even though the large mirrors on their long stalks were running with rainwater Ray was able to use them until he reached the stern deck of the ferry and here he had no option but to open his and my windows in order to hear the barked instructions from the crew. This of course meant that we both got faces dashed with salty spray but there was nothing else for it. After a couple of shunts we were positioned to the crew's satisfaction and we both jumped down from the cab clutching our cases. Luckily we were now protected from the rain as we crossed the cavernous vehicle deck.

"Nice truck!" one of the sailors shouted as we reached the companionway up to the driver's cabins. I saw him battening down our trailer with chains and wondered just how rough the crossing ahead might be.

We had been allocated to Cabin 5 which had four bunks in it together with a sink. There was a shower also available in the driver's quarters but we really didn't need it and after drying ourselves off we made our way to the messroom where we sat down with several other drivers for a couple of beers and a very welcome meal. Before we had finished, the *Celtic Ferry* had cast off and was chugging her way gently through the mouth of the river Orwell and out into the North Sea.

During the night I woke in the darkness and lay contentedly, feeling the North Sea swell lightly slapping against the sides of the ferry as the powerful Sulzer diesels relentlessly propelled us towards Holland. I was in heaven as I drifted in and out of a fitful slumber.

My continental dream was fast becoming reality!

5

Europe at Last!

EVENTUALLY I must have fallen into a deep sleep because I was suddenly being shaken awake by Ray.

"If you want some breakfast mate, you'd better get up. There's only one sitting," he was cajoling me. I turned to and discovered that, apart from me, the cabin was now empty. I retrieved my washing bag from my case and had a quick wash and shave at the sink before heading for the driver's messroom. I briefly sauntered out to the open deck which ran the width of the ferry behind the salt encrusted white accommodation superstructure and enjoyed watching the bubbling wake emanating from the ship's stern which subsided to streaks of churned salt on the surface of the gently undulating sea as it fell further and further behind us almost as far back as the horizon. I looked up at the black funnel spewing diesel exhaust up towards the heavens where clouds scudded westward on the breeze back towards England. Peering round the side of the superstructure I could see the low grey coast of Holland and what I took to be the mouth of the Oude Maas River into which the bow of our ship appeared to be heading. The wind was light and cold but not icy and the grey rain clouds gently drifted across our path but thankfully had the grace not to dump their cargo onto us just yet.

Passing back through the door into the warmth of

the accommodation I turned left and then right, down a passage with cabin doors on either side and a door at the end directly ahead marked 'Mess'. I entered into a babble of driver's voices and sat down opposite Ray at a table for six.

"You're only just in time mate," he said. "Eight o'clock's the limit and we dock at 9:30!" A steward in a smart white jacket entered the mess from what I took to be the galley, and Ray beckoned him over. "Sorry about my mate," he pointed to me. "I couldn't wake him up. Is there anything left?"

"There's plenty back there," the steward said. "What would you like? Full English, toast and tea?"

"Yes please," I eagerly agreed. The steward collected some empty plates and cups from an adjoining table and scuttled out of the messroom. Minutes later he was back with a full plate of bacon, eggs, sausages, tomatoes, baked beans and a couple of slices of black pudding which he carefully placed between the knife and fork in front of me. Within another couple of minutes a rack of toast and a pot of tea were also plonked on the table and I tucked in to enjoy the meal.

There were two other drivers at our table and looking round the messroom I could see six other tables all well occupied with drivers discussing all manner of things from best routes to avoid Rotterdam town centre to latest specification diesel engines and even to a little light politics.

"Your first trip is it?" one of the other drivers on our table enquired.

"Yes, I'm *makey-learn* with Ray here," I said. "He was supposed to have tested me out on the Mack before we boarded but we were so late there wasn't time so he's taken quite a risk in bringing me over."

"You'll be alright," Ray interposed. "You've driven crash boxes before haven't you?"

"Scammell, Foden, Guy, one or two of them gate crashes," I answered.

"Reet boogers, them gate crashes," the other driver said. "Miss a gear and you've no option but to stop and start again."

"There's no gate on the Mack," Ray explained, "but with 24 forward gears and four reverse the main problem is remembering which bloody gear you're actually in!"

After breakfast and with my overnight case packed ready to disembark I went back out on deck and watched as the ferry nosed her way through the ever decreasing waves as we entered the wide mouth of the Oude Maas. You could see the muddy river water pushing its way out into the North Sea and it was quite amazing to think that this same mud had been scraped from the banks of rivers rising as far into Europe as Switzerland. The container cranes at Europoort could be clearly seen on the right and behind them the outlines of a vast array of chemical plants. On the left the land was flat, relieved only by the docks at Hook of Holland where I could see the funnel of a British Rail ferry with its dominant white arrows logo on its bright red background. We swung to the right before we came abreast of the Hook and headed into the natural harbour at Europoort. Now the container cranes were initially on our left but as the vessel rotated 180° and commenced to reverse onto the ferry berth they were on the other side in front of mountains of containers and behind them the vast tanks of the Dutch petrochemical industry, most of them seemingly owned by a company called Pakhoed whose name and black hat logo were emblazoned on the side of each white tank. Looking over to the shore side I could see that we were very close to the berth and just at that moment the Tannoy burst into life: "Calling all drivers. Calling all drivers. Would all drivers please rejoin their trucks for disembarkation? Do not start your engines until requested to do so by a member of the crew and please remember no smoking on the vehicle deck."

I re-entered the accommodation and found Ray in the cabin packing his case. Both of us made our way down the narrow companionways to the vehicle deck and we shuffled our way through the parked trucks looking for his Mack. The main sounds which could be heard were the throaty roar of the ship's diesels presumably now with forward thrust to slow the vessels progress towards the ramp and the clink and clank of restraining chains being detached from the trailers and allowed to fall onto the deck.

"Don't know why they bothered to chain us all up," Ray remarked. "That was one of the smoothest crossings I've had!" Suddenly the diesels revved up to maximum and the deck throbbed as the vessel was brought to a halt on the ramp. Then they died down and within a minute or two were switched off and we were left in relative peace with only the background hum of the diesel generators and the clanking of the last chains being released.

We found our truck now squeezed between a Ferrymaster's unaccompanied trailer and a Spiers and Hartwell Scania 110 with a green Davies Turner tilt trailer. We jumped in and sat and waited and waited. "We get this almost every bloody time," Ray said. "They load unaccompanied trailers in front of us and we have to wait for the shunters to get them off before we can roll. Bloody annoying, we might as well have stayed up in the mess having another cup of tea! Tell you what Art, you could walk off if you like. Just take care and keep on the raised section all the way along the deck and up the ramp. The offices are on the right on the ground floor of a big office block. Ron'll be in there waiting for you and he'll get you through customs and immigration. I'll probably see you in Hudig and Pieter's office before I take off up the road."

"Just in case I don't see you," I said, "thanks for all your help, Ray."

"Only following orders, old son." Ray laughed.

I gingerly climbed down from the cab, making sure that the Ferrymaster's trailer was not linked to a shunter and about to drive off, ducked under its front end and made it to the raised walkway running along the port side of the deck. Clutching my case I made my way to the vast door at the after end of the ship and waited while a shunter tractor backed over the ramp towards its next trailer. Seizing the opportunity I walked over the ramp and onto the continent of Europe! The feeling of elation was almost overwhelming but was mitigated somewhat by the awful chemical smell wafting across the terminal from the refineries upriver. I walked up the length of the ramp and made it to the top just as the shunter passed me towing a Chris Hudson trailer. It proceeded straight ahead towards the unaccompanied trailer park and I headed right, across the inbound truck park towards the brick and concrete three storey office block and a door marked Immigratiedienst, and underneath, Douane.

As I crossed the park a light drizzle started to fall and I wondered if this might be acid and if I might find holes in my clothes as a result but I made it to the office block without them falling off and entered into a long room with chairs on either side and windows at the far end through which could be seen the forms of uniformed officials and I guessed that this might be where I should present my passport.

"Arthur Jackson?" a friendly voice intoned.

"Yes that's me," I answered turning to face whoever it might be.

Ron Daly held out his hand and shook mine firmly. "Welcome to the club," he said. Ron had an air of imperturbability, something I found out as time went on to be his normal attitude to life and its vicissitudes. He stood about 5 feet 10 inches tall with a slight stoop, but this could have been caused by his relaxed attitude rather than anything physical and his lined weather-tanned face topped by a mass of curly dark blond hair bore an almost permanent smile. Of slim build, he was dressed in a country and western style checked shirt over which he wore a brown leather jerkin and the ensemble was completed by jeans, which looked like they could have done with a thorough wash, and a pair of extremely dirty brown winkle picker shoes. "Come with me and we'll sort out your passport and customs," he gestured towards the windows at the far end of the room. As we reached them he took my passport from me and presented it through the right hand window to a uniformed Dutch official. "One of our new drivers," he explained. The official smiled. He obviously knew Ron well and he ceremoniously stamped my passport and handed it back through the window. "Anything to declare?" Ron asked me as we shuffled over to the left hand window.

"Only a bottle of scotch and a pack of cigarettes which Ray told me were for you," I replied.

Ron put his fingers to his lips "Shh" he intoned as he put his face to the open window.

"One of our new drivers," he explained again to the Dutch customs official. "Just 200 cigarettes and a bottle." "No problem," the Dutch official stamped a piece of paper which he inserted into my passport and handed back to Ron. Ron removed the paper and gave it to me with the passport.

"You'll need that paper to get out of the compound," he explained as we left the offices through the same door we had entered earlier and skirted the building before walking on a kind of elongated pedestrian crossing without the Belisha beacons, which stretched out about two hundred yards to the gates. Apparently these markings had some kind of mystical power which prevented the shunters from running you down, but if that was indeed the case it wasn't working particularly well this morning because we had to dodge the crazy Dutch drivers weaving around the parking lot with their unaccompanied trailers. "I think they're on some kind of bonus," Ron said, "if they offload the ferry within a certain time. Then there's a lull and the whole thing takes off again as they race to reload it."

My case was beginning to feel a bit heavy as we arrived at the gate and I switched arms. "Want me to carry it for you?" he asked. I shook my head. At the gatehouse Ron took my customs paper and stretched up to reach the window situated to serve truck drivers rather than pedestrians. The unseen official took it and the gate lifted and we were out of the terminal. Ron and I walked over to a dirt topped lorry park on the right just outside the gates and there was parked his R600. "Taxi Mack," he laughed, "jump in." He swung himself into the cab and I walked around the front to the passenger side, hurled my case into the footwell and scrunched myself up on the passenger seat with my feet on the window, a position I was starting to get used to! He started the engine and we took off down the road to the end of the harbour basin where he took a sharp left and drew up outside an office building sporting a huge Europoort sign on the top. "Leave your case in the truck," he said. "We're just going up to the agent's office on the top floor so you won't want to lug that thing all the way up there. Nothing valuable inside is there?"

"No, only clothes and things," I said.

"Little tip," Ron said. "Always keep your passport, wallet and driving licence on you. It's not worth the hassle of losing them."

We entered the building and took the lift up to the top floor. As we emerged from it, the agent's office was to our right and we entered through a half-glazed door with the legend, Hudig and Pieters, Shipping Agents' written across it in black bold lettering. The main office was thinly manned with only a couple of clerks banging away on typewriters amongst the many empty desks this being Saturday of course. Ron opened the flap on the long counter in front of us and we walked through to one of the desks.

"Goede morgen, René," he stopped in front of the first manned desk. René looked up from the paper-work he was laboriously typing.

"Good morning Ron." he answered in the Euro American accent so typical, I was to learn, of the Dutch. "Just completing Ray Fagan's transit documents." René was a fair haired thin and tall young man of about 20 years old or thereabouts, wearing an open necked denim blue shirt and jeans. He seemed to have a most efficient air about him.

"Where's the boss man this morning?" Ron enquired.

"Oh, as usual playing golf. We work, he shirks," laughed René. "Who is this new driver?" he continued.

"This is Arthur," Ron explained. "Just off the boat, as we say," he winked at René. "Hasn't even driven a Mack yet but I'll give him a try out after we've had a coffee."

"Hope he's not like the two last week," René said. "Back on the same boat."

I extended my hand and shook his.

"Pleased to meet you," I said. "I have driven difficult trucks before," I pointed out.

"It's not the difficult trucks," René answered, "it's the difficult drivers."

Ron's eyes rolled and he made a "tsk" sound as he looked skywards. "Bane of my life," he said. "They keep sending over unsuitable idiots. Last week's two had only ever driven rigids – TK's with synchro boxes. They couldn't even get the damn tractors rolling without the trailers on. I sent them straight back!"

"Coffee?" René asked, as he pulled the papers out of his typewriter and removed the blue interleaved copy sheets one by one and placed them in a box on the side of his desk.

"Yes please. You OK with sugar and creamer, Art?" Ron asked.

"No sugar thanks." I replied.

René disappeared through a door at the far end of the office and I took the opportunity to look out of the windows which ran down the entire length of the right side of the office. There in the Europort basin was *Celtic Ferry* still with a steady stream of trailers offloading.

"What time do you think Ray will be over?" I asked.

"Could be one hour, could be three," Ron said. "We're getting really pissed off with the way they load the boat with unaccompanied trailers in front of the driver accompanied ones. It's losing us all a lot of time."

"Can't you complain?" I asked.

"We have. We made a written complaint a couple of weeks ago on behalf of several companies," Ron shrugged. "But they just said they have to maximise their loads and they can't be sure how much space they've got until all the drivers are loaded so we've just got to live with it."

René re-appeared with a small tray with three cups of what smelled like very strong coffee, typical of the continent I was to discover. "I'll down this one," he said, "then I've got to put Ray's papers in for clearance. If he's lucky and they're out by lunchtime he could make Frankfurt tonight. Gerhard told me he's got to be in Salzburg for Monday."

"Gerd's jumping up and down on this one," Ron said turning to me. "Oh, he's our boss in Salzburg, Art. You'd think him American but actually he's German. You'll like him. He's OK."

"Ray'll have no trouble getting there will he?" I asked innocently.

"Driving ban in Germany as of 10 o'clock tonight," Ron explained. "He can't get back on the road until ten on Sunday night. It's worse in the summer. We can't drive Saturdays either."

We finished our coffees and René swept out of the office with a sheaf of papers under his arm. "OK, Art. Now's your chance to shine or it's back to Blighty for you!" Ron motioned me out of the office and we descended in the lift to the ground floor. His Mack was parked next to the large cafe taking up most of the ground floor, which rejoiced in the name of The Amstel Pub. "We'll have lunch in there later," he said, indicating that I was to heave myself up into the driver's seat. I sat behind the large green steering wheel for the first time and looked through the windscreen at the iconic Mack bulldog perched menacingly on the front of the long bonnet, its chrome backside menacingly directed straight at me as if it knew I had never driven a left hand drive vehicle before. Ron swung into the passenger seat and inserted the key in the ignition.

"Now," he said, "I'll just run through the gearbox with you and we'll take a short run down the service road and stop at the end. First you've got your main box," he pointed to a map of the gearbox helpfully fastened to the dashboard. "Six gears, but one's crawler which you'll never use. So start off in second. Then your right stick is the splitter which chops each gear into four. Just keep in your head, main second, one split, two split, three split, four split. Main third, one split, two split, three split, four split. First we'll just see how you do in second gear. OK? Right, turn the key and start her up. Make sure both sticks are in neutral."

I started the throaty 240 brake horse power Mack Thermodyne turbocharged motor and gave her a couple of blips on the accelerator. "Right Art. Let her idle. Now, foot on the clutch, put her into main second with your left stick, OK, now select first split with the right. Do you know where the park brake is? It's that blue button."

"Just a second," I interrupted the flow of instructions before I selected first split. "Are you telling me that I have to use two hands each time I change the main box?"

"That's right," Ron winked. "You're catching on!"

I increased the pressure of my left foot on the clutch, slipped the splitter into first, pressed the airbrake button and gingerly started to release the clutch.

"Gently, gently," Ron shouted at me over the roar of the diesel as I increased the revs. "She'll pull away on idle without the weight of the trailer." I let the revs drop and continued to release the clutch slowly.

Then I felt the plates start to mesh and, as I used to do on the Scammells, pushed the clutch a tad down as she started to roll. She took off quite well and I let the clutch slowly out all the way. We were on the way! I pushed the accelerator down and within seconds we had gone from sixteen hundred up to two thousand one hundred revs.

"OK," Ron shouted. "Second split." I took my foot off the accelerator, and knocked the splitter out of gear as I pressed down on the clutch. As fast as I could I blipped the revs up and as they died, selected second split. There was a nasty grating noise and we shuddered to a halt. I pulled the engine stop and the parking brake. "You've got to take it slowly, slowly," Ron chided. "Besides which, the engine and gear-boxes are cold so you need to take it even more slowly, slowly! Don't blip the accelerator next time. Just wait while the revs die down and watch the rev meter. You should be able to slip the splitter in as she passes down through seventeen hundred revs."

I started off once again, reasonably smoothly I thought, and this time as Ron shouted "Second split" I took my foot off the throttle, pushed the clutch down and, waiting till the revs touched seventeen hundred, moved the split stick to second and released the clutch as gently as I could. This time she engaged and with slight jerking we continued on our way. Third split went well, fourth split was again a bit on the gratey side but she went in reasonably clunk-free. "Now," Ron shouted, "declutch, out of main second, out of split fourth. Foot off clutch, rev the engine, foot on clutch, let revs die to seventeen hundred, into main third and split first at the same time, foot off clutch!" Needless to say, I missed the last split and we ground to a halt!

"Back on the next ferry?" I asked.

"Keep at it," Ron said, and so it was that we spent the next hour traipsing up and down the service road, grating gears, kangarooing, juddering to a stop but eventually I did get her as far up the box as main fourth and split second. At this point we were passing the Amstel pub for about the tenth time. "OK," Ron shouted. "Bring her to a halt and we'll pop in for a beer." I have to admit that I was sweating buckets by this time and, jumping down from the cab, realised that my left leg had just about had it as well. I limped into the Amstel following Ron and sat down at one of the tables next to the huge picture windows as Ron summoned a waiter.

"Twee Biertjes, please," he ordered. The waiter departed behind the bar.

"Well, Ron," I asked somewhat tentatively. "How did I do?"

6

The Amstel Pub

AT that moment René, once again burdened with an armful of paperwork, entered the bar and made his way over to our table. "Ray's cleared and on his way." He said as he sat down at the table with us. "He might stop off here before he sets off."

"I hope so," Ron said. "I've got some paperwork for Salzburg he could take." Looking out of the window I could see Ray's Mack over in the terminal snaking in and out of the parked trailers which were waiting to be loaded onto the ferry.

"He's on his way out now," I helpfully interjected. "Shall we go out onto the road and wave him down?"

Ray looked at me somewhat witheringly rather like a kindly uncle to a presumptuous child. "No, he'll come in, don't worry," he cajolled. "Besides, here are our beers. Do you want one, René?"

"Yes, please," René said. "I've got a good half hour before I need to get back to the terminal." The waiter hurried off to fill the order and, looking once again out of the window, I saw Ray leave the main highway and head towards us down the slip road.

Within a couple of minutes he had pulled to an airbrake hissing stop behind Ron's tractor unit. He jumped down and made his way over to the Amstel Pub. Entering, he looked around the near deserted bar area before joining us at the window table. "Is he

49

alright?" he asked Ron, grinning at me, "Not going back on the ferry like last week's duo?"

"No, we can knock him into shape," Ron's eyes once again rolled up to the ceiling. "Been up into fourth already with all the splits. We're going into Rotterdam this afternoon so that'll be a bit more experience for him. You stopping for a beer?" he finished.

"I'll have a quick coffee," Ray said, "then I've got to get onto the road and as far into Germany as possible before the driving ban tonight." René sauntered over to the bar to order Ray's coffee. Ron gave Ray a quizzical look, and started to handroll a cigarette by unfolding a Rizla paper. His brow furrowed a little and he became seemingly lost in thought.

"It's only an Autobahn ban," he said. "If you can get down to Frankfurt tonight, you could get onto the old road and probably make Wurzburg or Nuremberg on Sunday. I'm not sure about the bridge heights. That'll be your main problem. Some of them are only 3.6 metres high so that might stop you." He lit his ragged little rollup, the threads of the Old Holborn tobacco hanging out of the lit end and glowing, the fragrant smoke drifting across the table towards us. "I can't see you making Salzburg by Monday midday unless you do that. It's 18 solid driving hours from here."

My stomach tightened considerably. There was the good news that I was staying but the thought of taking the Mack out into city traffic was inducing a rising panic. Driving up and down the service road had been one thing. Keeping up with heavy traffic on a main thoroughfare would be quite another. One other little complication that had added to the problems of my training so far had been negotiating the turns. There was no power steering and although the steering wheel was large enough, it was still quite an effort to turn her round at slow speeds. I thankfully gulped down the bottle of Amstel Pils and Ray drew out a map of Germany and spread it out on the table in front of Ron. René finished his beer and got up to leave.

"I'll see you two upstairs in half an hour," he said. "I've got a load of telexes to go through."

"Oh great," Ron answered. "I'd hoped we'd have a clear weekend ahead."

"They're mainly truck movements and some details of the next batch of Pitt trailers coming over," René said reassuringly. "There's nothing scheduled in on the next two ferries and Ian Scott is en route from Salzburg. Should be here Monday night," he added as he left the pub, still clutching his sheaf of documents.

Ron turned back to the Hallwag road map of Germany. "See there," he jabbed his finger at the map. "If you come off at junction 65 just before Wurzburg, you can take the old road round the town and pick up the A13 through Ansbach and Ingolstadt as far as Munich if the bridges don't get you." He took a deep draught of the Old Holborn and settled back to finish his beer.

"Thanks Ron," Ray said, carefully folding up his map. "I've not been off the autobahns on this route before apart from around Munich of course," he smiled ruefully. "I bet you can't wait for them to finish off the Mittlerer Ring!" Ron's eyes rolled to the ceiling again. This was obviously a trucker's bête noire I decided. "Anyways," he concluded, draining his strong Douwe Egberts. "I'm off. Good luck, Art. You're in good hands, mate. Oh, I've got this for you from Achemian." He handed a bulging envelope over to Ron.

"That's what I'm waiting for," Ron smiled.

"The geld to keep this operation going! Could you

give this envelope to Gerd in Salzburg? Have a good trip and watch out for the bridges!" Ray left the bar and I watched him walk over to the Mack and swing himself up the far side into the driver's seat. Great clouds of black smoke belched up from the stack behind the cab as he started the motor, selected his gear and moved off waving to us as he went.

"That truck needs a service," Ron commented. "Looks as though he's got injector trouble. Another beer?" he suggested.

"Have we got time?" I asked.

"All the time in the world," Ron said rolling another cigarette and gesturing to the barman for refills. "Can't move now till René returns from the terminal."

The second beer arrived and we enjoyed watching the world go by outside. Some local workers entered the bar and, ordering up beers, settled down on stools beside the counter. Several lit up and a hubbub of unintelligible, to me anyway, conversation ensued. More entered and soon all the tables were filled, some with office workers, others with stevedores still clad in their working gear. The smoke-filled atmosphere became lively and convivial with much laughter and raised voices making important points as forcefully as possible. Outside, drizzle was washing the cold pavement and the wind appeared to be rising, blowing light wafts of spray across the container parks and onto the massive tank farms nearby. Ron ordered yet more beers. "Four's the maximum when you're driving," he helpfully explained. "It's lunchtime. Would you like an Uitsmijter to soak up the beer?"

"My God," I thought. "If I have any more alcohol I'm finished!"

"Is that like a schnapps?" I asked.

"Nah, Uitsmijter, Strammer Max, Ham and Eggs" he smiled.

"Oh, OK, I could do with some food," I answered, feeling exactly like the first tripper I was. Ron gestured the waiter to our table and ordered. More port workers arrived in a minibus and hurried through what was now driving rain, into the warmth of the hostelry. Soon René himself drove up and parked in front of the minibus. This time he had to protect his sheaf of paperwork by holding it inside his coat as he sprinted from his dark red DAF Daffodil car into the building.

The waiter was delivering our Uitsmijters as the rain-soaked René strolled over to our table. "You going to join us?" Ron asked.

"I'd like to but I've got paperwork to complete for some Chris Hudson trailers shipping out on the next ferry," René explained apologetically. "Come up when you're finished. I need you to sign off the telexes please. I'll put the coffee on for you."

"We'll be there," Ron said. "Make sure you've got some cream."

"Only Carnation creamer," René said. "Cream, creamer what's the difference?" He turned to go and Ron grimaced.

"Can't stand that bloody creamer," he said. "It's like pure chemical. I'd almost prefer UHT milk."

The Uitsmijters turned out to be very nice indeed – two fried eggs on thick slices of ham on top of fresh Dutch brown bread. We finished them off and Ron sauntered – he never walked or indeed ran I discovered – over to the bar to pay the bill and we then took the lift up to the Hudig and Pieters office, Ron rolling up yet another cigarette en route. The aroma of strong percolating coffee was sneaking its way through the entrance door to the office as we left the lift and soon we were sitting around René's desk drinking from china cups with the Douwe Egberts logo emblazoned across them. Ron was riffling through the telexes passed to him by René and signing each one to prove he'd read and/or approved them.

"Looks like Ian'll be here in time for the container ship on Monday. He's got two 20fts of mohair. Have you booked space?" he asked.

"Yes, no problem. She's sailing half empty at the moment anyway," René replied. Ron explained to me that the normal method of shipment was for the containers to be transhipped at Europoort and then loaded in Felixstowe onto domestic vehicles for delivery and re-loading in the U.K.

"Any instructions for Arthur here?" Ron asked.

"None at the moment," René said. "There's nothing coming out of England until next Saturday I think. Gerd did say that you've got a contract loading out of a steelworks near Chambéry which needs about six trucks but there's nothing further on that yet."

"In that case we'll be on our way," Ron said draining his cup and making his way through the counter to the door. "See you on Monday René," he added as we made our way back to the lift.

Once outside we discovered that the rain was now pouring down, the drops bouncing off the shiny blue paintwork of the resting Mack. "OK Art, into the driver's seat you go," Ron yelled, jumping into the passenger side and leaving me to walk around the front of the cab in the wind driven rain. I reached up, opened the door and had mounted the two steps and into the cab almost before you could count the hands on a clock, but still managed to end up with rain streaming down my face. I swished back my straggly hair, inserted the key and fired up the mighty Thermodyne diesel. Two hundred and forty horses were now at my entire disposal, their only current purpose to deliver us to our lodgings in Rotterdam without the burden of a trailer and a 20 ton load.

"OK, Art, I'll leave it to you," Ron shouted. "Just remember – take it easy." I depressed the clutch and selected second main and first split, lifted the clutch until it started to engage, pressed the parking brake button and we started to move as I gently re-depressed the clutch ever so slightly before gently releasing it completely. Then it was through the splits, mains and splits, again double declutching on each change, and we reached the end of the service road in fourth main and third split. I took my foot off the accelerator and the unit slowed as we approached the junction onto the main Europoort to Rotterdam dual carriageway road on which we needed to cross the central reservation and turn left. "Nothing coming, keep going!" Ron yelled. I depressed the accelerator and we sped out onto the main road as I feverishly fed the steering wheel through my hands desperately trying to maintain the ten to three position. By the time we approached the De Beer Seaman's Mission I'd reached sixth main and second split and Ron indicated that we needed to pull into the hotel parking so it was back down through the gears and I'd reached third main second split as we turned right and then left into the long car park where were parked ten spanking new Pars Containers Macks. We came to a halt next to them.

"That's yours, Art. TEH 6822," Ron pointed out the second one in the row. "Take out anything you don't need for the weekend and stow it inside and we'll be on our way."

Prising my case from the footwell, I jumped down and made my way over to my new pride and joy. Ron tossed a keyring full of keys in my direction and I had to find the right one as I shielded myself from the driving rain sweeping across the unprotected parking area directly from the bleak North Sea. I unlocked the door and sat on the cold vinyl passenger seat, sorting through my case. Then with a change of clothes and my washing gear in my holdall, I locked the cab and raced back to Ron's tractor unit. I settled in behind the wheel and looked around me. This would be my life for the foreseeable future. In front of me was the reassuringly large green steering wheel through which I could see the twin dials of the speedo and the rev counter plus sundry light switches and the diff-locks. On the right of these outside the main binnacle was the red parking brake button and on the steering column were mounted on the left the indicator stalk with a pull out switch for the hazards and on the right the trailer brake stalk. This was basic stuff alright but the switch positions were all unfamiliar to me. To the right the dashboard continued underneath the right split windshield and there was a lockable cubby hole. The passenger seat, like the driver's, was unsprung but quite comfortable and everything was finished in a kind of muted green. I sat waiting for Ron to return from the hotel, feeling a buzz of rising excitement. Rain was now bucketing down and the hotel car park was awash but the trial was over. I'd passed the test. I was on the continent and about to enjoy a weekend in Rotterdam before work was to start on Monday!

7

'Press on Pantin'

THE rain was now plastering down and I was becoming somewhat nervous at the thought of driving this beast into Rotterdam through the traffic. Small lakes were forming in the car park and rivulets trickled and gushed between them and eventually disappeared into the overloaded drains. I started the motor and drove to the steps next to the hotel reception area just in time to catch Ron on his way back out, an overnight bag cradled in his arms to protect it from the weather. He jumped up into the cab.

"Thanks for bringing her over," he said. "Now before we set off just one thing. As we're not pulling a heavy trailer, you don't need to use all the splits, especially now since you've proved you can do it. Just go up or down through the box using second and fourth splits and start off in second main and second split." So off we set back out onto the Europaweg towards Rotterdam. This two way carriageway was built on top of a long dyke which separates the industrial area on the left from the dormitory towns and villages on the right. From time to time we crossed lifting bridges across canals and I noted village names like Brielle and Spijkenesse as we sped past. The heavy rain was now subsiding to the point at which I could switch the wipers to "slow" and I stopped worrying about losing traction at every bend in the road. Just after Spijkenesse was a huge chemical complex at Botlek.

"See that warehouse over there," Ron pointed. "That's the duty free store for the seamen on the tankers and container ships, but so long as you've got your passport you can get supplies in there and there's loads of parking even with a tractor trailer."

"Good tip," I thought. Soon we were running through the suburbs of Rotterdam, and after Rhoon we picked up the newly constructed A15 Rotterdam ring which we left at the very next junction and headed into the city centre over the Erasmusbrug. I was beginning to feel quite pleased with myself, not having grated a single gearchange for some time, when Ron indicated I should do a U turn at the next junction and take the service road which ran on each side of the main dual carriageway. We were now in the city and the road was lined with typical Dutch gabled terraced houses in long rows between each intersection. Ron instructed me to pull into the side and park and we found ourselves right outside our guesthouse just off Schiedamsdijk, number 47 to be precise, a guesthouse Ron explained which was run by a Mrs Vermeiren, an English lady who had married a Dutchman after the war. Sadly, he had died a couple of years before but Doris had stayed on, financing herself from the guesthouse which she specifically ran for British truck drivers.

Ron rang the bell and we entered a dark hallway which had the polished musky smell of an old but well-cared-for establishment. On the right side of the hallway were a desk and chair and a rack of city brochures which I was just starting to leaf through when the lady herself appeared. Doris Vermieren was a very neat and very attractive lady of some 60 years. Erring slightly on the plump side she was dressed in a flowery print dress over which she wore an apron featuring a map of the London underground system. Her round friendly face was not at all over made-up, a fault of so many other women of her age, and overall she exuded an air of bustling efficiency coupled with a palpable desire to ensure her guests were as comfortable as they could be. Ron took the key to the room and, as he was a regular guest, Doris left him to lead me up the stairs to the second floor where we found our room was on the street side with large windows uncluttered by the mesh curtains to which I was accustomed.

"The Dutch don't like to live behind curtains," Ron explained. "It's something to do with the war I think. As you pass their homes especially at night, if you wish you can see into all of them but of course, being a gentleman, you don't!" he finished with a wink.

The room was comfortable but a little Spartan with two white iron bedsteads, each covered with a colourful patchwork quilt. There was a small side table beside each one on which sat a reading lamp. In the corner was a washstand and mirror.

"There's a decent bathroom with a shower on the landing," Ron said, "but if you stow your gear we'll go down to the lounge where Doris will have left some coffee and cakes by now."

Sure enough, downstairs in the lounge, laid out on a coffee table between a couple of comfy leather chairs, was a pot of coffee and some very enticing muffins. Ron poured and I had a quick look around the room, which I guessed doubled as Mrs Vermeiren's parlour as there were family photos dotted around the substantially built wooden sideboards. Once again the heavy curtains at the windows were drawn aside so that we had a grandstand view of the passing traffic. As always in Holland, the coffee was superb and the muffins very welcome indeed. I had been expecting to go out on the town with Ron but he had other ideas. It turned out that he had an "arrangement" with a Dutch couple who lived in Vlaardingen. The husband apparently was unable for some reason to honour his marital duties and so Ron gallantly did the honours while the husband watched! This all took my breath away somewhat and then there was some further talk about the involvement of their daughter and my opinion of Ron was changing rapidly. So Ron was departing Vlaardingen-wards after a shower and brush up, leaving me to find my own way around the city.

"Try the Big Ben pub," he advised. "It's near the Central Station. You can't miss it. Turn left out of here, right at the lights, keep walking and it's just off that road on the right again as you come to a square with the central station on your left."

Following Ron's instructions, I set out later and by the time I was starting to think I should have taken the tram I could see the square ahead. Turning right, there was the Big Ben pub down on the next corner. It was quite a large affair complete with typically English clunky wooden bar furnishings which included the old style pot racks above the bar counter and behind elaborate art deco stained glass. I ordered a pint of draught Amstel, turned round as I took the first sip and noted that all the tables were occupied, but there was one, over by the wall and under the blackboard advertising such Dutch delicacies as Fish and Chips and also Nasi Goering, which only had one occupant. I made my way over and asked if the seats were taken.

"Help yourself," came the unexpected reply in broad Hampshire English.

"Thanks," I said, sitting down and taking a further swig. My neighbour at the table was an aged gentleman dressed in a suit which may well have been older than its wearer, slightly threadbare with shiny areas where limbs were often rested against chairs and tables, but showing signs of once having been a smart pinstripe.

"What are you doing over here," I asked, half expecting him to answer that he lived here and instructing me not to be so bloody nosy.

"I'm a road boss with Siddle Evans from Southampton" he drawled.

"Oh," I must have sounded a little surprised because he went on.

"Not a driver you understand, but they put me in charge of getting the real boary loads through to destination. On one at the moment. We're parked up at Ridderkerk waiting till after the rush hour on Monday for a police escort. Damn ridiculous if you ask me. Better for us to press on over the weekend when the roads aren't so busy. I phoned Frank in the office. I said 'get on to the Dutch police. Tell them the loads're urgent.' We've got two transformers, each 84 tonnes but we're almost in guage on this one. Only 10 foot wide, it's bloody ridiculous. Frank said 'Wait 'till Monday, there's nothing we can do. Then press on Pantin, press on'."

I toyed with the idea of heading back to the bar. Being saddled with a bore was not my idea of an evening out in Rotterdam, but the old boy had some character about him so I asked, "What make of tractors are you using?"

"Scammells, boy, Scammells fore and aft," he said. "We don't travel more than nine or ten miles an hour on the open road but if we press on you'd be amazed how far we can get in a day. What holds us up are the bloody escorts. Every police area we need a new one. They're never there when you arrive. These loads, we need one fore and one aft so getting these Dutchmen to organise that takes a month of Sundays.

We'd be better off getting off the ferry and pressing on without telling them if you ask me. Trouble is these Scammells stick out like a sore thumb so I don't suppose we'd get more'n a mile up the road and we'd be for it."

I drained my glass and offered to buy him a drink.

"Guinness boy, only ever drink Guinness," he said. "That's very civil of you, very civil indeed." He handed me his glass and I soon returned with an Amstel in one hand and his Guinness in the other. He took a sip and licked his lips appreciatively.

I gave him the once over as I started out on my beer. Sallow faced and with grey straggly hair which needed cutting but probably would have to wait because he treasured the remaining strands on his balding head, he gave the impression of a son of the road well versed in the mysteries of his craft. "Been on boary loads for over 40 years," he announced. "I'll probably die on them as well if they don't allow me to press on."

"Where are your drivers?" I asked.

"Oh them?" he started. "Gorn off into the flesh-spots, red lights, girls in the windows." He gave a deprecatory grunt. "Waste of bloody money, but they're young. They'll learn." His eyes were eerily almost black but were still full of life and they twin-kled when he embarked on one tale after another. Good company for one evening, but I could imagine that after a week or two on the road with him, the drivers would well need some respite.

"Last load we did, a chemical cracker," he went on. "Loaded it up in Salford, ferry from Hull to here, and then we took it through to Ludwigshafen, that's in Germany next to Manheim. Big BASF works. That was a boary load. They get a boary load they always call for Pantin to see it through. Main section, that was the cracker, 60 foot long, ten foot wide, ten foot high, 100 tonnes. They think it's easy 'cos they've planned the route for you. 'S'all on the paperwork, Pantin – press on,' that's what they say." He took a sip from his glass and looked at me a little conspiratorially. Seemingly taking me into his confidence he leaned forward over the table. "What they forget is I know what I'm doin'. You don't get 60 foot through Salford docks and out onto the A62 without moving the furniture. I always run it through on the road with the police before we set out. Paperwork, paperwork!!" He lifted his still smoking pipe from its ashtray and stabbed it at me. "Bloody paperwork. You tell me how those boys in the office with all their degrees in this and GCEs in that miss out the blasted keep left sign here and the corner lamppost there. Height's not usually a problem. Was in the tram days," he laughed. "I've grounded trams for hours on end with some loads where we had to lift the wires. Salford's got a lot of lamp wires though and they all had to be lifted. I phoned the office. 'Frank,' I said, 'we can go no further. You've forgotten that bloody keep left in the middle of Union Street at the dock end. Can't get the load round that until corporation move it.' What did he say? 'Press on Pantin. Call us from Hull.' No idea those boys. Two 'Constructors' on the front, one on the rear, sixty foot in between 'em. You don't get that lot round your average roundabout without a bit of planning. And you don't fool about with a 100 tonne lump five foot off the road," he finished, subsiding into a kind of reverie as he poked whatever evil shag he was smoking down into his nicotine stained old pipe. "You any idea how many axles you need to shift that lot?" he asked me. I hurriedly shook my head. "They say you can get away with ten tonne per axle, but I say five," he asserted, once more stabbing his pipe in my direction. "The problem's on the corners. You put too much side pressure on those tyres and they blow. I won't do it. If I'm road boss they do what I say. They get a boary load, they call for me." Then he said something that stayed with me throughout my time on the road it was so true. "Trouble with this job you're just rushing all the time to the next damn hold up."

I stayed with dear old "Press on Pantin" for another couple of drinks, both of which I bought, he wasn't that daft, made my excuses and left. Part of me felt that I should have been around the fleshspots with the drivers but I'd enjoyed the old boy's company. He had a fund of tales about a section of road haulage into which I never ventured and was one of life's rare characters to boot. Regrettably I never came across him again. I called in at another couple of bars on my way back to Mrs Vermeiren's and turned in well before midnight, pleasantly sozzled for a good night's sleep.

8

Mrs Vermeiren

I woke early the next morning to find Ron still not returned from Vlaardingen. The sun was weakly streaming through the thin flower patterned curtains and I turned over in an attempt to gain some extra sleep time as it was Sunday. I dozed and then smelt the familiar scent of an English breakfast cooking. The aroma of bacon and sausage was wafting up the stairs and under the door to the bedroom. My taste buds were alerted by the delightful smell and hunger assumed ascendancy over the desire for a morning's lie-in and I lumbered out of bed to find that the time on my watch was only 8 o'clock. I had changed it to continental time already so in fact my body was telling me that it was 7 o'clock on a Sunday morning and no time for any self-respecting driver on his day off to be up and about.

After a shower I descended the stairs and entered the lounge where, on the right behind the easy chairs, was a long table with place settings for six, already occupied by two men finishing their meals. At that moment Mrs Vermeiren bustled into the room. "Ah you're up already Mr Jackson," she said. "Hadn't expected you before about 10 after a night out on the town."

"I didn't want to miss out on breakfast," I explained. "The smell was too enticing."

"Oh, I serve breakfast until 12 o'clock on a Sunday,"

she smiled. "These two are off back today so needed an early start. That's Greg, he's here every week, and Jim who drops in whenever he's in Rotterdam. This is Arthur Jackson," she continued, to the seated drivers as she cleared up their breakfast plates. "He's new, on his first trip. Ron Daly brought him over from Europoort yesterday. So now you all know each other. Full English for you, Mr Jackson?" she enquired as she swept out of the room not waiting for an answer.

"You with Pars?" Greg asked as I sat down opposite him.

"Yes, first trip so I'm learning the ropes," I replied.

"Ron's a good bloke he'll see you right," Greg affirmed. "We don't see him a lot. I spend two nights a week here tipping and reloading. Regular run, outbound with air conditioning trunking and usually backloaded with vehicle parts. But Ron pops in for coffee then we don't see him again. I don't know why he bothers to take a room really!" He winked knowingly at Jim. It seemed that Ron's domestic arrangements were well known to the driving fraternity.

"He might get kicked out in the middle of the night?" Jim suggested. "Anyway he's a jammy bugger whichever way you look at it."

"Ah well, whatever," Greg sighed. "Time we hit the road if we're going to catch the 15:30 ferry from Zeebrugge. Take care of yourself Arthur, and don't believe everything that Ron tells you. He'll get you into trouble in no time."

"Or into the special diseases section at the hospital," Jim added as they both left the room. I could hear them settling up with our landlady in the lobby. Then the front door opened and banged shut and they were gone leaving me with a few things to think about. It appeared that life over here could be quite colourful. I was new but not too wet behind the ears to be on my guard against allowing situations to get out of control.

Mrs Vermeiren glided back into the room with a tray containing bacon, tomato and eggs, toast, butter and marmalade which she carefully laid out in front of me. "You can thank Greg for the bacon" she said. "Brings it over to me every week regular. Can't buy it here try as I might. I want to make you boys feel at home and this," she gestured to the bacon. "Does help. Tea or coffee?"

"Oh, tea please," I said.

"That's one thing you can buy here," she said. "Liptons mainly. If there's one thing that reminds me of home back in Winchester, it's a simple thing like tea. There's Friday's *Mirror* on the table if you'd like a read." She rustled back out of the room, her skirts brushing the chairs and sideboard as she left. Too old for me, I thought, but in her day she must have been quite a catch. The only thing that interested me in the *Mirror* was Garth. Lumiere was still being held prisoner by the Androids but Garth was getting closer and it looked as though the next issue might have news of his protracted rescue. There was also a Dutch paper on the sideboard, *Algemeen Dagblad,* but apart from a photograph of the Beatles it was all double Dutch to me!

Once I'd finished the toast and marmalade I moved over to one of the easy chairs and watched Mrs Vermeiren clearing the table and generally tidying up.

"How did you settle in Rotterdam?" I asked her.

"Oh!" she said with an audible sigh. "That was the war you see. Jan, that's my late hubby, had been in the Dutch army and had managed to escape to England in '43 when things really were becoming unbearable what with the Germans trying to draft the young Dutch men into their own army and the problems with the Jews disappearing and his friends in the resistance. He'd been a driver in the army and eventually joined a resistance group escorting some British bomber crew I think. He never spoke all that much about it. Anyway, he was driving a stolen ambulance with the crew in the back, I learned just a few years ago from one of his old friends. They had arranged a rendezvous with a canal boat. Someone had given their game away to the local Gestapo and they got badly shot up. Jan was quite badly injured but his mates gave as good as they got and the airmen and a couple of the resistance managed to get away. The others were killed but they say that all of that German patrol were dead. Anyway, they got them all through down to Antwerp, God knows how, and from there they escaped on a fishing boat and over to England. Jan finished up in my hospital, I was a nurse by the way, and we fell in love."

I could see a tear forming in her eye. "What a wonderful story," I said. "And after the war you came over to Holland?"

"Yes," she replied. "Jan made a reasonable recovery but his injuries left him with a limp for the rest of his life and of course he only had the one lung but that was OK. His family were still here, father and mother survived the war and they were comfortably off. This was their house. So we settled here, Jan ran a small taxi company and we were very happy. He died a few years back, the war injuries didn't help, my folks in England were gone so I had nothing to go back to and I had made quite a few lovely Dutch friends so I decided to stay here and this little B&B has supported me quite well." One thing I had learned was never to take people at face value or to judge to easily. Everyone had baggage accumulated and most had wonderful tales to tell if only you took the trouble to ask and more importantly to listen.

"Would you like some coffee?" Mrs Vermeiren enquired as she picked up some old magazines.

"Yes please," I answered. "Why not?"

On her return, just as she was placing the coffee pot, the cup and the milk on the table, Ron walked in through the door. "See you've made yourself at home," was his greeting.

Not half as much as you have, I thought to myself!

"Doris looking after you?" he asked.

"Coffee, Ron?" Doris enquired somewhat wearily as she placed my one in front of me. I got the impression that she didn't approve of Ron's weekend activities.

"Yes please, Doris." Ron said, sitting down opposite me. "Good night at the Big Ben?"

"Great," I said. "A few beers and I met a real character, road boss for a heavy haulage outfit."

"Not 'Press on Pantin'?" Ron smiled. "He's in De Beers almost every month. Great guy but does he go on!"

We had a pleasant coffee together. Ron didn't say a thing about Vlaardingen but we talked about the company and what I'd be doing.

"You'll be your own boss once they've given you instructions. Always follow them to the letter," Ron advised. "If they're wrong, it's their fault. If you misinterpret them it's yours! Anyway, you choose your routes and so long as you make reasonable progress there'll be no complaints. They don't nitpick and so long as your expenses look genuine," he winked at me, "they'll pass them."

The rest of Sunday was very pleasantly spent in several bars in town and Ron gave me a tour of the fleshspots to boot. "Don't even think about it," he laughed spying me ogling a particularly attractive "model" standing in a window dressed in the almost standard black stockings, suspenders and a wispy negligee. "They don't look half so good once they step out of that special lighting. They'll fleece you for everything you've got in your wallet and you'll probably end up with something even the NHS will have difficulty sorting out," was his wise counsel.

After breakfast on Monday morning, we paid our bills and Doris waved us off in the Mack, hoping, she said, to see us again soon. I drove back out on the Europaweg to Europoort and once again the stench of chemicals and smoke permeated the cab. Looking down to the left from the dyke I wondered how the Dutch people living in those clean and tidy little villages along the neat shiny canals must have felt about this monstrosity foisted upon them. "Most of them work either in the docks or the refineries," Ron reckoned. "I guess it's a bit of a trade-off. They get well paid but have to put up with the pollution."

We arrived at the offices of Hudig and Pieters by 9:30. René was there and we were soon sitting at his desk with our cups of fragrant hot coffee steaming in front of us. He had a thick batch of interleaved papers and carbons in his typewriter and was busily typing with two fingers. As he typed I could hear in the background a throaty diesel roar and looking out of the window saw the unmistakable outline of a Mack pulling a 40 foot blue container behind it swinging into the service road. "Must be Ian," Ron said. "No one else is due." The Mack parked up behind Ron's tractor and I could see a lanky figure jump out cradling a briefcase. Within a couple of minutes Ian strode into the office. Ian was tall, over six foot I would think and he wore a peaked bus driver's cap which added to the impression of height which itself was augmented by the fact that he was quite skinny. His face was long and ruddy, pitted with the remnants of smallpox and the indents in his cheeks gave an impression of someone who either starved himself or perhaps chain smoking had killed his appetite. Indeed a cigarette now hung from his lips and he took a deep breath, inhaled the smoke, and removed it from his mouth stubbing it out in the Transport Ferry Services ashtray on René's desk. He was dressed in a black denim jacket under which was a blue denim shirt with a remarkably frayed collar, and the regulation set of dirty blue jeans set off with a pair of brown Doc Martens.

"You've had a good run," Ron remarked. "How d'you get here so fast?"

"Cross country," Ian smiled putting a finger to the side of his nose indicating trade secrets it was better not to enquire about.

He opened his briefcase and pulled out a wad of papers which he handed to René. "Have I got time for a cup of coffee with these jokers or do I need to get the container off for it to catch the ferry?" he asked.

"Stop for coffee," René said. "It's booked on tonight's ferry. We weren't expecting you until this afternoon at the earliest."

"Anything for me to take back?" Ian enquired.

"No sir," René answered. "Nothing scheduled from U.K. this week and no loadings on the telex."

"So what's all the rush for?" Ian demanded. "I might as well have taken my time instead of busting a gut through the back doubles."

"That's Gerd," Ron observed. "There's no 'take it easy' as far as he's concerned."

René whisked the paperwork out of his typewriter and removed the carbons before distributing the copies among four filing trays. Then he took the top two copies over to a dock runner on the far side of the office who scurried out with them. Returning to his desk and the trio of Pars drivers, he turned to Ian.

"Sugar and creamer?" he asked.

"Sure thing please," Ian affirmed and René turned on his heel and marched off to the kitchen. On his return with the coffee he also had a roll of telexes for Ron. Ron glanced through them and started to sign each one off. "Nothing to load," was his comment as he handed back the roll to René. "Looks like you two are marooned here for a bit. Once we've finished our coffee we'll go and look at the new batch of Pitt trailers and check them over while Ian takes his container down to the terminal."

"Ah, Mr de Smet, good morning," René stood to shake the hand of a smartly dressed newcomer. "He's the big boss," he explained to me.

"Another new boy?" Mr De Smet asked in a thick Dutch accent. "All you boys do is sit around in my office and trink my coffees." A dapper if slightly plump figure, Ronnie de Smet stood about 5 foot 5 inches in his highly polished two tone brown black shoes. His dark grey business suit was pinstriped and he wore what looked like a Royal Engineers striped tie and an immaculately ironed light blue shirt. His face was round and again slightly but not overly plump. His ruddy complexion I put down to the rounds of golf he allegedly played while his minions were hard at work. "Well," he continued, extending his hand to me. "Welcome to, what do you call it? Ah yes, the funny farm!" He laughed loudly as he shook both Ron and Ian's hands. "I've a meeting at 11:30 down at the Botlek so can't stop," he finished, as he turned round and disappeared into his office.

René winked and whispered "Brielle golf course is a better possibility!"

Ian, Ron and I descended in the lift and went our separate ways. I noticed that Ian raced his engine and almost spun his wheels as he took off for the terminal. "He's really pissed off," Ron said. "Driven all the hours God gave and along the old roads to get here and then there's no load for him. Only thing is," he suddenly became serious, "we're all on a weekly wage so whether you're driving or sitting in the Amstel, you're being paid. Don't knock it!!" What Ron didn't mention, and as he was the road boss it was understandable, was that the more miles you got under your belt the more fiddled money there would be but that was to surface later as part of my initiation into the secret rites of the company.

9

Marching Orders

"WE'LL drag your trailer out of the terminal and put a number plate on it. I've got them all in the room at De Beers so we'll risk running without a plate for the few klicks to the hotel," Ron suggested. We climbed up into his tractor and took the service road back up to the Transport Ferry Service terminal reaching the gate just as Ian was moving off to the container offloading area. Ron received a stamped paper from the gatehouse and instructed me to hang a left behind the terminal buildings where there was a large parking area for unaccompanied trailers and next to this were parked various vehicles, trucks, cars and buses waiting for importation into Holland. On the far side of these vehicles, almost at the end of the compound and at the river's edge, were parked the new dark blue Pitt skeletal trailers. I reversed onto the first one and Ron motioned me to stop a couple of feet from it.

"You'll have to get used to this when you drop one of these," he said as we clambered round onto the rear of the Mack chassis. "I'll show you why in a minute. See, we've got two continental air couplings, not three like in England. We always connect them up before backing under the trailers because the manual parking brake won't always hold them and the air reservoir's more than likely to be empty and we're not fitted with spring brakes on the trailers."

Ron connected the two air lines and the electrical susie.

"One more thing sent to try us," he smiled. "These trailers don't have wind up legs. They've got a weird cheap system whereby you knock out a holding bracket and lift each leg manually to the top of its travel. You then put the bracket back in and secure it with a spring loaded retaining clip. It's a mad system. We never had this on the Crane-Fruehaufs." Little was I to know that it was this stupid system that was to be the reason for my only accident involving a fatality but that was to occur a lot later in my career with Pars. Ron jumped down to the ground and I followed him to look at the legs. "We also have to drop the trailers low," he explained. "Once the tractor's underneath, the legs have to be off the ground or you can't lift 'em. They're not too bad while they're new but I've had at least one with a slightly bent leg and the only way to lift it was with a sledge hammer. There's no option really but to get it repaired. First they send us bent drivers then we get bent trailers. Jump up in the cab and reverse under the trailer. Put your trailer park brake on first by the way and don't spare the horses. No great problem when it's skeletal like this but you get a container and 24 tonne load on and you've got to give it some welly!"

I started the motor, pulled back the trailer brake on the right side of the steering column, selected reverse and second split and took my foot off the clutch a bit more sharpish than I should have done. The tractor leapt back and under the trailer and smashed into the pin, locking it on contact. I just saw Ron out of the corner of my eye jumping back as I stamped my foot down on the clutch pedal and applied the brakes.

"Bloody hell, Arthur. I said not so heavy on an

empty trailer!" Ron grimaced as I jumped down from the cab.

"Sorry," I replied. "My foot slipped!" Ron's eyes moved skywards as he motioned me under the trailer and showed me how to lift the legs.

"This is a damn stupid arrangement," he muttered as he twisted the holding pin back on its spring and pulled out the retaining bracket which was not a problem with the legs a few inches off the ground. He then lifted the leg, reinserted the bracket and twisted the holding pin back home. Then he told me to do the other one which went without a hitch. "Hopefully," he said, "there'll be very few occasions when you need to drop the trailer. I can see us having massive problems with these legs. They're just not strong enough for the job, bearing in mind that some of our loads gross out at 44 tonnes."

After securing the fifth wheel safety lock, we both jumped back up into the cab and Ron instructed me to do a circuit of the trailer park with my newly acquired trailer before we risked the open Dutch roads. I moved off in first main and second split and soon had her up into fourth and third. The trailer without its container load looked a lot longer in the mirrors than its actual 40 feet and I was enjoying manoeuvring the rig around the park. "OK," Ron said, "let's take a trip down to Hellevoetsluis. There's a nice bar there, we can get a beer and some lunch." Leaving the trailer park after handing in our paper-work at the gate, we saw Ian's tractor parked up outside the Amstel Inn so we took a left turn down the slip road and drew alongside to find him still in the cab. Ron lowered his window and shouted across to him, "Fancy a beer?"

"Why not?" came the reply and Ian locked up his tractor and joined us in the cramped confines of the cab sharing the passenger seat with Ron, each having one cheek on the cushion!

"No pressure, Arthur," Ron laughed. "Just go right up through the boxes as if you were fully loaded." Ian's face assumed a look of curiosity as he peered directly across the cab at me.

"Sorts out the men from the boys," he commented as I selected first main and third split.

"Tsk, tsk," Ron hissed. "Right through the boxes, Art, and you buy the drinks if you miss a split." Crawler, first main and first split, was a ridiculous gear and by the time we were hurtling along at four miles an hour I was already moving up to second then third then fourth split. Then with both hands off the steering wheel I floored the clutch and selected second main and fourth split. The engine had lost revs so I gave her a little blip and slid the main box in just ahead of the splitter and the revs started to die again. It was either luck or judgement but the dreaded grating didn't occur and the change went smoothly as I retook control of the wheel and almost immediately started up through the splitter box again.

"Very good," Ian nodded. "Ron's on the first round by the look of it!"

So it was right up to sixth main and fourth split and then I could relax and concentrate on the road. I have to admit to a couple of near misses on the jamming front but in essence I was doing alright. I was lucky with the first set of lights which we were able to cruise through at 60ish but the next set pre-dictably were red. I started the change down process and was in fourth main fourth split when they turned to green. Then it was back up through the box and so on until we reached Brielle. Here we turned off the main Europoort drag and onto a country road leading down from the main dyke to Hellevoetsluis. This was the real Holland with small fields surrounded by water filled dykes and linked by rickety wooden bridges some of which were cantilevered to allow barges to pass underneath.

Ron guided me into the old centre of the town and indicated I should park up on the right, outside a hostelry which rejoiced in the name of Cafe de Hommel. We jumped down from the cab, locked up and I gazed at the rig with a kind of satisfied proprietorial air. She looked great and I was proud to be identified as her driver by the clutch of locals sitting inside the bar's windows. I walked in with a certain swagger following Ron and Ian to the bar counter which ran down the right side of the room.

"What're you having?" Ron said.

"An Amstel please," I replied. "Does this mean I did alright?"

"You'll do," Ian smiled.

"Best I've had this week," Ron concurred.

"How many have you had through this week?" I was stupid enough to ask.

"Only you," Ron replied drily.

Cafe de Hommel was a nice homely bar, basically two rooms, the first housing the bar and then a wide archway into a back room where there was a stage with microphones, amps and speakers. I gathered that "Hommel" must be Dutch for bumblebee by the number of depictions of the insect all over the room. The decor was Dutch ancient and modern, lots of browns and beiges, old Dutch Genever adverts, barrel ends stuck to the walls advertising beers, and the archway itself appearing to be clad in raffia!

"Great music bar," Ron said. "Something on every night, trad jazz, blues, rock and roll. Plenty of girls and loads of wacky backy."

Ian sat down beside me at a table against the wall

and opposite the bar. He pulled out a pack of Old Holborn.

"Wacky backy?" I asked.

"Not at this time of day," he laughed as he started to expertly roll a cigarette using only one hand. I expressed my admiration for this feat.

"Ex BRS," explained Ron. "Can't get a job on there unless you can roll up with one hand and steer and change gear with the other!"

"Unless you're Makowski," Ian interrupted. "Uses both hands to roll his spliffs but on the plus side doesn't put either on the steering wheel or the gearstick while he's doing it."

"Who's Makowski?" I asked.

"Oh you'll meet him soon enough," Ron said. "Great guy, never knowingly not spaced out of his brain but one of our best drivers. He's been trunking in the U.K. for the past couple of weeks but he'll be back over here next week. Takes a bit of getting used to but a heart of gold."

"You know what happened at Rainham depot last week?" Ian asked.

Ron rolled his eyes. "Oh God, what's he done now?"

"Trundled in from Glasgow at about 6 a.m.," Ian continued, "after driving non-stop. Parked up on the loading bay and turned in. Warehouse manager tried to wake him at 9. Banged on the door like crazy. No reply. Decided to let him have a bit more shuteye and tried again at 10. Bang, bang, bang on the door, nothing, driver's door locked so he went round to the other side and banged again. This time there was movement. Makowski blearily wound the window half down. 'Yeah what you want?' he muttered. 'You off the bay,' shouted the warehouseman.' Makowski squinted at him and thrust his bearded face through the gap. 'No way,' he announced, 'I'm an orange.' And that was that. He wound the window back up and turned in. So they offloaded him and reloaded him while he slept. He finally turned to at about 4 o'clock. Clambered down from his cab, and without a by-your-leave calmly walked over to the washroom, took his papers to the office, picked up the paperwork for the new load and was gone!"

"Don't know how he gets away with it," Ron said.

"Oh they all think he's a nutter but he keeps his job because he's the fastest and most reliable driver in the company," Ian finished.

After a couple more beers we ordered another round and some cheese and ham sandwiches liberally sprinkled with mayonnaise and with salad even more liberally sprinkled with French dressing.

"Not a bad old life is it?" Ron remarked as he too rolled a cigarette.

"Any idea where we're off to?" Ian asked. "And when?"

"Not a clue mate," Ron replied. "There was nothing on the telex this morning. We'll have a look when we get back to Hudig and Pieters. In the meantime, prost!" he raised his glass and we followed suit.

"Hi boys!" a smart suited Dutchman walked over to the table.

"Meet Theo," Ron said. "He's the owner."

"You coming over tonight. We've got the Dutch Swing College Band. No entry charge. Best jazz band in Holland."

"I'll have to give Elkie a ring," Ron said. "I'm supposed to be taking her and her husband out for a meal."

"Come here," Theo insisted. "I'll buy you a drink." He swung on his heel and left to accost another table-ful of lunchtime drinkers. Being a jazz fanatic, the promise of hearing the best jazz band in Holland had me hooked.

"Think I'll come over if it's alright," I said as we piled back into the Mack.

"You and Ian can get a taxi," Ron suggested.

Back at Hudig and Pieters, Ron discovered nothing on the telex from Salzburg so we took our respective Macks out onto the Europaweg once again in driving rain and into the parking area at De Beer Seaman's Mission. De Beers was one of those late-fifties concrete and brick monstrosities thrown up quickly to fulfil the needs of itinerant seamen whose accommodation had largely been taken out by allied bombing during the war. It was a T-shaped building with all the accommodation in the crosspiece, and the bars, restaurants and lounge in the tail. Reception was at the junction of these two and we entered through large glass and aluminium doors. Ron already had a room permanently reserved by Pars, so Ian and myself were booked in after completing the register and the police papers. The rooms themselves were basic but clean, warm and ensuite. Once I'd arranged my gear and laid out my toiletries in the bathroom, I sauntered back downstairs to find Ron in the lounge.

"Do we have to pay for this?" I asked him.

"No way," he replied. "All on the company account." It turned out that Ron was off to Vlaardingen to his ménage à trois but after dinner Ian and I shared a taxi and Ron set off in another. Watching the Dutch Swing College Band was a great treat. They played all the old standards – Doctor Jazz, Basin Street, St Louis Blues and I was totally absorbed in the music – so absorbed, in fact, that I didn't notice Ian departing with a lady friend until I was buying a beer at the bar in the interval.

"Your friend left," the barman said gesturing

towards the door. "Don't think he'll be back." So I was on my own but in my element with the music and the camaraderie of other jazzers. Later I took a taxi back to De Beers and turned in. At breakfast in the morning, Ron and Ian joked about their performances the previous evening and I filled them in on the performance I had enjoyed, viz the Dutch Swing College Band!

After breakfast we took one truck back to Hudig and Pieters where once again, there were no instructions waiting for us. Ron sent a telex to Salzburg and we drank a couple of cups of the strong coffee before repairing to the Amstel Inn for beer and lunch. So the days passed, endless cups of coffee with René and his boss continually moaning about what our habit was costing him, lunches at the Amstel Inn and evenings for Ron in Vlaardingen and for us in Hellevoetsluis after one of which we did get to an extremely herbal smoky party and it was not until Friday morning that we got our marching orders. Ron held up the telex as we sat once again sipping coffee at René's desk.

"It says both of you are to proceed immediately to Notre Dame de Briancon to load steel for Tehran," he read.

"20 foots or 40s?" Ian asked.

"Doesn't mention containers," Ron replied. "You'll go down there skeletal."

"Are you sure?" Ian asked somewhat incredulously.

"I learnt long ago to follow orders to the letter," Ron said. "Since the time I got a telex with an address in Bamberg which I decided didn't exist so I used my initiative and drove up to Hamburg. After the bollocking I got from Gerhard on that one I don't second guess them any more so skeletal it will be. After all, they know that both of you don't have containers loaded and if they'd wanted you to take any they'd have given us fleet numbers." So that was that. René organised running money for us and handed me my first set of documents in a black plastic document folder. Tryptychs for the tractor and trailer, and permits for France and Germany. That was it.

"You'll get your export documents for the steel at the mill. The agents are Gondrand," he said. "Ian'll look after you. He knows the ropes. Good luck!"

"By the way," Ron interposed. "The telex says that owing to height restrictions you need to travel via Chambéry not through Grenoble." We looked at our maps and Ian traced out the route. Rotterdam to Breda, Antwerp, Brussels, Lille, Paris, Lyon, Chambéry, and Albertville. "We'll be there by tomorrow night," he promised, rolling up yet another cigarette. "I shouldn't worry too much," Ron said. "Loading's not until Monday afternoon."

Back at De Beers we checked out and stowed our gear in the cabs. Ron wished me luck again and I climbed up into the cab just as Ian's smokestack belched black fumes as he revved his truck and swung out of the car park and onto the Europaweg. I followed behind him as close as possible. I had my own maps but I was determined not to lose sight of him as I skip changed up through the boxes. With no weight to speak of, we built up speed quickly and I have to admit to the excitement and a little trepidation welling up inside me as the two Macks and skeletals sped purposefully along the Rotterdam highway to our assignment in the Alps.

10

Les Girls

AND then it started to rain! Just as we breasted the small hill before the Botlek petrochemical conglomeration the heavens opened. Small dashes of splattered water on the split windscreens rapidly accelerated into streams and then rivers as I turned the wipers from slow to fast and watched cascades of water disappear off the edge of the glass. The road ahead glistened and then shimmered with the attack from above and soon we appeared to be sailing on a canal rather than speeding down the Europaweg. Luckily our tanks were full so we were not going to have to stop to refuel just yet but Ian's truck was now slowed to a sensible 30 miles per hour as we traversed this dangerous road knowing that if we touched the brakes too fiercely aquaplaning would all too probably take place. I caught up with Ian at a traffic lights as he slowed down well in advance using his gears sensibly, just briefly touching his brakes to signal to me what he was doing. I had gone down to third main and second split as they changed and we glided safely through the intersection but Ian slowed gently to a halt after the lights and I stopped right behind him on the hard shoulder. In the gloom ahead I could just discern Ian's lanky figure descending from his cab with a coat over his peaked cap protecting him from the worst of the downpour. He ran back and climbed into my passenger side, water streaming off him and dripping onto the floor.

"This is ridiculous," he said. "I was going to hang a right through the back doubles through Spijkenese but I think we'll keep going through to the E19 and if it's still bad there's a small service area about five klicks down the motorway where we can get a coffee while the worst of this blows over."

I looked at my watch and found that it was already 10:30. "How about some food as well?" I asked.

"Good idea," was Ian's riposte as he jumped down from my cab into the unrelenting rainstorm. I watched him run back to his cab and clamber up into it. Seconds later his left indicators were flashing and he pulled straight out onto the highway with me close behind. His taillights all but disappeared in the spray even though he was maintaining a steady 30 miles an hour. A description of the surroundings on either side of the dual carriageway would be errone-ous since it was impossible to see further than a truck length by this time. However, from my previous trip into Rotterdam, I knew we were in an industrial port zone area with warehousing, chemical plants and oil storage facilities and the stench of these entered the cab even through the driving rain!

I did know that a new motorway system was under construction on the right side of the Botlekweg which we were now on. We passed an intersection for Schiedam and as we approached Barendrecht we joined the fledgling motorway, a section of which was now semi-open but heavily coned off and down to one lane. A few kilometres further on was the turning for the E19 southbound with large blue signs across the carriageway for Rotterdam and Utrecht to the left and Dordrecht and Breda to the right. Ian's right indi-cators started winking, he pulled over into the feeder lane for the right turn and I faithfully followed. There was a gentle right turnout and then we were feedering left onto the E19 with our left indicators flashing our intentions to the steady stream of southbound traffic from Rotterdam and the north. Within about five kilometres by the Zwijndrecht exit we came upon a small Shell station whose sign indicated a coffee cup as well as fuel and Ian swung to the right and we both crawled around the back of the fuel station and into a small parking area which luckily just had room for us. We stopped and Ian's lanky figure once again ran back to my cab.

"Bring your map in with you," he shouted as he disappeared into the cafe. Tucking my atlas beneath my reefer jacket I exited the cab, locked up and legged it into the damp steamy warmth of the small coffee shop. While eating our Uitsmijters and drinking our Douwe Egberts, we pored over my map. The route down to Lyons was very straightforward but east of the city, up into the Alps towards Notre Dame de Briancon was a different matter. We had already been told that the route via Grenoble was out because of height restrictions.

"Maybe that only applies if we've got containers on," I ventured.

"Well, don't forget our smokestacks are at least 3.6, possibly even 3.8 metres high," Ian said. "And we don't know where the height problem is. Could be a tunnel or just a bridge but we'd better not risk it."

We also looked at a possible route via Bourg en Bresse but that petered out into questionably narrow and circuitous routes nationales southeast of Anberieu-En-Bugey and then we noticed the Tunnel du Chat with a 7.5 tonne weight limit near the Lac du Bourget north of Chambéry so that was out.

"Looks like Lyon, then hang a left onto the 1006 through Bourgoin-Jallieu, fork right at La Tour du Pin then on this mountain road down to Les Echelles where we hang a left up to Chambéry. Then we take the 1006 again up to Albertville and then the 990 south to Notre Dame de Briancon. That's the only route open to us," Ian finished as he took a final puff from his wafer thin rollup and emptied the last dregs of his black coffee. "Doesn't look quite so bad out there," he remarked. "Let's hit the road!"

It seemed just as bad to me as we jumped into the Macks and fired up the diesels. I set off in second main and third split right behind Ian's smoke belching steed. Within 500 metres he skidded to a halt and I anchored up just in time, clouds of steam emanating from the brake drums. I sat there for a good five minutes wondering what was up, not really wanting to venture out into the inhospitable outdoors. I sat and looked around the cab. In front of me the instrument binnacle with its two main black dials and four ancillary black dials with their brushed chrome surrounds sitting on the black surrounds. The numerals and needles were all in white and very easy to read at a glance. I rested my hands on the large flat three spoke steering wheel coloured green matching the rest of the cabs decor. Lack of power steering was the reason for the size of the wheel, in the middle of which was a silver and black metal Mack Bulldog emblem once again outlined in that same green. On my left, attached to the outside of the driver's door, was a black metal assembly holding the mirror which, owing to the cab not running the width of the chassis, had to jut out a long way as did the one on the passenger side. In fact the step up to the cab was inset in the black fuel tanks on either side. I then looked through the screen at the Mack bulldog sitting on the front of the engine cowling and watched the rain splashing off his chromium plated back. Luckily so far I had not bothered to clean off the transit wax protecting all the brightwork so my little dog mascot was protected from the weather, I was thinking with some degree of satisfaction just as Ian appeared with someone following him. I leaned across the cab and opened the door.

"Couple of hitchhikers want a lift to Paris," he shouted up at me, rain spattering off his peaked cap and the shoulders of his black donkey jacket. "OK if this one rides with you?"

"No problem," I shouted back thinking a bit of company would help to while the hours away, there being no radio in the cab. The hitchhiker climbed gingerly up into the cab and sat down on the seat, pulling a backpack behind which was deposited in the footwell. The door slammed shut and it was at that point I realised that there was a shock of long straggly blonde hair under the sodden hat!

She took off her hat and shook her head and droplets of rainwater jetted all over the cab including onto me. I just had time to note the beautiful hair so suddenly and unexpectedly exposed when Ian's left indicators flashed and he was off. I started the motor, jammed the gears into second main and third split and we were off back into the thronging traffic on the E19. Once I was safely onto the road I allowed myself time to look at the hitchhiker foisted on me by Ian. She was in the course of shedding her dark blue coat.

"Can I hang this up?" she asked.

"Yeah, sure, use the wardrobe," I rather facetiously replied.

"The wardrobe?" she asked. "Where is that?"

I could just see her looking around the cab and taking in what a cramped space we were occupying. She laughed. "Ah, you funny guy eh?"

"There's a kind of hook you could use above the rear window," I said. "See if you can prop it up there."

Taking quick glances to my right I was building up

a picture of this intruder into my workspace and I was rather taken aback. She was stunningly beautiful but not at all in a brash way. She wore very little make-up. She didn't need to. Her features were classically angular with an intelligent countenance, not the vacuous look you get with so many blondes. Her nose was a cross between snub and aquiline and her eye-brows were blonde so presumably she was genuine! I was one of those guys who always wondered why so many blondes dyed their pubic hair brunette. Her eyes were blue and she was wearing a bulky woollen sweater and baggy jeans but you could tell from the way she sat that she was slimly built and I felt that it would be very interesting to find out and her lips looked quite inviting even without lipstick.

"Sorry if I'm in the way," she ventured after I'd said nothing for a good five minutes of concentrating on keeping up with Ian while we negotiated the tunnels at Dordrecht.

"Really," I blustered. "You're not in the way at all. What's your name by the way?"

"Annatje," she replied.

I had to ask her to spell it a couple of times. We exchanged some information about each other as we sped down the motorway. With the weather improving we were soon able to bat along between 60 and 70 miles an hour on the straight flat Dutch roads through the straight flat Dutch countryside. Annatje knew the route quite well so told me about the Hollandse Diep as we traversed the long bridges over the vast expanses of water underneath. On the left were the bridges carrying the north south railway lines, cantilevered steel affairs which boxed in the railway lines and had inclined banks at each end raising the track up to the height needed to allow ships to pass underneath.

"We're now in North Brabant," Annatje announced

as we descended from the last of the bridge complexes. It transpired that she and her friend often hitchhiked their way around Europe on weekend breaks from their jobs as nurses in a Rotterdam hospital. They would aim for a distant destination such as Paris but would settle for somewhere closer if the lifts were few and far between, so long as they could return for work on Monday morning. With us they'd hit gold since we could take them all the way. Normally they did not like to be split up and they had taken some convincing from Ian but the size of his cab had meant that the two of them couldn't be transported in any degree of comfort and the relentless rain had decided the matter as they didn't want to continue hitching.

"Also you are English so we can trust you," she explained. I didn't quite know how to take this. Luckily she had no idea that she had sent my pulses racing. Her Dutch accent with its slight American intonation was a turn-on alone without the additional pleasure of actually enjoying the way she looked.

The uninteresting flatlands of southern Holland were starting to give way to some lightly wooded areas on either side as we passed Breda and Ian turned into the freight section of the customs at the Hazeldonk border, cruised straight through the parked lines of trucks and came to a halt at a lowered gate at the far end of the compound. A customs officer approached him and I could see Ian gesturing back to his skeletal trailer and then to my truck. The barrier was raised and Ian sailed through. I gingerly followed him and was ready to stop but the customs officer waved me straight through so I followed Ian back onto the E19 under gantries reading Anvers-Antwerpen. The route from the frontier down to Antwerp was very similar to the Dutch terrain, wooded areas on each side giving way to flat feature-less farmland enclosed by dykes as we approached the city. We then came to a huge intersection with signs for Antwerpen Haven and exits for various groups of quays in the port area. Ian expertly negotiated his way through and seemed to be heading for the Kennedy Tunnel, putting us on the Antwerp ring road which mid-afternoon was just starting to get busy. Soon we were heading in a constant stream of traffic in about five or six lanes on occasions and then we started the descent into the mouth of the tunnel under the river Schelde and about ten kilometres further on Ian swung right into a BP station and we parked side by side, Ian on my left in the parking lot. Looking out of my window I could see the other hitchhiker descend from Ian's cab and they both came over.

"We're going to get a coffee," Ian said. "And the girls are going to decide what they're going to do apparently," he smiled and winked and the four of us walked over to the restaurant building on the right side of the parking. This modern concrete block was a long flat roofed affair with the main restaurant facilities on the first floor, a large shopping area at ground level and toilets in the basement to which we all thankfully repaired.

"I've drawn the short straw," Ian complained as he dried his hands after washing. "Katya's very nice but you've got the looker."

"Beginners luck?" I joked as, after tipping the concierge lady, we made our way up the stairs to the restaurant. This was arranged in small booths with high-backed bench seating upholstered in red leatherette but surprisingly comfortable. Katya and Annatje joined us and Ian ordered up coffees and croissants. Katya was a bubbly vivacious and not unattractive girl, slightly dumpy but not overly so. Her dark hair was parted in the middle and fell to shoulder length, and her brown eyes sparkled with fun.

"Katya reckons she'd like to come down to the Alps with us," Ian announced. Annatje gave her friend a withering look and then initiated a somewhat heated conversation with her in Dutch.

"Katya thinks we should take a week off," Annatje explained turning to me. "But we have to be at work on Monday and it won't look good on our records if we both call in sick."

"Personally speaking, Annatje, I would love you to come down to Notre Dame de Briancon with us," I said. "But don't forget we won't be coming back the same way. We're off to Germany and Austria so you'd have to come back without us."

I could have kicked myself for saying this. Annatje was someone I could really fall for and I could feel myself in the first instances of that stupidity but I knew we had to play fair with the girls. It was Ian's turn to give me a withering look and the girls launched into another intense conversation in Dutch while we sipped the hot coffee and munched the warm croissants and Ian rolled yet another cigarette with one hand which impressed the girls.

"The problem is," Annatje said looking directly into my eyes which I found extremely disconcerting, mine are grey green and I thought what a good match they would make if they were merged with her vivid blue ones, "Katya is a staff nurse and I'm in charge of a ward so it's easy for her to take off a 'sick' week but I'm supposed to be more responsible." She said this with a naughty smile and I got the feeling that her resolve might be wavering.

"From here to Paris will take about four to five hours depending on the traffic," Ian interposed. "Why don't you girls have a think about it and make a decision at our next stop."

There was another furious conversation in Dutch

and Katya said, "OK that's a good idea. If it was me I would come with you. A weekend in the Alps sounds fun. Maybe we could get some skiing. But Annatje is my boss so I have to do what she decides." I smiled at Annatje and she smiled back, a secret, shared, rather wicked smile just for me, I thought!

11

Decisions! Decisions!

AFTER our coffee and croissant stop, we re-joined our trucks to find the rain had almost stopped and this time I accompanied Annatje round to the passenger door which I unlocked with my key and helped her up into the cab – any excuse to get my hands on her! What I did get my hands on were the layers of soft clothing sheathing what I guessed would be an exquisitely feminine body underneath. I could smell her delicate perfume and her leg brushed my face as she mounted the steps. When I sat down in the unsprung driver's seat, she was in the process of hanging her wet coat up on the hook by the rear window.

"Katya is crazy," she said. "Did you see the way she was looking at Ian? She gets herself into stupid scrapes. She doesn't think about what she's doing. I think we must leave you in Paris. Do you know the Boulevard Périphérique?"

I shrugged. "My first trip," I explained.

"I'm sure Ian knows it," she replied. "If you can drop us off on the east side at the Porte de Montreuil we have some friends who live near there on Rue Belgrand. We can walk. It's not too far."

"I can't see a problem," I said. "But I really hope to see you again sometime. Maybe the next time I return to Rotterdam."

"That would be really nice," Annatje said smiling at me. "I'll give you the phone number of my apartment.

At the moment I'm on my own there," she finished with what I took to be a quite meaningful tone in her voice. However I could see another problem to my left in Ian's cab. Two heads were perilously close together.

Annatje saw it too. "Gott verdoemen, she is so crazy," she whispered through clenched teeth. On my left above the window was the cord to my twin airhorns. I pulled it and a loud blast was emitted throughout the parking area. The two heads separated and, smiling out of the window, Katya shook her fist at me as Ian blasted his air horns, started his motor and pulled out to the left smoke billowing from his stack. I followed him closely back out into the early afternoon E19 traffic.

"You're very busy driving this truck," Annatje remarked. She had been observing my constant gear changing using two splits on each main as we were empty which meant eight changes up to sixth main and fourth split from starting in second main and third split. By now I could knock both sticks out of gear with my right hand but needed both hands off the steering wheel to put them back in. As well as this I was constantly checking the offside and nearside mirrors and keeping an eye on the air and oil pressure gauges.

"It's not like driving a car," I observed. "Cars drive themselves nowadays especially if you've got cruise control. With a truck you've got to be on top of the situation all the time. One mistake and something really serious can result."

"That's what I tell Katya," Annatje laughed.

We were humming along at 60 now on the newly dried out road and I had time to note the names of some of the passing trucks – Wim Vos, Rijnaart, a lot of Norfolk Lines and some English Chris Hudson trailers pulled by various Dutch and Belgian tractors. Once again the terrain was very low country and we passed signs for St Niklaas, Gent/Gand Nord, Centrum and Zuid, and Oostende. We were following the signs for Lille and just before that conurbation Ian pulled into the freight area at the French border near Courtrai. We parked up and Ian and Katya sauntered over with what I took to be a rather jaunty air, full of the joys of spring no doubt.

"We've got to take our papers into the agent for entry to France," he said. "We use Frans Maas at this border so bring your folder with you. Shouldn't take too long."

Katya climbed into my seat, no doubt to confer with Annatje while we were gone. We walked past the lines of parked trucks and through what looked like the frontier divide into a parking area on the other side. On the right of this area were parked a number of old grey and green caravans which turned out to house the offices of the freight agents. There were offices for Kuehne & Nagel, Gondrand, Atramef, SCAC, and eventually we came to that for Frans Maas. Inside there was just room for a couple of tables replete with typewriters, document trays, and sheafs of carbon paper. In the far corner was a telex machine and sundry phones were scattered around the room.

"Good afternoon," Ian said. "Pars International Containers. Two trucks – deux camions – vide."

"Ah, yes, Mr Ian?" one of the clerks rose from behind his desk. "We have a telex from René. You have your triptychs and permits?"

Ian handed his paperwork over and I offered up my file.

"OK, 15 minutes come back and all finished," the clerk said.

"We'll go over to the restaurant and have a look

at the road report," Ian said as we left the caravan. "Getting around Lille ain't easy. They're building a big motorway ring system. Parts of it are finished but sometimes it's faster just to go straight through the town centre. Anyway we'll see." We entered the low concrete block structure situated between the truck parking area and the lanes of the motorway, one end of which housed the customs and passport offices of both the Belgian and the French authorities, and the other a small restaurant and shop, mainly for truckers since the cars only had to stop momentarily for their passports to be checked and a random selection pulled over for a customs control. Even so, you could see that this was leading to lengthy delays and there was quite a long queue of cars, motorhomes, and coaches leading back from the booths.

Inside the building and on the wall in front of the restaurant was displayed a large scale map of the Lille/Tourcoing/Roubaix area with suggested routes mapped out to cater for trucks heading down to Paris, or east to Luxembourg and Brussels or west to Dunkerque or Calais. The motorway to Tournai was semi-operational but that landed you too far to the east and you were doing two sides of a triangle to get back onto the Paris road, Ian explained. It looked as though we were going to have to follow the Route Nationale to Tourcoing and then get on the Lille inner ring.

"Don't worry," Ian said. "Just follow me and you won't go wrong. By the way," he continued, pointing his latest smoking roll-up at me, "don't discourage the girls from coming all the way with us. We'll have a fun weekend and I'm not above bringing them back up to Paris on our way back. Also Katya said that Annatje reckons you're alright so you're in there as well."

I started to protest, pointing out that they were really nice girls, not just roadside pickups but Ian stopped me.

"First trip, you've got a lot to learn," he finished, as we made our way back over across the French side parking lot to the Frans Maas caravan.

"All finished. Allez, mes amis," the freight clerk smiled as we entered. "Just get your passports stamped."

The passport office was at the extreme right hand end of the customs building complex but, as we didn't have the girl's passports, we had to walk back to our trucks on the Belgian side. Katya had returned to Ian's cab and as I jumped up into the driving seat I could see that Annatje was not looking particularly happy. Ian's truck moved off down the centre of the lines of trucks and I followed.

"You've not had a row have you?" I said.

"Yes," Annatje explained furiously. "I told her I'm her boss and we have to get back to Rotterdam for Monday morning. We're both due on shift at 2 o'clock. She of course mentioned that I'm only her boss in the hospital. Outside we're just friends although not so much at the moment." She gave a wry smile.

"Don't worry," I said as the two trucks came to a halt outside the passport office. "I'll make sure we drop you off at the Porte de Montreuil."

Annatje smiled a conspiratorial smile. "You're a nice guy," she replied.

"I know," I said. "Unfortunately girls normally go for the nasty guys." I crossed round to the passenger side and opened her door.

"Really?" she said as she slid down from her seat and I momentarily held her in my arms. "You're not right at all." And she gave me a very brief kiss on the cheek!

After passport control and a knowing wink from the French passport officer at the two truck drivers with the two Dutch girls, we were back out on the motorway. Ian took the first exit signed Roubaix and we were immediately onto an old stretch of cobbled road which shook the life out of us but this turned back into tarmac and we were in the suburbs, quite heavily trafficked, and then a stretch of dual carriageway and the south western part of the new ring road which led us all the way to the A1 autoroute. Once back on the open road I was able to relax as we passed signs for Douai and Arras and Annatje started to tell me about herself. Her parents lived in Reuwijk which was a small town near Gouda where there were lots of lakes with sailing and fishing. She had matriculated at the high school and attended university in Haarlem. After university she had gone straight into nursing which she loved and was pursuing a career which she hoped would end with her becoming the Dutch equivalent of a hospital matron. She had no boyfriend at the moment and preferred being a free spirit. She didn't like one night stands and never went to bed on the first date as a matter of principle.

"Do you think sex is part of love?" she asked. "Or just a physical pleasure of the moment?"

"Well, it's certainly pleasurable," I affirmed, "but it's much better with someone you can really relate to." I could see us getting into a philosophical discussion here but the subject was appealing especially when it was being discussed with such a beautiful companion.

"Everything in Holland is very free," she continued. "I think it's too free. We have drugs, we have sex shops. Anything you want but no one thinks about the price you pay. I see the drug addicts with their wrecked bodies in the hospital. The highs they got cost them more than they know. They don't die from the drug, although some do, but from diseases their bodies can no longer fight. And the sex. It's great for men but we have to live with the results. The diseases, the babies, the abortions. Life for women is unfair I think."

"You're right," I agreed. "But I'd hate to go back to what we call the Victorian era where everything was hidden below the table and there was so much hypocrisy, lying, and also exploitation. They say it's bad enough now with the rich capitalists exploiting the workers but at least in western Europe it's paradise when you think of the child labour, prostitution and illnesses which used to exist."

At this moment I glanced in my mirror to see a flashing blue light back in the distance and soon we were being overtaken by a police car and a couple of ambulances.

"Oh dear. That doesn't look good," I remarked.

"Probably an accident," Annatje said and almost instantly the traffic was slowing and within a couple of kilometres we had ground to a complete halt next to an exit sign which read Exit 12, Roye, Noyon, Soissons.

Our conversation continued and Annatje told me she was 26 years old, had once been engaged but had luckily been able to call the whole thing off when she caught her fiancé in flagrante with a friend. She loved working in the hospital although it did get very hot in the summer.

"Sometimes we wear nothing under our uniforms," she announced rather unexpectedly and without any consideration whatever for my blood pressure. Why was she telling me these intimate details? I wondered. Either she was a tease or she was just being friendly and exchanging information or was it a come-on?

Once again she had my pulses racing when, after talking about her apartment which had a nice comfortable lounge, a large bathroom which was unusual she maintained, and a big bed.

"I can't sleep in a small single bed," she explained. "I like to move around and also I don't wear anything at night. Do you?" she asked looking at me with such an innocent face that I burst out laughing.

"You," I said, looking straight into her deep blue eyes, "are too much. But just for the record, no I don't wear anything in bed either."

"Why not?" she asked once again with the feigned air of innocence.

"Because it saves time," I answered. She laughed and I turned towards her. "One day I would really like to get to know you," I said once again gazing into those infinitely deep eyes. I was just about to kiss her deeply, intensely and longingly when she said softly, "We're moving." I looked through the screen and saw that Ian was already 50 metres ahead.

"Damn," I expleted as I quickly brushed my lips against hers, as soft as I had expected and every bit as yielding. My heart was pounding as I turned the key, switched the engine on and bumpily managed to take off in second main and fourth split. Once we were cruising again I felt her hand extend to touch mine and we remained like that for some long time communicating physically rather than verbally.

It was now pushing 5 o'clock and I reckoned we had another couple of hours before we reached Paris. We did not see what had caused the delay, presumably whatever wreckage there might have been had been cleared up. About an hour later we turned into the Elf services just after the exit for Compiegne. Ian pulled up next to a rank of trucks on the right and I deliberately joined the parked trucks on the left.

The airbrakes hissed as I lifted the park brake button, pulled the engine stop and took my foot off the clutch pedal. Within seconds I was locked in an inseparable embrace with Annatje and our lips met and melded and the strength of her passion vibrated through me. How long we remained thus I do not know but Ian pounding on one door and Katya on the other roused us from our reverie.

"To be continued," I smiled at Annatje.

"Soon," she replied. I knew why Ian had stopped. Apart from the constant requirement for coffee, there was an important decision to be made by the girls. Were we to have their delightful company for the weekend or were we soon to part, perhaps never to see each other again?

12

Denouement

"WE'LL see you in the restaurant," I yelled as I opened and quickly shut my window. I watched as Ian and Katya made certain gestures in our direction and then turned back to give Annatje another kiss which we shared and enjoyed for a few minutes until she broke away.

"We must go in," she protested. "This is a bad example I set for Katya!" She was firmly in my arms now and my pulses were racing but I could see that she was adamant so I kissed her nose and forehead again, her blonde hair swishing across my face as we disentangled.

"I hope we meet again," I said.

"I hope so," Annatje replied. "You are a nice guy and I like your kissing very much."

I was near the top of the world as hand in hand we walked across the parking lot to the restaurant opposite the filling station complex. On entering I could see a look of triumph on Ian's face. He obviously thought that his seduction of Katya was going to succeed and that Annatje would now be in agreement about accompanying us all the way. His current roll-up was half smoked and he placed the burning remains in a Perrier branded ashtray in the centre of the table. The restaurant was busy with weekend tourists journeying to Paris and a few truck drivers dotted around conspicuous by their overalls or donkey jackets contrasting sharply with the casual attire of the tourists. There were about 30 or so tables, some seating four and some seating six arranged on each side of the oblong shaped room at the far end of which was a bar area with a few high seats for inveterate drinkers including a couple of autoroute employees in their dark blue overalls. We were positioned right in the middle of the room and as I sat down with Annatje on my right side, Ian gave me a conspiratorial wink. I had a feeling he was going to be sorely disappointed. Annatje was a feisty young lady and I reckoned that her mind was made up. She was a professional career girl and was not likely to put that career in jeopardy by going absent without leave, especially as her story would look pretty suspicious when allied to that of her friend on the same shift in the same ward at the same hospital. For myself I would be overjoyed if she decided to spend the weekend with us but as the song says, "I fall in love too easily", and there was no way that I wanted to compromise the future of this delicious woman, for whom I had developed a great degree of respect, just to extend my pleasure of the moment. There would be plenty of time in the future to meet again in Rotterdam or elsewhere. On the other hand, a bird in the hand is worth two in the bush and there had been similar previous occasions where I had gambled on the future and lost.

It's amazing how, looking back, memories are jogged not so much by facts and timelines or even events, but often by smells, tastes or even music which evokes the atmosphere of the moment. I knew that Ian was about to initiate a discourse on a certain subject and I was frankly feeling happy about whichever way it would turn out. I had sitting next to me an incredibly attractive member of the opposite sex with whom I had found I could converse for hours on end. Her smile, the faint aroma of her perfume which I later found to be *L'Air du Temps*, the smell of roasting coffee wafting through every time the kitchen door opened blowing a draught of warm clammy air through the room, and a piquant hint of aniseed or liquorice from the aperitifs, underlined the moment. What was playing on the jukebox I can't remember but it was almost certainly Johnny Hallyday or Sylvie Vartan. I have to confess that I was feeling quite happy and relaxed and convinced that the life of a continental truck driver was the "right one I had chose!"

"I'm going to phone Ron," Ian announced. I was just wondering if Ian was going to request Ron to arbitrate with the girls when he explained "He'll be at Hudig and Pieters right now and I'll check out the loading times." Ian disappeared through a side door which had a telephone symbol on the window. I now had my sophisticated Annatje on my right and the impetuous fun-loving Katya on my left. Annatje was glaring at Katya and Katya was glaring defiantly back.

I was just about to excuse myself, when Annatje said, "Katya I'm really sorry but I at least have to be back for our Monday shift. Arthur is going to drop me off at Porte de Montreuil. If you wish you can stay with Ian. All I'd point out is that although I'll cover for your story, you'll have quite a job to get back from the Alps. It's going to add at least another day or two to your journey and you may end up having to catch the train."

Katya then lapsed into a tirade in Dutch at the end of which Annatje calmly looked at her and said, "Please, Katya, speak in English so Arthur can understand you."

"All I'm saying," Katya somewhat resignedly and shamefacedly explained, "is that I'm not going to leave Anna but we've both got first class records at the hospital and maybe we can make up another story, not about us being sick but we could get stranded or something. Maybe have our money stolen. I don't know. Maybe we got lost or the person who gave us a lift forced us to travel further than we wanted," she finished lamely.

"That's not exactly what you said, Kat," Annatje interposed. I looked at the two girls. Annatje looked naturally beautiful snuggled in her thick polo necked cardigan. She'd have looked stunning in a bin bag I thought. Katya, still slightly dishevelled in layers of clothing under a blue duffel coat, had a different kind of attraction. She was by no means a stunner as Ian had already remarked but she made up for this with her outgoing personality and apparent sense of fun which at this particular moment had left her. Ian returned.

"Got through," he said. "Ron was there. Said there was no further news despite telexes he'd sent to Austria. Said I was to remind you of a Mr Pantin and you'd know what to do."

"Press on," I replied. "Press on!"

Just at that moment sirens were sounding from the autoroute and blue lights could be seen racing southbound.

"Looks like another hold up," Ian remarked as he embarked on another rollup even before his previous one had burned out in the ashtray. "Well," he said licking the edge of the Rizla and smoothing it down between his thumb and forefinger. "Looks like we're stranded here for some time. You girls decided what you want to do?" He looked at Katya with some degree of confidence which I knew was about to be dashed.

"We'd love to come down to the Alps with you but you must understand that we have jobs which are important to us and we can't take the risk that we won't be back for Monday," Annatje said. "Katty wanted to go with you anyway but I think she now sees sense and I pointed out to her that we can all meet again in Rotterdam anyway." Katya was looking down at the table and Ian shot me a glance which showed a degree of annoyance that I had been siding with Annatje.

"You sure?" he said. "We're quite happy to bring you back up to Paris probably by Tuesday or Wednesday."

"Or Thursday or Friday," Annatje interrupted. "Please look at it from our point of view. We just came out hitching for a weekend's fun, not to get involved with a couple of truck drivers." The way she said this with a slightly disparaging tone in her voice stung me, but I thought about the strength of her kisses and knew that she was merely strengthening her negotiating stance with the still recalcitrant Katya.

"So do you want to leave us here and hitch a lift into the centre of Paris?" Ian asked. "Because we take the Périphérique which is some way from the centre."

"I've already suggested to Arthur that you drop us at Porte de Montreuil which should be on your route," Annatje explained. I looked out of the window and through the Elf service station to the autoroute where the traffic was now stationary. Ian was looking crestfallen as the waitress at last came over to our table. I asked her to come back in a couple of minutes and she retired back behind the bar.

"Why did you do that?" Ian asked. "I'm gasping for a coffee."

"Because I have an idea which might suit all of us. The motorway is blocked at the moment. Even if we were to move immediately how long would it take us to get to the Périphérique?" I asked.

"About an hour at least possibly an hour and a half,"

Ian answered, suddenly looking at me a little quizzically. I could see that both the girls were suddenly paying attention. Annatje's eyebrows raised and Katya looked like someone for whom a ray of hope was about to shine through from an unrelentingly gloomy and threatening sky.

"It's now 6:30," I reasoned. "Even if we get going now we couldn't drop you off before about 8 and actually it will probably be 9 or 10 or even later. We all seem to like each other so why don't we check in to the hotel. I'm quite happy to pay for Annatje's room and I'm sure Ian will pay for Katya's." Ian nodded a little gravely just starting to take in what I was trying to organise. "Then once we're checked in we can all have some drinks and a good meal. In the morning the motorway should be clear and we can run you straight into Paris after breakfast," I finished.

I looked around the table as the idea began to sink in. I knew that what Ian really wanted above all was to get Katya into bed. I wasn't sure what Katya wanted. She was a little fun bundle and probably just up for a good time. Her outlook on life seemed to be a devil-may-care existence with no sense of responsibility. She needed someone with sense and a bit of foresight to guide her and protect her from the calamities which would so obviously be strewn across her path and she had certainly found that someone in Annatje. And what of Annatje? She was out for a fun weekend but not at any cost. She was someone who weighed things up in her mind before taking action. Someone who would check the swimming pool to ensure it was full of water before she dived in. I looked at her now and gave her a questioning smile.

"I can pay for my own room," she asserted. "And if Katya agrees she can share it."

First of all, that seemed like a good compromise because the girls would not feel beholden to us and I knew that Annatje would not want that scenario. Second, and most importantly it also meant that the girls would have dinner with us and we had the prospect of a convivial evening ahead.

"Maybe you should check that they have rooms available," Annatje suggested, so, as I spoke some French, I volunteered to walk over to the Novotel and investigate. Outside, darkness was fast descending but the air was clear and there was no sign of the torrential rain we had suffered earlier in the day. I turned right outside the restaurant complex and headed through the car parking area towards the hotel which was perched at the far edge of the service area. Looking over to the autoroute on my left I could see signs of movement in the traffic but it was still wall to wall as far as the eye could see southbound towards Paris.

The hotel itself was a two storey, white, featureless structure which looked as if it had been prefabricated and re-assembled on site, room by room. On the top was a huge Novotel sign in neon blue and at the left side on the ground floor was a sign also in neon blue which announced the reception. I entered and rang a bell at a small desk situated at the right of the room. A door opened behind and a middle aged woman emerged.

"Est ce que vous avez des chambres libres?" I asked in halting schoolboy French.

She looked me up and down. "You are English?" she asked, a little haughtily I thought, but it was probably just her French intonation.

"Qui nous voulons trois chambres pour la nuit s'il vous plait," I explained once again somewhat haltingly.

"I speak English a little," the lady replied. "But sorrowfully we have no rooms. It is Friday. The traffic is great and the accident sent more people."

"Merci, Madame," I said resignedly. "À bientôt!"

"À bientôt," she replied as she vanished back into her office. "Et bonne route."

Ian and Katya looked up expectantly as I sat down.

"No luck I'm afraid, they're full," I said raising my eyebrows as I looked at Annatje who I have to say had a look of relief on her face. Katya on the other hand was crestfallen.

"On the bright side," I said, attempting to breathe some lightness into the suddenly depressed mood. "The traffic has started to move. Why don't we have a meal anyway and we'll drop you off at Porte de Montreuil." Ian appeared to be quite put out but it was now obvious that the girls, very sensibly in my view, were not coming down to Notre Dame de Briancon with us and I wanted to reinforce Annatje's decision before Ian could come up with any further blandishments via Katya. The waitress returned at this juncture and asked if we were ready to order. I asked her for the menu as we decided on beers for us, red wine for Annatje and white wine for Katya.

After what can only be kindly described as an interesting initiation into French motorway cuisine – patés, crudités, steaks frites, côtes de porc and some tartes tatins which were actually quite good – we finished the meal with cafes crèmes and repaired back to the trucks. I could see Ian and Katya indulging in some pre-journey intimacy silhouetted by the headlights of passing cars as they entered the parking area. I turned to Annatje.

"I'm so sorry, I would have loved to spend the night with you. One day, not today obviously, not tomorrow, maybe not even next week but soon I want to really express how I feel about you," I breathlessly stuttered as our mouths met and my hands held her far too generously clad body tight.

"In bed do you mean?" she asked, once again flashing me that look of complete innocence that would have wrecked the defences of a weaker spirit.

"In bed, out of bed, in the garden, up against a wall. You've got through to me but unlike Ian, I'm happy to wait because I think there is something genuine between us, not just lust," I finished, once again cuddling her tightly.

"Oh," she said. "I don't think anyone spoke to me like that before."

"Not even when you were engaged?" I asked incredulously.

"I'll tell you a secret," she confided, as her lips continued to pepper little kisses across my face. "I was still virgin when I broke it off."

"Maybe that's why he slept with your friend," I suggested jokingly as I started up the engine, and slipped the gears into second main and third split.

"Maybe," she said thoughtfully, "but it was for the best."

We followed Ian back out onto the autoroute which was now completely clear again and soon we were traversing the tunnels under Charles de Gaulle Airport, a 707 taxiing overhead as we entered the first of them. I kept glancing at Annatje.

"Thanks, Arthur," she said, "for backing me up with Katya. She was really stupid if she thought we could just take a week off like that."

"I know," I replied. "I would have loved to have your company for a few days but the time will come."

After Charles de Gaulle we were fast approaching the Paris suburbs. I saw a sign for Le Bourget airport and then the autoroute, which by now had four or five lanes on each side, was plunging through a series of long underpasses and the signage was becoming confusing. Signs flashed by for Le Havre and Dieppe and traffic was leaving and joining at an alarming rate but Ian appeared to be steadfastly hugging the second lane and then he switched to the third lane apparently guided by Porte de la Chapelle signs. A kilometre further on there appeared a blue sign for Périphérique Est above the Port de la Chapelle sign and it was obvious that Ian knew what he was doing. There was a complicated junction as we passed under an interchange and then a marked left turnout onto the legendary Paris ring road. Views of central Paris there were none, just the lights from countless apartment blocks and neon lit industrial states with their advertising signs glaring out of the gloom. Porte de La Villette, Porte de Pantin interestingly enough, Porte des Lilas, Porte de Bagnolet and then the sign I was dreading, Porte de Montreuil. We exited the Périphérique down a steep hill on the slip road and onto a large roundabout. Ian managed to stop after the turn into Rue d'Avron and I came to a halt behind him. I jumped down and walked round to the passenger door as Annatje was gingerly clambering down the steps with her small rucksack. We embraced and she pushed every curve of her body into me as we kissed giving me all sorts of clues as to what she would look like without her bulky clothes on. Eventually we had to break off and Ian and Katya joined us.

"Well you know what the French say when lovers part," I whispered into Annatje's deliciously soft ear. "Ce n'est pas adieu, c'est au revoir. We'll meet again!" I was also stupid enough to say, "I love you" as Annatje pressed a small piece of paper into my hand, but that's how I felt. Ian and Katya shared a last hug and we watched the two girls disappear down the

Rue d'Avron in the direction of Paris until they had vanished beyond a street lamp.

"Well, that's that," Ian muttered. "Could have had a great weekend."

"Yes," I answered, "but the girls would have had to pick up the pieces. Besides, we'll see them in Rotterdam."

"I forgot to ask Katya for her address," Ian remarked. "Anyway, time to hit the road. It's 9:30, we'll give it another hour or two and park up somewhere like Auxerre." So saying, he gruffly turned on his heel and within seconds smoke was pouring from his exhaust stack once again and I was desperately jamming gears to keep up with him, tears welling up in my eyes. So near and yet so far. I switched the cab light on once we were back on the Périphérique and unfolded the piece of paper Annatje had given to me. On it was written, in clear precise handwriting, her full address and telephone number and, at the bottom, several kisses!

13

Southbound and Down

THE Périphérique was not nearly so busy now and our journey around to Porte d'Italie was an easy one. Once up in sixth main and fourth split I was able to relax a little. The Mack cab was not the world's quietest but the Thermodyne engine was very smooth running, the constant modulated whine from the turbocharger was a comforting sound and now I had got used to the gears there were very few bad changes. The main problem was simply remembering what gear you were in with 24 to choose from. Once you put your hands on the sticks of course you knew where you were, especially as you slipped them into neutral, and then you had to make the decision how many splits to go up or down. With experience you mastered the art of skip changing and even when you missed a gear and the revs had died down or you were descending a hill and the truck's speed had increased more than you were anticipating, you learned how to blip the accelerator or apply the brakes and then blip the accelerator to achieve smooth changes. Right now, I was still a novice and was improving fast but as my old science master would have noted on my school report: "He could do better if he were to apply himself!" The other enjoyable feature was the Mack bulldog mascot sitting on the front of the bonnet, a constant companion through thick and thin. He could be baked by the sun, lashed by the rain or icebound in snow but he never complained. Each journey was almost like taking him for a walk. I'd also ensured the survival of his shiny chrome exterior by my policy of not removing his original factory fitted wax coating.

The A6 south of Paris was a joy at this time of night. What did take a bit of getting used to was the headlights of the cars, most of which, being French, were a kind of yellowy orange, white headlights being forbidden. The weekend traffic deserting the capital had died down, all sensible people having dossed down somewhere for the night already. I was wondering if Ian had a hotel in mind or if we would be cabbing it. Luckily I had my sleeping bag including a washable cotton insert. I had experienced the joys of overnighting at a transport cafe bed and breakfast only once. I had been driving unit only up to Newton Aycliffe to collect a brand new car transporter and had to overnight at a transport cafe with "accommodation" on the A1 north of Leeds. I put accommodation in 'inverted commas' because what it was in fact was a room sleeping around ten drivers farting, snoring, burping and worse through the night. The smell was truly awful, and actual, meaningful sleep scored less than one star. I vowed there and then never to repeat the experience. However, I did a series of trunks as an agency driver for BRS contracted to Thorn Lighting and shared a room with one other driver up near Huddersfield but that was not so bad. What was bad was the amount of time we spent parked up in laybys in order to comply with the TGWU's idea of legal trip times, my first experience of mid-morning and afternoon siestas. Otherwise it was a room of my own or cabbing it which, in those days before sleepers, was apparently technically illegal but it did stand me in good stead for the Mack R600.

By 10:30 we were past the industrial estates and

urban sprawl of the capital and heading down the A6 at a good lick, having stopped to pick up a toll ticket at the péage booth. The next exit was for Montargis but was passed and I was beginning to wonder if Ian would ever stop. I for one could have done with another cup of coffee to keep the old eyelids from drooping. 45 minutes later we pulled into the services just south of Auxerre and parked alongside the rows of other trucks, quite a few of them British, in the truck area. I pulled the parking brake button up and sat with the diesel idling for a few minutes, as I had been instructed by Ron, to allow the turbocharger to cool down and then pulled the stop button. There was a wonderful moment of complete silence broken only by the ringing in my ears and then the gentle hum of traffic on the autoroute cut back in as I opened the door and slid down onto the tarmac. Ian emerged from the dark bulk of his truck.

"Fancy a beer before we turn in," he said. "It's round midnight so too late to book in to a guesthouse."

"OK, just one though," I emphasised. "I'm knackered."

"Help you to sleep," Ian pointed out as we crossed over to the restaurant building.

"Quite a few Brits here," I remarked, noting in passing some Fretitalias, SKIs, SCAs, several Cawthorne and Sinclairs and a lone Scottish Christian Salvesen fridge revving away.

"Quite a few of them park here," Ian said. "It's an easy trunk down from Calais and gives them a good start up Mont Blanc in the morning."

We entered the services and headed for the restaurant once again with its bar which I was surprised to see was still open.

"Closes for beer at midnight," Ian said. "Just have time to get one in so buy two bottles," he winked. He wouldn't accept my offer to buy a round. "Get's too complicated," he said. "Out on the road I always buy me own, then there's no long running dispute about whose turn it is and no one gets a reputation." He touched his nose significantly and turned his attention to the next roll-up as we sat down on the bar stools. The beers came and the barman made a great show of his largesse in allowing us a couple of beers each right on closing time. He slapped the bottles and glasses down in front of us together with the bill.

"Please pay now," he insisted. "I'm just finishing." He then busied himself with a great show of tidying up the bar area round us.

"He's playing for a tip," Ian remarked. "Well Art, what did you think of your first day on the job?"

"To be frank," I said. "It's been great. The truck is fantastic, especially after my old Dodge, I don't have to load and offload, or get soaked chaining down cars in the rain, we've had some fun on the way down and we're on the continent."

Ian laughed. "New boy," he said. "You'll soon get used to it and become as raddled and disillusioned as the rest of us. Little thing I'd better explain," he continued confidentially and dropped his voice. "We get a reasonable wage on this company but what makes it worth all the hardships, long hours and time away from home is the 'extras'." He stopped to see my reaction.

"Go on," I said. I was used to certain fiddles in the U.K. where you could claim for non-existent expenses and non-existent nights out when the motor was actually parked around the corner from the old homestead.

"Well," Ian drew a little closer to reinforce the secrecy of this mystery of the road. "We're lucky because we pay cash for all our fuel. So you get to know, shall we say, the friendly gas stations who're willing to do deals for our custom. There's one down at Mâcon. Basically we fill up with a couple of hundred litres. They invoice us for three hundred and we share the difference."

"Oh," I said. "I'm not sure about that. Seems a bit blatant to me."

"If you're going to stay on the company you'll have to do it mate," Ian said matter of factly. "Otherwise the rest of us start to look stupid. See," he paused looking me over trying to ascertain whether I would comply or, as I later found out, have to be outed from the company, "the office boys in Salzburg are not transport people so they don't figure out miles per gallon or in our case kilometres per litre. One day they may get round to that but they've so much on their plates at the moment what with expanding the company and fulfilling all the loadings they're getting, they don't have time for the, shall we say, fine tuning." I nodded. Frankly I'm no angel and there was no way I was about to upset the apple cart in my new posting. "Anyway, I'll do the negotiating, just follow me in the morning and I'll fix it." Ian finished as he slid off his bar stool, puffing to eliminate his latest roll-up and mulching the remains into a clean ashtray on the bar. The barman tutted, picked it up and disappeared.

Back in the truck I stuffed my suitcase in between the two seats as Ron had shown me so that I had a level bed of sorts, right across the five foot wide cab. I laid my sleeping bag across it and, stripping down to vest and pants, slid into it using my sweater as a pillow. It was best to lie with your head on the passenger seat and your feet on the driver's seat as the steering wheel restricted movement at that end. Even so, it was near impossible to straighten out but as I'm only 5 foot 6 it wasn't that bad. I lay there and

118

thought about the events of the day and especially about the lovely Annatje. Would I ever see her again? I certainly hoped so. She was an exceptional girl. If only there had been rooms in the Novotel things might have been very different. First, I tried to get comfortable on my left side but the case in the middle was jarring against a bone. Then I tried my right side and that was a little better. I then found I could lay on my back relatively straight if I raised my feet up and rested them against the side window. It crossed my mind that in the summer I would be able stretch out completely by leaving the window open. Eventually, however, I drifted off, the rigours of the day and the nightcap having their effect at last.

Morning shone brightly through the truck windscreen. There were no curtains and the dawn light woke me. Looking at my wristwatch I saw that it was 7 o'clock and that it was not just the daylight which had roused me. Diesels were starting up all around and the truck park was emptying as sleepy drivers pulled themselves out of their bunks to get as many kilometres as possible behind them before the breakfast stop. I blearily regarded the unfolding scene and saw Ian walking towards me carrying his washbag.

"Just going for a wash and brush up," he shouted up at me. "Then a quick coffee and we're on the road."

I hurriedly pulled on my clothes, trying to keep as low a profile as possible which was not easy inside the small confines of my cab and I followed Ian into the toilets which had that stench almost unique to France. Either it was a lack of cleanliness or it was a perfume beloved of the Gaulish race which the manufacturers of toilet cleaning products added to their wares at great expense. Either way it was pretty horrible and, after a quick face wash and tooth clean, I threw my washbag back up into the cab and joined Ian for a coffee and croissant. Crossing the parking area back to our two Macks, Ian reminded me to play it carefully at the filling station we would be visiting later on. We were briefly accosted by a couple of Brits as we reached the trucks.

"You Irish?" one of them asked as if about to provoke a fight.

"No we're English," I answered.

"How come you're driving Irish trucks?" the worthy continued.

"They're not Irish, they're Iranian," Ian butted in.

"So how come you've got IR nationality plates," our antagonist ploughed on.

"IR is Iran," Ian said rather testily. "Look at the outline map on the door with the company name."

"Oh," our friend responded. "I thought that was a map of Ireland."

"You're not Irish yourself are you by any chance?" Ian responded as he climbed the steps into the cab.

I swung up into the driver's seat closing the door behind me, stowed my washbag back in my case and folded my sleeping bag into the passenger footwell. Then I heard the roar of Ian's diesel, saw the familiar plume of black smoke burst from his smokestack, heard the hiss of released air brakes, and watched his brake lights glow red and then off as he released his footbrake. I was going through the same motions and soon both Macks, with their skeletal trailers, were out on the autoroute carving up the lines of heavily laden French wagons, spending more time in the centre lane than the nearside. By 9 o'clock we were passing Chalon-sur-Saone and 45 minutes later Ian pulled onto the exit road for Mâcon Nord, stopping at the péage to pay our tolls. We skirted the main town and pulled into a Total garage where Ian filled with diesel while I waited my turn. He then drove his truck off the pump and I pulled forward.

"Fill both tanks," he yelled as he walked over to the pay booth. I slung the fuel pipe across the chassis and filled the nearside tank, followed by the offside which was next to the pump, 380 litres in all. I was approaching the pay booth when I saw Ian waving to me to get back into the truck and a couple of minutes later he ambled over.

"No problem, all paid," he said. "I'll settle up with you when we do our accounts."

With that he turned and climbed back into his truck and we were off, but within 500 metres he swung his truck off the road to the right into a large parking area at the far end of which was a *Relais Routiers*. He stopped and I could see the dust flying in little twisting eddies under his truck as he applied his parking brake.

"Coffee and snack," he said, as we crossed over to the old brick built building with its cobbled tile roof. Inside was cosy with cushioned banquettes in the bar area and at the far end a glass door which led into the restaurant from where inviting wafts of cooking emanated. "Best to have a snack now before the lunch crowd descend on the place," Ian explained. "Just a ham baguette for me, but you have what you like. If we get roped into lunch it'll be wall to wall free wine and that'll be us out of it for the rest of the day." I looked at my watch. It was 11:15 but I was feeling quite peckish so ordered a croque monsieur and some tea which arrived without milk.

"Du lait s'il vous plait, monsieur," I pointed to the tea and the waiter promptly brought me a small jug of steaming hot milk.

"You'll get used to it," Ian smiled.

Back on the road we re-entered the autoroute

almost immediately which came to its end as we entered the Lyon suburbs. Ian did seem to know what he was doing because he guided us effortlessly around the eastern ring road, weaving through the heavy Saturday lunchtime traffic and by 1:30 we found ourselves heading east on the N6 passing through a myriad of small villages until we reached the town of La Tour du Pin where there was a fork in the road and Ian headed to the right, signposted to Les Echelles and, in brackets, Chambéry. The countryside which had been pure French rolling agricultural with very few hedges but with many copses dotted here and there, now started to become hilly and I guessed that essentially we were in the foothills of the Alps. The N6 now appeared to be hugging contour lines as it swung this way and that but always routed us straight through the centres of the tiny villages where traffic had to stop to allow us to pass. And then we came to Les Echelles.

I was following right behind Ian as we entered the small bustling market town where once again the streets were becoming too narrow to allow us to pass cars and I was beginning to imagine that we were in one of those dreams where you're driving a huge truck into an impossibly small village and the road is becoming narrower and narrower and, as you take an S bend, you're thinking "There's no way I can back out of this if it gets too narrow to continue!" and then you wake up in a cold sweat. As we approached the town centre I could see a sign for Chambéry point- ing left with a gendarme controlling traffic, and as Ian swung wide to get round the narrow crossroads he stopped dead. I also came to an abrupt halt and, after a few minutes, it became obvious that Ian was not about to take off again and no cars were coming out of the turning either. I saw Ian jump down from his truck and disappear down the road he had been about to enter so I decided to join him, imagining that there must have been some sort of accident.

Looking back up the road I could see a long line of cars and vans, their drivers already sounding their horns and shaking their fists. I locked up my truck and strolled down to the front of Ian's rig, now obviously parked right across the town's main intersection. Ian was nowhere to be seen. The road to the right was blocked with cars. The road ahead was blocked with cars and the road to the left where we needed to go was also jammed solid. We were going nowhere and for one moment of blind panic I harboured the terrifying thought that Ian had done a runner!

14

Chaos Theory

ANOTHER person who was absent was the gendarme who had been controlling the traffic! I assumed that he had scurried off to obtain help to sort out the mess. I stood there for several minutes before I was approached by an aged local sporting a rather loud tweed jacket and, of all things, a deerstalker hat.

"Excuse me," he enquired. "Are you Iranian?"

"No," I replied. "We're English, driving Iranian trucks."

"Why are you here with such big trucks in such a small village?" he persevered.

"Because there is a height restriction on the Grenoble route and we have to get to Chambéry to load French exports for Iran." I patiently explained. He gave a Gallic shrug and shuffled off tapping his walking stick on the pavement. By this time, drivers were getting out of their cars and descending on the crossroads from all four intersecting carriage-ways. Discussions were taking place with much gesticulating, shrugging and pointing in my direction. I decided to state my position in my best possible French.

"J'etais suivant mon chef," I started out, determined to put the blame on Ian rather than myself. I had heard what the French mob could get up to when roused. Any moment now I would be carried off shoulder high to their equivalent of the Bastille I felt. "Il cherche les gendarmes pour ouvrir la route," I finished holding my hands up. Rather than stand my ground in the middle of the ever-increasing crowd of malcontents I decided to follow in Ian's footsteps to discover what was causing the chaos. Our road out of town was straight for about two hundred yards then it turned sharp left. I rounded this corner only to be confronted with a line of traffic as far as the eye could see. Luckily the motorists here did not associate me with their predicament so the harassment had stopped and in the distance I could see Ian's lanky figure striding back towards me.

"This," he gestured to the line of cars, "goes back at least a couple of kilometres. There's only two side roads and both of those are jammed. We'll have to get back in the trucks and wait for the gendarmes to sort it out. It's their fault anyway," he said accusingly. "That bloody point-duty gendarme waved me forward when he must have been able to see I couldn't get round. If you look, that first car is way over the white line." Sure enough as we returned to the trucks I noted that the first car in the queue, which was effectively bumper to bumper with Ian's Mack, was indeed a good couple of car lengths in front of the painted white stop line. However, without the gendarme to confirm that he had waved Ian through, we had no argument. Might was always right in these situations and we were vastly outnumbered.

"Where is the gendarme, by the way?" I asked.

"I dunno," Ian replied. "He sodded off down the road opposite as I was jumping out of my cab. I thought he'd be back with some more *flics* to sort this out."

As we passed the first car the driver shouted something out of his window. I sauntered over to him.

"What are you saying?" I looked directly into his

eyes and he looked blankly back at me. "Que est-ce-que vous avez dite," I repeated in my schoolboy French.

"Vous etes fou a conduire ces gros camions dans ce ville. Vous devez etre enferme." Which I took to mean: "You are mad to drive your big trucks through this town. You should be locked up."

"C'est votre faut," I accused him. "Votre voiture est en face de la ligne blanche." (It's your fault. Your car is in front of the white line) "You stupid git," I added under my breath as I turned to join Ian who by now was sitting serenely in his cab. We discussed our situation at length while during the next quarter of an hour absolutely nothing happened. Looking out of the windows I could see a myriad of drivers and pedestrians standing in groups waving their hands about accusingly in our general direction and formulating their own plans to sort us out. Eventually there was a knock on the door on my side and an extremely polite voice asked in perfect English.

"What is the problem? Why can you not move your trucks?" If he had asked in a thick French accent I think we might have not been responsible for our actions but his voice was so perfectly modulated and he was so softly spoken that we wound down the windows to find an elderly gentleman grey of hair, full of face and short of build peering up at us.

"I'm sorry," I said. "This is not our problem. The gendarme waved this truck to turn left and that car over there," I pointed an accusatory finger at the offending off-white Renault Dauphine whose driver and wife were now out of their car and appeared to be engaged in a furious argument, "drove over the white stop line making it impossible for us to take the bend. The gendarme has vanished and we are waiting for him to return to deal with the traffic."

Our elderly friend laughed. "Ha, you will wait all day. It seems he has made a big mistake and won't want to take any blame. What can we do to help?"

Ian had dismounted from the cab by now and walked round to the passenger side. I also jumped down and faced our possible saviour.

"Thanks very much indeed," I said. "All we've had so far is a load of abuse about us not being supposed to drive trucks through here but there is no restriction on this road as far as we know."

"You are correct," our new found friend agreed. "We are always getting problems like this because of the height restriction on the Grenoble road. You are going to the steel mill?" I nodded. "Yes it is often the same although this is the worst I have ever seen it. You are quite allowed to be here. By the way my name is Claude. I was an English teacher and lived in England during the war," he finished.

"The only way out of this," Ian interjected mournfully, surveying the scene as he rolled up another Rizla and Old Holborn, "is to back all those cars up by about two car lengths so we can get around the corner. Then we should be able to proceed and everything should get back to normal. Trouble is the road is so narrow that I think we will have to go right to the rear of the queue and back them all up."

"That seems like a good idea," Claude said. "I will come and help you explain." Ian locked up his truck and the three of us set off down the road only stopping for Claude to let off a stream of what I was sure would be the most polite abuse at the portly red faced Dauphine driver who was now looking rather shamefaced, especially as it was obvious that his rather stuffy wife was also about to have a go at him. This episode would probably cost her reputation dear amongst the neighbourhood circle.

"Can we not just pull a few cars across the road, back up the frontrunners, bring our trucks round so the queue can move and then wait while the mess sorts itself out?" I helpfully suggested. Ian gave me a look which would have made a novice nun feel guilty.

"Are you mad?" he asked. "We could do that but it'd take ten times as long for us to get away and also don't forget that the road past that bend is little more than single track!"

As we walked along the line of cars Claude met several enquiries with what appeared to be being accepted as a reasonable excuse fully exonerating us poor innocent truck drivers so far from home. It transpired that Claude had been a French exchange teacher in Southall at the outbreak of war and unlike many of his compatriots had decided to stay in England until it was too late for him even to consider going home.

"I had no family, you understand," he emphasised. "I was an orphan brought up in an all boys boarding school near Aix les Bains," he shook his head. "A very bad place. It was a Catholic school and the priests … I will say no more but you will understand I am no longer religious." He had eventually joined the Free French and proudly told us how he had met and shook hands with de Gaulle. "A great man," he announced. "A fine man. Good for France." He was explaining how he had been sent to Marseilles in 1944 with orders to combine the resistance into a group capable of governing once the Vichy regime had been defeated, when we reached the end of the line at a road junction signposted Chambéry to the left and Voiron to the right. In effect, this appeared to be a bypass if you had the luck to be travelling between these two towns. Anywhere else and you had to go through the centre of Les Echelles. Claude approached the last car and explained things and the driver dutifully backed up onto the roundabout at the junction. Then the next car was approached and did the same. I could see that this was already creating a good deal of space. The third car reversed without us having to ask him and so we went back down the queue helping several drivers to reverse in a straight line and having to explain the situation to the occasional trouble maker who couldn't see why he would have to *derange* himself even though everyone else had got the message.

"What did you say to him?" I asked Claude after one particularly recalcitrant fat rustic in a beret and Citroen 2CV had eventually complied.

"I just said that if he didn't do as the rest he would be there all day and what did he think these Englishmen would think of his ungratefulness for their country-men's assistance with the Boche. I also showed him my resistance badge," he smiled at me as he proffered his lapel. It took a full 45 minutes before we had reached the front and M Portly and Mme Furious reversed their Dauphine virtually to the next bend giving us plenty of room to swing round. We both thanked Claude profusely.

"If you ever pass this way again, and I hope you won't," he smiled, "look me up. They all know me here. I taught most of them. Claude Vranjes is the name. Good day to you and I wish you a safe journey."

"Shall we have a cup of coffee before we continue?" I ventured. "Especially as we're already parked up?"

Ian gave me another of his disdainful looks and rolling his eyes climbed up into his cab and started the engine. A small crowd had now gathered and they actually waved, whether good riddance or an expression of sympathy for our plight, I will never know. Claude waved and I waved back, a brave courteous man, typical of many of the French who had survived the rigours of the war. Unfortunately, I never saw him again. Ian's truck negotiated the turn and needed every inch of the road to do it. At the next bend he stopped again. M Citroen 2CV had managed to stop his car right on the bend making it impossible for us to pass him. Ian waved him forward onto the straight which he eventually managed to achieve and we gingerly skirted past him and round the corner where Ian stopped and waved the whole line of cars through. Once the tail ender had passed we were fully mobile again and by 4 o'clock we were clear of the village.

We were now travelling in a valley on the left side of which were foothills and on the right, steep pine-forested inclines leading up to snow covered mountain slopes. As the light deteriorated, we switched on our lights and in the beam of the headlights could be seen flurries of snow beginning to descend onto the roadway. Within a couple of kilometres the snow was lightly covering the road but the traffic was preventing it from building up; on either side of our route the trees were now turning white. By the time we had skirted Chambéry on an outer ring road it was coming down thick and fast and worries started to formulate about whether we would be able to get through, especially as we had no chains with us. However, as we passed through Albertville and took a sharp right turn over the river signposted to Moutiers, the snow had built upon my bonnet and windscreen and the wipers could only just cope, but once outside the town the snowfall stopped and the gritted roads were clear. However, it was obvious the higher we climbed that we were now above the snow line and winter already reigned in this Alpine region. The road we were now on was what in England would be classified as a B road but it was a route up to the ski resorts on the other side of Moutiers and to the Petit St. Bernard pass into Italy so was kept as open as possible. We passed through several small villages with their warm lights, smoky fires and thronged cafe bars welcoming their weekend visitors to come in from the cold. After another half hour we entered the village of Notre Dame de Briancon, on the far side of which we encountered the massive steel mill complex straddling the road. Ian pulled into a layby on the right, next to a glowing blast furnace. Production was in full flow and the noise of the various processes, the hum of machinery, the cracks and booms from the furnaces and the clanking of unseen wheels and cranes gave the whole area a feeling of a set from Dante's Inferno. We trudged through the slush to a small gatehouse where sat an old pensioner, probably a survivor of some awful steel mill accident, who glowered out at us. Seeing the trucks he muttered a curt, "Premier a gauche, monsieurs," and returned to his newspaper. We drove another couple of hundred yards up the road and Ian guided his truck to the left through a massive pair of gates and I followed into a large parking area with offices on one side and more steel processing plant on the other.

We sloshed our way through the snow-covered yard and into the reception where Ian reported our presence to another old functionary manning the desk. Luckily he spoke some English.

"You load Monday," he said.

"Yes we know," Ian replied. "We need to park our trucks here and find a hotel for the weekend. Can you help please?"

"The nearest hotel is Moutiers," the receptionist volunteered. "You would like I call them?"

"Merci, thank you very much," Ian said and the old man lifted the receiver of an ancient black bakelite phone and, with his pencil, carefully and slowly dialled the number. After a conversation with the hotel he held the receiver away from his ear and turned to us.

"Is one room for two of you OK?" he enquired. We agreed and he made the reservation. "Hotel du Commerce," he explained. "In the centre of the town near memorial to the maquis."

Thanking him, we left the warmth of the office block and trudged out into the parking lot. It was obvious how much the temperature had dropped during our relentless climb into the mountain valley, the wind whistling up between the hillsides chaffing our cheeks.

"We'll drop my trailer and take my tractor up to Moutiers," Ian said, and I helped him decouple, drop the legs down and stow the susies.

Once out on the road, the snow started to fall again. This time it was serious, and the wind, accelerated by the narrow valley, was blowing it up into a veritable blizzard. The road was now covered with slushy, freshly fallen snow and Ian reduced speed.

"These things skid about all over the place when there's no weight on the rear wheels," he said. "By the way, did you see that bloody gendarme in Les Echelles?" I shook my head. "Propping up the bar at that cafe on the right just before the bend," Ian said, rolling up yet another Rizla Old Holborn.

15

L'Assomoir

THE snow was falling relentlessly now, great white flakes slapping against the windscreens and lying there momentarily before the wipers consigned them to the icy mass building up at the limits of their stroke. Both the driver's and the passenger's windows were now covered and we were constantly opening and closing them to keep them clear. I was in some discomfort because the cramped conditions of the cab necessitated me having my overnight case in my lap, every other space being taken up with Ian's belongings stuffed willy nilly wherever he could place them.

"We'll be bloody lucky to make Moutiers," he remarked as we entered the aptly named village of Aigueblanche. "Fancy cabbing it?"

"What and die of smoke inhalation during the night?" I replied. "How many times do you roll-up by the way?" I asked.

"Every time I wake up," came the dread reply. "Only way I can get back to sleep."

"Guilty conscience?" I enquired.

"Must have done something wrong years ago. I've led a blameless life ever since," he declared.

"Oh yeah," I countered. "What about Katya?"

"All in the mind, all in the mind," Ian laughed. Just at that moment we were approaching the centre of the village with what looked like an S bend around a church and Ian eased right up on the revs, skip changing down as we bore down on the ninety degree right turn. "Main thing is, driving in snow," Ian said, "don't put too much strain on the drive wheels either braking or accelerating. Just take it easy." We had slowed right down to about 15 miles per hour as we took the right hander and I could feel the rear bogie slide to the left. Ian immediately corrected this by steering left towards the church momentarily and then right and we were round the first corner. Within 20 yards there was a 90° turn left which we rounded smoothly as Ian had not touched the accelerator since correcting the slide. We were now skirting the side of the church at the far end of which could be seen a dimly lit square with a PTT on the right and almost immediately in front, the road took a slight left to avoid the Cafe du Sport with its neon-lit Tabac sign shining through the murk. Slipping past this edifice I could see that the road was now ascending out of the village and we were having trouble maintaining traction. "No weight on the bogie. Bloody nightmare," Ian observed, dragging on his latest roll-up and holding it between his nicotine stained thumb and forefinger as he changed up a couple of splits. "The higher the gear the better the traction," he explained. "Got to keep the wheels turning. Once they stop you're lost," but stop we did. Straight ahead a Simca 1100 had entered the road from the right and had skidded to a halt blocking the road completely. "Shit!" was all Ian had to add to the situation as he allowed the Mack to come to a halt. "See if you can find a stone or something to wedge under the rear wheel," he shouted as he exited the cab. "Otherwise we could slip back with the road in this condition."

Once on the ground, my Doc Martins were also slipping and sliding all over the place. With a coating of snow it was impossible to find any loose stones and with a knowing touch of the side of his nose he beckoned round to the back of the cab where a spade was located lashed to the susie mounting. "Dig out about six foot back from the rear wheels on each side," he instructed. "Then we'll reverse onto it, which will stop us from sliding back down the hill and it'll also give us a hard surface to start off from. I'll go and see what we can do about shifting the car." In fact the snow was not that deep but what was causing the loss of traction was that it had not been gritted and several vehicles had already compacted it into ice. I dug a trench a good ten feet behind the tractor unit, jumped up into the cab and reversed onto the exposed tarmac. Back at the scene of the obstruction, Ian was pushing while the driver was revving the engine of the Simca for all he was worth, spinning his front wheels like crazy and doing nothing to get himself unstuck. Ian stopped pushing as I flicked snow away from my eyebrows and surveyed the road. The driver got out and Ian offered to take the wheel.

"Merci mes copains, vous etes trop gentils," the local worthy said, making to throw his arms round Ian's shoulders. That was the stage at which we realised he was in his cups. Ian side-stepped which was a little unfortunate because the inebriate had little sense of balance in the first place. Having decided to place his trust in Ian and having decided to utilise him as a means of support he was sorely misguided and he stumbled as we stopped him from crashing to an inevitable limb fracture.

"Ah merci, merci mes braves," he insisted. "Je suis tellement chanceuse d'avoir de si bons amis dans mon heure de besoin!" ("It is good luck to have such friends in my hour of need!")

"You're damn lucky we're not the police," Ian muttered as he got into the car, leaving me to support the drunk. Within a couple of minutes he had reversed the car back into the side turning, parked it neatly and locked it up. "We'll take him down to that cafe," he said, "and hand the car keys to them. We can't leave him to drive in this condition."

"You're all heart," I replied. "Saving this poor sod from himself."

"It's not him I'm worried about," Ian said. "It's some other poor bastard who might wander across his path."

"Anglais?" the drunk intoned thickly.

"Bon chance nous ne sommes pas les gendarmes," I pointed out.

"Tres bien, tres bien," he gabbled. "God save the Queen!" and those were the last words he spoke to us because he then slumped to the ground and we had to half drag and half carry him the couple of hundred yards down to the cafe.

Opening the door a mixed smell of coffee, beer, Pernod and Gauloises slammed into our near frost-bitten faces and accusatory looks were flashed in our direction from the assembled Saturday night throng around the bar.

"Votre ami est ivre," I announced as we sat the near lifeless body into a chair where he sprawled as if he were a rag doll.

"English?" the barman enquired, not mistaking my accent for that of another far flung French *departement*. I nodded and handed him the car keys.

"Thank you, Messieurs, for bringing him back. We told him on no account to drive. He has been drinking since lunchtime. You would like a small cognac before you continue?" he asked. In the circumstances, chilled to the marrow as we were, there was no way we could refuse this kind offer and we joined in the bonhomie and general merriment occasioned at our unknown friend's expense. They called him *l'assomoir* which I think means habitual drinker or drunk and I began to feel sorry for him. He was probably drinking to forget some awful personal tragedy or other I thought and didn't really deserve being the butt of the hilarity surrounding him. We drank up and said our farewells.

"Take dinner in the Auberge de Savoie," the barman advised. "Very good food ... oh, and good wine, too! Thanks again, Messieurs," and we left the warm intimacy of the cafe to trudge back up through the windblown snow to our truck which now had a good layer of the stuff on top of the cab and bonnet. We climbed up onto our respective top steps and brushed away all the snow and ice from the screens before Ian started the motor.

"I'll try second main second split," he said. "The secret is to move off as gently as you can and not allow the wheels to spin." These last few words he formed slowly as he gently released the clutch and I could feel the rear wheels bite.

"Have you got the diff-lock on?" I asked.

"More steering control with it off," Ian asserted. "We may have to use it. There's about a couple of hundred metres to the top of this rise."

We passed the last of the sparse village street lighting and the headlights now picked out the falling snow driven down the valley by the wind from Moutiers directly into our path. The wipers once again were finding it difficult to keep up but Ian proved an expert at keeping the wheels turning and was even able to change up to third main and second split as we gained momentum.

"Highest gear you can, highest gear you can," he intoned as we breasted the crest of the hill and safely coasted along the level. It was not too far before we reached Moutiers (twinned with Verres in Italy apparently), just a couple of kilometres of gently undulating and, thank goodness, unchallenging road. The route through to the Petit St. Bernard passed straight through the centre, and just before the main square, aptly named Square de la Liberté, was the Hotel du Commerce on the left. We were able to stop right outside and, with a swish of airbrakes, parked and climbed down from the tractor unit, clutching our cases. Once on the pavement I had a brief look around before entering the hotel. There was not a great deal to see with the snow billowing on down, mottling the neon street lighting. The hotel itself was a garish 50s concrete excrescence, not at all what one might expect in this lovely Alpine environment. There were four stories, each with an identical array of evenly spaced characterless windows, the casements standing slightly proud from the walls but fabricated in grey concrete. Once inside, however, the mock low beams and custard and brown coloured walls of the reception area were a little more attuned to the region. We rang the bell on the reception desk and a very pleasant middle-aged lady, slightly but not overly plump, with greying hair and rosy windblown cheeks, bustled out from her lair.

"Bienvenue," she welcomed us and then continued in English. "You must be the chauffeurs from Carbone de Savoie."

Ian looked a little puzzled.

"Moulin a Notre Dame de Briancon," she further explained.

"Ah, yes," Ian understood.

"Anyway," she continued. "We have no other visitors arriving because we are full and with the snow, most roads are almost impassable. Did you come from Albertville?"

"Yes we actually started in Auxerre this morning," I interjected.

"You have done well," she asserted. "The road is now blocked so you are very lucky to be here." She handed us the French interior ministry forms to complete our registration.

"They have to hand these in to the gendarmerie every evening," Ian said. "They keep tabs on all foreigners staying the night." We also had to sign the register before Madame escorted us up to our fourth storey room. She unlocked the door into a room with two beds sporting the regulation white duvets. It was a sparse but clean space and proved to be a corner room with a view of the road and the square.

"The salle de bain, bathroom?" she asked, checking on her English translation. "It is opposite this room, so very convenient for you. In fact, you are very lucky. There are no other rooms available in the whole of Moutiers. We have a small convention for French travel agents before the ski season and everywhere is full. Now," she continued, "petit dejeuner," she smiled and said haltingly, "breakfast is served downstairs from 7 until 9:30. We have no restaurant so you will need to go out if you wish to eat. Perhaps the Auberge in the square?" With this she disappeared leaving Ian and myself to unpack.

"I think we'll give that Auberge place a go," Ian declared, much to my annoyance twisting another roll-up between his fingers.

"I think I'll go and have a shower before we go out," I said hastily.

"Me too," said Ian.

"Not at the same time though I trust," I joked.

"No, you go first while I finish this fag," he agreed.

After freshening up and the first decent shave in a couple of days I sat at the window gazing up at what I imagined to be a superb Alpine vista but at the moment obscured by the snowstorm raging outside. The room however, was warm even though it was not fully carpeted, there being only a large rug positioned next to each bed. The windows were thick wooden secondary glazed affairs which opened inwards, a fact I only discovered when I foolishly decided to try them. The immediate blast of freezing wind driven snow highlighted my mistake and I had quite a struggle to close them tightly again against the thrust of the storm.

Once we had both freshened up we made our way down to the lobby and out into the blizzard. Turning left we found the war memorial at the bottom end of the square and across from that on the far side was the Auberge de Savoie, a typical alpine inn, half-timbered, gaily lit and a welcome bolt hole from the cold. Entering, we were immediately confronted by an atmosphere of warm conviviality, made even cosier by the low height of the ceiling beams. Ian had to watch his head as he walked under them. Immediately on the left was a snug bar area and to here we repaired for what I thought was a well-earned reward for a hard day's trek and our charitable act at Aigueblanche. We ordered a couple of beers and sat down in a corner by a roaring fire. This, I thought, is pretty close to paradise.

"You are eating, Messieurs?" the barman called over to us. We nodded and he brought over menus. We had a delightful meal and an even more delightful bottle or two of local plonk and were well fortified for our journey back through the frozen square to the hotel. Turning in, I snuggled under the duvet as Ian rolled his last of the day. Where would I rather be, I wondered, halfway up the A1 marooned at a transport cafe offering a meagre fare of chips with everything and the prospect of a drive through the autumnal drizzle in the morning to a thankless drop at yet another haughty car dealership or here in the Alps in a comfortable bed having enjoyed French cuisine, French wine and good company all at the firm's expense? People at home paid to come on holiday to places like this. The whiff of Old Holborn drifting across my bed ended this idyllic reverie. Ah well, does anyone ever really find Shangri-La?

16

Moutiers

THE previous day's efforts had taken their toll and the previous night's apology for sleep across the seats of the Mack had left me with sore spots and an aching back so the luxury of a comfortable bed, in which I could actually stretch out and turn over at will, meant I slept like a log. The tolling of a church bell summoning the faithful to get their butts out of the sack woke me and I checked my watch to find it was 7:50. Laying back on the pillow listening to the bell I realised that there was no other noise. Here in the centre of the town there was no traffic. I made my way over to the window and drew back the curtains allowing bright sunlight to strike the opposite wall of the room and evincing a groan from Ian who turned over but did not wake. Outside there had been a considerable fall of snow. Looking down to the street I saw a good six inches or so on top of Ian's Mack. The road was covered and remarkable for there being no tyre marks through it. I guessed that the night's blizzard had indeed closed off all the roads around the town. The skies were now that special shade of lucent blue that you find in the clear pure air of the alps. There was the odd puffy, unthreatening cloud but otherwise the sun was indeed falling on the righteous as small groups trudged their way to pay their respects to their religion. They were all well wrapped up, almost without exception with hats, coats, scarves, and were well booted against the elements. I was not, I suddenly thought. I had my reefer jacket, I had a jersey and I had a pair of the good Doctor's boots but that was it. I could see that with winter ahead I would have to buy something more substantial if I was to survive. Gazing out over the rooftops I could see the mountains entirely white with the occasional outcrop of black granite where the snow had been unable to gain a foothold. They rose up with high peaks behind lesser ones seemingly close together but actually miles apart, the shadows they cast continually changing the visible contours of their rock faces. High above, wide winged birds were effortlessly circling, riding the updraughts created by the vertiginous slopes. In the town to the left I could see the square surrounded by chalet style buildings with steep roofs designed to easily bear the weight of the deep snow which would probably rest upon them for the entire winter period. They were mainly half-timbered, some painted brown, some black and their windows were latticed and small, a common feature in cold climates before the advent of double glazing. It was an idyllic sight and so quiet now that the church bell had ceased it's urgent insistent summons to herd in the flock. I opened the window and a delicious waft of clean mountain air sidled through. I breathed it in deeply. It was indeed good to be alive on such a morning and in such a setting!

"Bloody hell, Art," a voice emanated from the depth of the other bed. "Are you trying to freeze my bollocks off?"

"Sorry, Ian," I apologised. "It's such a beautiful morning,"

"Maybe beautiful for you," Ian said grumpily. "I've been awake most of the night. Those bloody bells!"

"What bloody bells?" I asked innocently.

"That damn church clock clangs away every quarter of an hour," he complained. "You get dong on the quarter, dong, dong on the half, dong, dong, dong on the three quarters and on the hour, do you want to know what midnight sounds like?"

"I didn't hear a thing," I confessed. "Slept like a baby."

Just then a rumble could be heard and the chink of chains and round the corner from the Albertville road thundered a snow plough attached to the front of a long nose Unic gritter. Clouds of snow hung around the vehicle as it trundled on its way through the square and salted sand cascaded from the vents at the rear and scattered across the road splattering against the parked cars and Ian's Mack. Then the sound died away and it was gone and peace and quiet descended for at least five minutes when the noise of light traffic took over and cars started to arrive in the street outside and that was the end of the idyll.

We got washed and dressed in shifts and wandered down to the reception area and through to the restaurant which was positioned on the street side of the building with lace curtains drawn across the large picture windows to afford some degree of privacy. It was a rather bare room, cream walls with a few nondescript prints of alpine vistas, a long table at the far end with some buffet items laid out, and ten tables, half of which I assumed were occupied by travel agents on their freebies. We luckily found a table by the window and sat down and almost immediately the middle-aged receptionist was with us.

"You would like coffee or tea?" she asked. We agreed on tea for two.

"Eggs we make boiled or fried or mixed," she continued. I assumed by mixed she meant scrambled. We both chose boiled.

"You can find some croissants, or bread and some meats on the table," she explained, waving in the direction of the buffet before she bustled out to the kitchen. It was while we were happily ensconced with our breakfast laid out on the table in front of us that we heard the sound of a diesel engine.

"Good God," Ian said. "That's a Mack or I'm a Dutchman." Within seconds, not one but two Pars International Macks sidled slowly into the road outside and managed to park behind Ian's truck. "One of them's Maltese Joe," Ian observed. "But the other one, I've not seen him before." Both trucks were dripping with ice, windblown with road dirt and blackened by slush kicked up by the wheels. The drivers now approaching the hotel entrance were little better, looking for all the world like a couple of down-at-heel vagrants. Ian went out to the reception area and brought them back to our table.

"This is Joe, Joe this is Arthur on his first trip and this is Steve Vargas on his second trip apparently," Ian introduced us. We all shook hands and Joe and Steve sat down. Our hostess hurried back in with an inquisitive look on her face.

"Two more drivers from Carbone de Savoie," Ian re-assured her. "Can you find a room for them tonight and is it OK if they have breakfast? We will pay," he added.

"Breakfast is not a problem," she replied. "Anyway Carbone will pay but tonight we have no rooms and there are no rooms in the town. But we will find something don't worry. Teas or coffees?" she asked. Once the breakfasts had been settled she hurried back to the kitchen.

"You lads look in a state," Ian remarked.

"So would you if you'd been stuck in a layby about five miles this side of Albertville all night,"

Joe explained. "Steve and me, we kept the engines running otherwise we'd of froze to death! Got taken off the road by the gendarmes about 7 o'clock and that was it. No food, no drinks no nothing. Started moving a couple of hours back, saw your trailers parked up so we dropped ours and came up here."

Joe had a swarthy middle-aged Mediterranean complexion with black slightly curly hair topping a full face, dark bushy eyebrows over brown eyes and a slightly turned down mouth which gave him a rather sullen appearance. I guessed he was about five foot six in his stockinged feet, rather plumpish and dressed in a blue parka with jeans and a pair of strong light brown leather calf length boots which impressed me greatly. Steve, on the other hand, was, like Ian, a tallish sallow figure. Of ruddy countenance, he looked like your typical central European farmer and I had already guessed that with a name like Vargas he was probably Hungarian. His blue penetrating eyes were a remarkable feature and I noticed that he tended to fix anyone he was talking to with an unremitting stare which could be quite disconcerting. I reckoned his age at around the mid-thirties. His dress was almost standard British driver, black donkey jacket, blue jeans and black unpolished boots. Both of these new arrivals looked like they could do with a square meal and a good wash and I could see that the freebie travel agents were looking at our little group with disapproving glances. Madame returned to the table, laden with tea, coffee for Steve, eggs and toast. The new arrivals set about their breakfast as though they hadn't eaten for a month.

"By the way," Joe observed, "we noticed your trailers were skeletal. How're you goin' to load steel ingots, lash them to the chassis?"

"We're only following orders," Ian replied.

"Well, there's no containers at the steelworks," Joe asserted.

"Maybe they're sending them down with the other trucks," Ian retorted a little testily. "Anyway, we'll see on Monday morning."

I asked Steve how he was getting on with the company.

"Two trips so far," he replied. "First one was from Europoort up to Salzburg, then I wait for a week. Snow in Turkey so the Iranian trucks are late. Now I get load for Le Thilot. Bales of cotton. Unload and then Joe and me, we come down 'ere." Steve had a thick Hungarian accent but I guessed he had lived in the Midlands as there was a definite Black Country burr running through it.

"Usual nonsense at Le Thilot," Joe interjected. "Got there on Wednesday for tipping. Directed up to Epinal for customs. Time we got there customs shut. Didn't clear 'till lunchtime Thursday. Time we got to Le Thilot mill, no offloading crew 'till the morning. Offloaded Friday, back to Epinal for the clearance papers and then Salzburg send us here."

Ian called Madame over to the table. "Is it alright if these guys use our room to wash?" he asked. "They've been stuck in the snow all night on the Albertville road."

"Ooh, la la," Madame cried. "You poor boys. Yes, you must use the bathrooms upstairs. Tonight we will do something for you, not to worry," she smiled concernedly almost like a mother hen looking after her chicks and the skirts of her alpine dress rustled as she attended to a large table of freebie travel agents and I could see her explaining our plight to them as she cleared their dishes. Her explanation must have been convincing because the disapproving glances now turned to looks of admiration for the plucky truckers who had struggled through the blizzards to load essential exports for the glory of La France!

After breakfast, Joe and Steve retrieved their cases from their trucks and went upstairs to our room while Ian and myself had a look around the town. Moutiers was situated at the top of the valley from Albertville and at the bottom of the valleys to Bourg St Maurice and Courchevel and Meribel, right on the edge of the Les Trois Valees ski resort area. It had evidently grown from its position at the confluence of the valleys, its consequent railway hub and the abundance of local coal and iron ore which had led to the construction of the steelworks. Today it was a lazy Sunday morning that greeted us as we left the cosy warmth of the hotel into the biting chill of the alpine air. The wind had dropped and the sun was now blazing down as we turned left out of the hotel and headed into the square. The klaxons of trains, their metallic clear notes echoing around the surrounding mountainsides seemingly coming from the other side of the buildings on the far side of the square indicated that the railway, too, was open to traffic. Straggles of snow-covered cars and the odd small truck were now making their unsteady way in both directions and people were now food shopping, all other outlets being closed on Sunday of course. The bells from the cathedral which seemed to be on the Bourg St Maurice side of the town rung out, no doubt to summon more of the faithful to even more services during which even more money could be wrung out of them to fill the coffers of the mighty Roman Catholic industry, sorry Church! We circled the square and returned to the hotel. During the rest of that day we hired a taxi and travelled up to one of the lower ski resorts and found a restaurant where we had lunch and spent most of the afternoon lounging by a picture window halfway up an alp, sipping our beers, exchanging the odd tale of the road and discussing the minutiae of the company I had just joined. It did seem that so long as you did your job and kept your nose reasonably clean, so to speak, you were left to your own devices so that was good news. On our return to the hotel, Madame accosted us in reception.

"Ah, the English drivers," she announced rather portentously. "Unfortunately we 'ave not found a room for your friends but we 'ave put two small beds in your room so they can sleep there tonight." She beamed in expectation of the grateful thanks she was about to receive. Joe and Steve retraced their steps, collected their suitcases from their trucks and took them upstairs. We again dined at the excellent Auberge de Savoie and it was past midnight by the time we turned in.

After breakfast the next morning we checked out and the three Macks made dramatic three point turns in the street before heading out of town, black smoke soaring from the stacks, the motors thundering and the turbos whistling. The road had been well gritted by now and the Monday morning traffic had no problems negotiating the hairpin in Aigueblanche. I noticed that the Cafe du Sport was full of morning trade, its clients sipping their coffee cognacs and reading their newspapers as we passed by. Soon we could see the massive corrugated iron structures which were the enclosures of the steel mill and then Ian steered to the right into the truck park. We backed on to Ian's skeletal and I helped him attach it while Joe, who had a 40 foot open top and Steve, who had a 40 foot box perched on his trailer also hitched up their wagons. The four of us sauntered over to the reception where we were asked to wait while the export manager was summoned. Within a couple of minutes an expensively suited and, I thought, expensively attractive, brunette entered through the swing doors which linked the reception area to the offices. She marched over to us, her heels clicking on the parquet.

"Bonjour," she greeted us. "Vous etes ici pour?"

"Sorry," Joe interrupted. "We're English. We don't speak French."

The delicious brunette looked a little nonplussed.

"Sprechen sie Deutsche?" she suggested. The receptionist, the same ancient one we had encountered on our arrival on Saturday intervened.

"I will translate," he suggested. It transpired that there were ten loads to go to Iran during the next five days but on our enquiry it was confirmed that they had no containers to load onto our skeletals.

"Can we telephone Salzburg please?" Ian asked.

"Yes, of course," the brunette replied through our interpreter and she left us in his hands as she sashayed her trim frame back through the swing doors.

"Whew!" Ian exclaimed, followed by a sharp audible intake of breath.

"Nice girl, eh?" the receptionist whistled suggestively then lowering his voice he chuckled as he added. "Be careful, she's our boss!"

It took 20 minutes for us to be connected with Salzburg and Ian was handed the phone.

"Hi Helga, Ian here," he announced. "Can I speak to Gerhard please?" There was a pause then, "Hi Gerhard, it's Ian here. We're at the steel mill and they say they have no containers for us. What? No, we had no instructions to bring containers. We only have the skellys!"

17

The Waiting Game

THE atmosphere in the reception foyer at Carbone de Savoie had suddenly become tense. Ian was seated in the accommodating receptionist's chair. Joe, Steve and myself were standing in front of the wooden desk which itself stood in front of a wood panelled wall on which were hung photographs of the original plant when first built. Some were sepia, others faded black and white and there were also some in colour of a certain general with a big nose visiting the factory in the 1950s. Ian was now getting an ear bashing from HQ.

"But ... but ... but," was all he was getting into the tirade. Eventually he was able to explain. "Gerhardt, we're very sorry about this but I've got a copy of the telex and there is no mention of loading empty containers. Ron also confirmed this was the case and we assumed there would be containers here on our arrival."

There was a stream of what sounded to us like pinky and perky coming out of the earpiece and Ian held it out to us so we could listen. "Ian, you son of a gun, whatdya think we're gonna do?" came Gerhardt's fluent American English. "I've got ten loads outta there this week. We gotta load them." Ian put the phone back onto his ear so we could only hear his side of the conversation from that point on.

"How much loadspace do the ingots take?" he answered. There was a pause.

"Just a second, I'll ask him," Ian said, then putting his hand over the mouthpiece he turned to the receptionist. "How much space do our loads need?" he asked. The receptionist shrugged but then picked up an intercom and gabbled away in French.

"We will load 22 tonnes on each truck" he answered.

"Thanks," Ian replied, "but I need to know how many metres of container space you need." Once again there was a flurry of conversation over the intercom.

"Normally we load 22 tonnes in a 20 foot container," the receptionist replied.

"Hey Gerhardt, they can load 22 tonnes in a 20 foot," Ian said rather excitedly. "Could you send down a couple of trailers carrying two 20 foots each? Then we could tranship one 20 foot onto each of our skeletals. OK, Gerhardt ... OK, Gerhardt ... OK ,we'll wait for you to call," and he handed the phone to the receptionist. "Could you put this through to your export manager please?" he asked. The old man put the call on hold, and slowly dialled a number.

"C'est pour vous. Transports Pars," he said and carefully replaced his receiver.

Ian vacated the receptionists, chair, thanked him for his help and the four of us repaired to a plush leather seating area at the side of the foyer meant for visiting customers or suppliers.

"Gerhardt's checking with them that they can tranship the containers. Then he's checking truck positions to find trailers with double 20s. Then he's going to call back and either we wait for them to arrive or we're back to Rotterdam to collect containers," he sighed, scratched his head and removed his peaked

Figure 1 *PS Lincoln Castle* which plied the Humber estuary between New Holland Quay and Hull

Figure 2 Carrimore car transporter trailer

Figure 3
Controls of the
Mack R600

Figure 4 Mack
dog bonnet
mascot

Figure 5
The Mack
Thermodyne
240 BHP
turbocharged
diesel engine

Figure 6 The author with his Mack outside the Amstel Pub in Europoort

Figure 7 Near Moutiers

Figure 8 Auxerre Cathedral

Figure 9 Moutiers today with the Auberge de Savoie in the background

Figure 10 The notorious left turn in the centre of Les Echelles

Figure 11 The Doubs Valley at Besancon

Figure 12 Pension Fenninger, Walserberg, Austria

Figure 13 The container terminal at Vogelweiderstrasse, Salzburg

Figure 14 The author in Bremerhaven

Figure 15 Bremerhaven container terminal

Figure 16
Eastbound on the
autobahn near
Bremen

Figure 17 Bob
the Salzburg yard
manager

Figure 18 Loading
a front positioned
container

Figure 19
Relaing outside
Pension Fenninger

cap. "I love this job," he commenced another roll-up, "but they can't have it both ways. Either we do as we're told and follow instructions to the letter or we start to use our brains which I reckon are probably sharper than the wooden-tops in the office." A young clerk appeared through the office door carrying a sheaf of paperwork.

"Deux camions, s'il vous plait." He suddenly realised from our blank looks that we were English. "Two trucks for loading please," he said.

Steve and Joe stood up, smiled at us in a superior kind of way, the sort of way that wise virgins who had remembered to fill their lamps with oil would have smiled at the foolish virgins who hadn't bothered, and followed him out of the glass entrance doors and into the yard. Soon we heard them start their motors and watched them move off to the loading area. Ian puffed thoughtfully on his cigarette, ringlets of smoke rising into the air and disappearing up to the triple-height ceiling of the imposing foyer.

"You know what they say," he observed. "Doesn't matter how fast you make the trip, you'll be held up by the paperwork or the organisational geniuses back in the office."

"Yep," I replied resignedly. "I heard that from a certain heavy load road-boss in Rotterdam!"

We sat in the warmth and comfort of the foyer riffling through old copies of *Paris Match*, some copies of *France Soir* and the previous day's *Le Monde*. Unfortunately that latter publication did not carry a franchise for the Garth cartoon strip so I had now completely lost touch with the latest story. The ancient functionary rose from his desk at about 11 o'clock and shuffled through the office entrance door. Looking out of the ceiling to floor windows onto the parking area enveloped in misty cold I noted that light snow was now falling. Ten minutes later the old man opened the door before disappearing again momentarily and re-appearing with a trolley.

"You would like some tea, gentlemen?" he asked as he arranged the trolley alongside the low table in front of our comfy chairs. He placed a pot of near boiling water, a jug of hot milk, some Lipton's tea bags on a small silver tray, a couple of cups and saucers and some biscuits on the table. We thanked him profusely and he ceremoniously pushed the trolley back through the office door.

"Ah," said Ian, immediately plopping the tea bags into the hot water, "the ancient French tea ceremony!"

"Very good of them," I observed. "They're treating us very well considering that we're just a couple of truck drivers."

Ian touched his nose. "Ah, but they think we're taking their loads all the way to Tehran so we're kind of special. Never let them know we only go as far as Salzburg," he advised as he stirred the pot to strengthen the brew. "Just wish they'd get the hang of putting the tea bags in the pot before they add the boiling water," Ian said, shaking his head at the perceived idiocy of the foreigner with regard to such basic elements of English culture. "One problem we've got," he continued, "is that we've no room to carry food or drink on the trucks apart from the odd Coke or beer. The Iranians on the Salzburg-Tehran run all have large food and equipment boxes fitted to the Crane Fruehaufs. These Pitts have got absolutely sweet FA on them."

At about 12:30 Steve and Joe parked their laden trucks next to our skeletals and joined us.

"Gondrand in Moutiers are bringing the paperwork after lunch," Joe said. "So we may as well get the cards out, eh?"

"Would you gentlemen like some lunch?" our receptionist friend called over to us.

"Yes, please," we chorused as one.

"Follow me then," he instructed, taking us through the open plan outer offices with their ranks of typewriters, comptometers and telex machines all unmanned during the sacred French lunch hour. We then traversed a corridor on the right of which were single offices, presumably for the top brass I surmised. I took-in names like M Dupont, M Lesurier, M Lazarus, all engraved on brass plates, and peeped momentarily into plush wooden walled offices with large desks, huge executive chairs and green topped directional desk lamps. It looked like a very cosy world indeed. At the end of the corridor we entered the dining hall.

"This one's for the office staff," Joe remarked. "You wouldn't have wanted to eat in the worker's canteen. It was pretty basic compared with this."

"That's because the steelworks itself is a pretty filthy place to be working in," Steve observed. "I had a look while they were loading us. It's superhot, the floor is covered in black ash and when they pour out the molten steel it's like a volcano erupting!"

We were seated at a table for six with a brightly coloured check plastic table cloth on top of which was a paper cover torn off from a roll from which the waiting staff replenished the table tops after each sitting. There were menus on each table and soon, advised on which food to choose by our receptionist friend who had now become our translator, we all chose the set meal. A bottle of red wine was plonked on the table together with a carafe of water and a sliced up baguette. We then embarked on the *dejeuner* which turned out to be a coarse paté followed by a plate of raw vegetables, mainly shredded carrot, and for the main course, slices of roast pork with some

155

kind of garlicky creamy potatoes and then a sweet of either ice cream or a chocolate mousse. At the end the waiter brought us coffee and cheese – a slightly different selection from your average English work canteen.

Back in the foyer, Steve and Joe found their paperwork waiting together with a pimply teen runner from the Gondrand office in Moutiers whose *velo*, little more than a bicycle with a tiny two stroke motor attached to the top front wheel, was parked precariously outside the door. He handed over the ready stamped-up paperwork and in halting English instructed Ian and Joe to present them without fail to Gondrand at the Strasbourg border. He then mounted his cycle, pulled a cord to start the engine and sped off towards Moutiers. There were two envelopes for each truck.

"One's the French export docs," Ian explained. "And the other's the T-Forms. Don't know why they double them up. They could start the T-forms at Strasbourg if they wanted to. They take us through to Salzburg. Then it's local documents for the containers into Salzburg central customs and they all get redone when the Iranian trucks tranship them. At the moment Turkey is not on T.I.R. even though Iran is, so all the documents get renewed at every border point."

We said our goodbyes and watched the pair of them check round their trucks with the now sealed containers before they jumped in the cabs and with much revving of diesels, smoking of exhausts and jamming of gears they swept majestically out of the parking area and onto the road towards Albertville. Once again we were experiencing a snow storm outside but inside in the warm centrally heated foyer we settled back into our armchairs and stretched out for a post prandial snooze. I woke to hear Ian gently snoring and the reception phone ringing.

"Carbone de Savoie" the receptionist muttered into his mouthpiece. "Oui, oui, bon, un moment s'il-vous-plait." He gestured to me.

"Salzburg," was all he said.

I woke Ian and he wearily lumbered over to the desk, the effects of the lunchtime red biddy not yet worn off. He picked up the receiver.

"Ian," he affirmed. "Ah, Gerhardt. How are things?" There was then a lengthy conversation of which I only heard Ian's "buts", "maybes" and "OKs". Ian then asked the receptionist to connect our office to their export department and he joined me back at the waiting zone. "Looks like we're here for a day or two," he announced as he sat down, pulled out his Old Holborn and Rizlas and commenced rolling. "They've found a way to tranship the empty contain-ers using forklifts so Gerhardt's got Ron to double up in Europoort and get down here as fast as possible and there's another double offloading now in Bordeaux which should be here by Wednesday lunchtime. In the meantime, he's agreed to pay our hotel bills so the steelworks will organise our rooms again." Ian lit up and noticed my frown. "What're you worried about. We're here in the warm, tea and coffee on demand, food provided and we're on weekly wages. Just lay back and enjoy it."

We spent the next couple of hours in the foyer until our receptionist friend beckoned us over.

"I've booked two rooms for you at the hotel, gen-tlemen." He informed us. "Also tonight our export manager wished to have dinner with you if possible,"

"But she doesn't speak English," I exclaimed.

"She does," our friend asserted. "Very well indeed but she has a funny sense of humour you understand."

"OK," Ian agreed. "Where shall we meet?"

"Veronique will call for you at 7:30," he confirmed.

Wow! We looked at each other speechlessly. The prospect of a free dinner in the company of a beautiful Frenchwoman was indeed a pleasurable one.

"She wishes to speak to you about the journey to Tehran," Our friend explained. "She is very interested in such things."

I must have looked a little crestfallen at this news but Ian took it on the chin.

"No problem," he said. "We'll look forward to it."

We thanked our friend for his help and opened the glass doors.

Back out in the parking lot the snow was now blizzarding once more and we climbed back into Ian's Mack. He turned the key and cranked the icy-cold engine for a minute or so before it spluttered into life. Soon all six cylinders were firing and Ian let the Thermodyne fast idle for a few minutes.

"Don't like the sound of that," he remarked. "She's either misfiring or there's a fuel delivery problem. Probably some shit in the pipes or the pump." I listened carefully and sure enough there was an irregular misfire. "Can't risk it getting worse out on the road," Ian continued. "And I'm not going to bleed the bloody thing through in this weather. We'll have to take your tractor – give you some experience of driving on the ice," he smiled.

We both lifted our cases into my cab and made our way underneath my trailer – me to let down the left leg and Ian the right. It soon became apparent that we would need a hammer to release the retaining sprung pin. It was seized tight in the cold. Luckily, Ian had one and very quickly we had the legs down and the pins back in. I then removed the safety clip and pulled the fifth wheel release and clambered up on the ice covered tractor chassis to disconnect the two airbrake susies and the electrical susie which stowed onto attachments behind the cab when out of use. I was just about to re-enter the cab when Ian shouted over to me, "Have you forgotten something?" I shrugged. "Parking brake on the trailer. You can't rely on the air reservoir and it hasn't got spring brakes." So I had to traipse back under the trailer and pull the brake lever back as far as I could manage until it clicked.

Re-entering the freezing cab I cranked the engine which started after about 30 seconds and was about to engage gears when Ian told me to let it run for a few minutes. "Get the oil circulating and lubricate the turbo," he explained. After a couple of minutes I released the airbrakes and made a slightly juddery start. "Bit of icing up," Ian said. "Nothing to worry about."

It was now dusk as I turned left onto the N90 which was once again carpeted with fresh snow and I felt the rear bogie slide just a little as I accelerated up the hill outside the steelworks. The wind had changed direction and the snow was now horizontally hitting our screens from the top of the valley at Moutiers. The wipers were just managing to clear at each sweep and I was skip-changing up for all I was worth to prevent wheel spin. What was contributing to a rougher ride than that before the weekend was the fact that the snow was lying over frozen ruts of slush which continually attempted to throw us either off the road or in the direction of the few oncoming vehicles. My frozen hands were now beginning to thaw as hot air at last trickled from the face level vents on the dash and I turned the fans up to increase our comfort level now that engine heat was reaching normal. I was dreading the S bend at Aigueblanche but as we descended the slight hill into the village, we passed a gritter coming in the opposite direction, its yellow lights flashing through the teeming snow and the road visibly cleared before we reached the church. I slowed as we passed the Cafe du Sport which looked busy but the windows were steamed up and we couldn't see whether *l'assomoir* was propping up the bar or not.

Madame welcomed us back into the Hotel du Commerce.

"It is terrible, the weather," she tsked and shook her head. "But now the hotel is empty. The travel agents have left for Meribel so you can each have a room."

She handed us the keys and we ascended the stairs to the first floor, clutching our overnight cases. In expectation of our assignation with the beautiful French export manager we both scrubbed up and tried to present ourselves as immaculately as possible in our respective reefer and donkey jackets, although I felt that ironing a crease into my jeans might be a little over the top!

At 7:30 prompt we were sitting in the warmth of the reception area.

"How're we going to handle the questions about Tehran? Have you been there?" I asked. Ian touched his nose again.

"No, but I've heard all the stories, so no need to panic!"

Just then the street door opened and in walked our glamorous hostess, a vision in a fur coat and glossy two toned leather boots. She wished us good evening in perfect English.

"Thank you for having dinner with me," she smiled and her lips parted to reveal rows of sparkling white teeth. "We have a chauffeur who will drive us back to my house where I have prepared a typical regional meal for you."

Oh wow! Things were starting to rise and blood was coursing. How could I get rid of Ian? She shook her luxuriant shoulder length black hair and drops of water and snow scattered.

"The roads are not too bad," she asserted "and my chalet is only a couple of kilometres from here." She opened the street door and ushered two excited drivers across the pavement to a black Citroen DS Safari where we took our seats in the back and she closed the door and walked round to the front passenger seat. She sat down and her perfume permeated the suddenly enclosed space. She turned round to us and said. "Oh, my name is Veronique by the way. May I please introduce you to my husband, Claude?"

18

Veronique (and Claude!)

SPIRITS dampened. The prospect of unbridled sex in the snow, the thoughts in my overactive brain about divesting this beautiful woman of her fur coat and discovering no knickers but almost certainly stockings and suspenders, the rising sap and the promise of fulfilment, all dissipated in an instant at the mention of Claude. He turned in his seat to shake our hands and luckily the looks of pure hatred on our faces mixed with unmitigated envy could not be seen in the dark interior of the DS Safari. Claude started the motor, engaged the column shift and we moved smoothly off. To be frank, we had a thoroughly enjoyable evening *chez* Claude and Veronique. They had a lovely chalet on a steeply winding mountain road above Moutiers and the sparkling lights of that town formed a charming background through the large picture windows of their lounge. Veronique was professionally interested in the route and the hazards of the journey through to Tehran and Ian was able to answer almost all of her questions and to fend off the rest quite expertly I thought.

Veronique, once out of her fur coat, was wearing a tight, figure-hugging little black number which had the unfortunate habit of riding up, giving tantalising glimpses of dark tan stocking top every now and then but that is as far as the sexual side of the evening went. As soon as we entered the comfortable lounge area with its deep pile carpeting and sofas replete with a copious supply of squashable cushions, we were treated to a local aperitif of vermouth from Chambéry which our hostess informed us also contained chicory, gentian and lemon amongst other ingredients.

"We have a lovely local wine here," she said. "You do both drink wine I suppose?" she asked.

"Yes, indeed," we choroused.

"It is called Mondeuse and made from an old traditional grape which almost disappeared from France because of disease," she explained. "It is very fruity and quite dry."

"Or we 'ave a Pinot Noir, also local," Claude butted in. His French accent was much more marked than Veronique's, who almost spoke Queen's English.

We insisted on the Mondeuse and Claude went off to uncork a couple of bottles while we continued sipping the Vermouth.

"You must tell me about the journey to Tehran," Veronique said. Ian flashed me a leave-it-to me look, a course of action with which I was extremely happy. "What route do you take from here," she enquired.

"Well," Ian drawled, once again taking out his pouch of Old Holborn and his pack of Rizlas, almost a nervous reaction I concluded. "From here we make our way up to Strasbourg, then across Germany and into Austria. From Austria we take the route down through Graz and then into Yugoslavia near to Maribor. From there we pass through Belgrade and Nis and then we turn east and into Bulgaria passing Sofia and Plovdiv before the Turkish border at Kapikule. After that we go through Istanbul where we take a ferry across the Bosphorus, and then through Ankara and eastern Turkey to the Iranian frontier at Bazargan. Once we've cleared customs there it's a one and a half day's drive to Tehran," he finished as he lit up his freshly rolled cigarette. I was deeply impressed. For someone who had never driven the route, I thought that he had given a masterly performance. He gave me a sly knowing wink and then Veronique turned her flashing dark eyes on me.

"And how long does this normally take?" she asked.

Nonplussed, I answered, "Well it does depend on the time of year."

"You're right, Arthur," Ian saved me from total humiliation. "In the summer we can do it in ten days from here but in the winter you can take anything from a couple of weeks to a month."

"Oh!" she replied. "I was informed it should take only two weeks."

"Absolutely, dependent on the weather," Ian cut in. "If the roads are snowed up there's nothing you can do, rather like your Albertville road at the weekend. On the other hand our overland route is much faster and reliable than sending the goods by ship. You get a lot of damage and losses, especially at Bandar Abbas where they tranship the cargo onto the quay and then you can wait more than a month for a truck just to take it on to Tehran. What you load into our trucks is what arrives at the destination. That's why we're picking up so much business!"

Veronique thought about that and eventually nodded her head in agreement. "Yes you are right, we have had a lot of problems with shortages and delays," she affirmed. "But now we must start our dinner. First we have some local charcuterie with smoked mountain hams, some salami with walnuts, hazelnuts and blueberries and some paté and for this we have a chilled white Chignin wine. It is made from Jacquere grapes which is also quite rare." She seated us at the dark pine table which was at the back of the lounge area in front of the kitchen. The wine was already poured. "Just help yourself," she said encouragingly.

The rest of the meal consisted of a Potée Savoyard, which turned out to be a delicious pork, ham, sausage and vegetable stew and with this we made short work of a couple of bottles of the deliciously smooth and fruity Mondeuse wine. The sweet was a kind of tart made from blueberries. I noticed that Ian had managed to refrain from smoking throughout the meal which was some kind of record but our hostess had been plying us with questions about the border posts, the customs documentation and the clearance procedures in Tehran.

"Can't help you on that one," said Ian in between mouthfuls of the Tarte Myrtylle. "When we arrive we hand the documentation to our customs man and he returns it when we are ready to offload. One good thing is that we have our own terminal situated just before Tehran airport so we don't have to join the general mayhem in the central customs offices."

Once the meal was over we repaired back to the lounge area for coffee and finally some Remy Martin cognac was offered and accepted. Veronique said something in French to Claude and he burst out laughing. I looked at her with eyebrows raised.

"Ah," she explained. "I was just telling Claude about the look on your faces when I asked on Saturday if you spoke German." Truly this lady had a strange sense of humour!

"May we drink a toast to our hostess?" I asked.

"No, we should drink a toast to you guys. You have been very helpful and also good company," Veronique laughed.

"Why don't we just drink a toast to company present," Claude suggested and that is what we did before the pleasure of a couple of perfumed pecks on the cheek from Veronique as we left her for the journey back down the seemingly treacherous mountain lanes to the hotel, driven by Claude who was evidently expert at avoiding the vast drops to the fairy-lit valley below that beckoned at each hairpin. As we tottered up the stairs to the first floor I remarked on our unusual treatment as drivers.

"I've had similar things happen a few times," Ian said. "It's because the route is quite new to them and they want to pump us for information. That's why it's a good idea to mug up on what happens once the trailers leave Salzburg. I'm afraid it's something that you just have to put up with!"

"Sing for your supper?" I suggested.

Next morning we had a late breakfast before driving back down to the steel mill through the now gently falling snow, the wind having substantially died down. Once there, we passed the day in the warm comfort of the reception area largely reading a couple of last week's English *Daily Mails* we had bought in Moutiers before leaving. We were treated to lunch in the office canteen once again and the lovely Veronique came and sat with us for a short while, delivering a telex to Ian.

"Ron left Europoort yesterday teatime," he read out loud. "And Peter Stevens is leaving Bordeaux round about now. That means they'll be with us tomorrow morning I reckon. Two Iranians will be here on Thursday, and two more of our lads are detailed to load on Friday."

After lunch the snow had stopped so Ian decided to bleed through his fuel lines. There was no problem with waxing he reckoned because the temperature was only reading minus five, so the problem had to be dirty diesel or possibly air leakage into the system though that was quite unlikely. He started the engine, which operated in the same way it had previously, missing unpredictably every so often. "It's OK at the moment but once we put a load on, that'll misfire like mad," he asserted. He opened the huge fibreglass bonnet which tilted forward on its hinges exposing the entire majesty of the Thermodyne engine. "Very easy to work on, these conventionals," Ian said, puffing his roll-up while selecting spanners from his toolkit. "I'm going to drain and refill the filters and then bleed through the whole line." First of all he opened the vent screw on the first filter and manually pumped the lift pump, noting the steady stream of fuel emitting through the screw. "No air in that," he said turning his attention to the second filter with the same results. He then detached both filters and emptied them of fuel and shook them, banging them against the diesel tank to detach any dirt that might have accrued. Then he fitted them back on and painstakingly bled the fuel through the first filter and then the second. "Got to bleed it through the pump now," he announced. "Bleed screw at the intake and then I'll do each cylinder." All was well at the pump, a good spurt of diesel coming through each time he operated the lift pump lever. So he then cracked open each of the six injectors, tested them for flow, this time with me cranking the engine over, and tightened them up. Lastly he checked the return line but diesel was free flowing there as well. I then started the engine and she ran as smooth as clockwork. "Well," said Ian, scratching his forehead with his oily fingers, creating black marks across his furrowed brow. "I'm blowed if I know what the problem was but somewhere or other we've managed to clear it!" I was deputed to ask our receptionist friend if there was a workers toilet where Ian could clean up but he directed that we use the office facilities and Ian walked across the foyer

with a can of Swarfega attempting not to touch anything on his way.

That night we again slept at the Hotel du Commerce
and in the morning checked out, signing the bill for
the factory to pay, and returned to the mill. Halfway
through the morning there was a throaty roar of a
diesel revving as gears were engaged to slow progress and Ron appeared through the gates with two
20 foot containers on his chassis. The airbrakes hissed
and Ron engaged the park brake before sauntering
over to the reception in his laid back, unhurried way.
After a couple of phone calls, the yard foreman was
summoned and our friend on reception had to translate for us as the foreman spoke no English whatsoever but appeared to have a good command of French
profanity. His heated exchanges were peppered with
such phrases as "Quelle bordelle!" and "Merde alors!"
He was not a happy or co-operative man. He was
adamant that they had never transhipped containers and were not about to start now. In addition,
his union were against the use of such monstrously
labour saving equipment and he had only loaded the
previous two containers under duress. He was sorry
he had lived to see the day when the railhead so
expensively built at government expense was being
compromised by the use of road transport. Eventually
he calmed down and Ron explained how the transhipment should take place, as apparently agreed by
Gerhardt and Veronique. Needless to say, the yard
foreman had not been patched in to this loop so had
to be convinced that the operation was safe.

"Two forklifts, one on each side of the rear container, just lift it above the chassis," Ron patiently
explained. "The first truck drives out and the second
truck reverses his chassis under the container and the
forklifts gently lower it down onto the twistlocks. But

remember, as they are only 20 foots, they have to be at the front of the trailer so most of the weight will be on the tractor bogie."

"So how will we load our ingots into them?" I could sense the foreman's sense of triumph that he had spotted a flaw in the English idiot's plan.

"The container doors will be at the front of the chassis," Ron ploughed on. "So we then either drop the trailer or preferably jack-knife the tractor so the forklifts have direct access to the containers." The upshot of this masterclass in container handling was that the short surly foreman stomped off in his blue dungarees swearing that he for one would have nothing to do with this insane operation and threatening to call his union office for advice. Our receptionist was visibly embarrassed at this outburst and Veronique was called.

"I do not know why they have this attitude," she sighed. "This was all agreed with the despatch manager and I assumed that he had cleared it with the workers." There was then much telephoning and it was evident that a meeting had been called between management and staff, which Ron was asked to attend in case there were any technical questions. He then disappeared with Veronique and we were left in the foyer. Tea was brought in and, miracle of miracles, the tea bags had actually been placed in the pot already, giving them a good chance of a proper infusion.

"I am so sorry," the receptionist said rather shame-facedly. "We have always labour problems in France. You can do nothing unless the unions agree. The tail wags the dog you see."

Within 15 minutes Ron re-appeared, a smile on his face. "No problem. They all agree to do the transhipment," he said. "I think the foreman had over-reached himself. Got a rap on the knuckles from his union. They've just had a strike here which was resolved a month ago and no one wants to upset the apple cart. Anyway I told them we do this in Holland and Germany all the time." He winked at us as we returned to our trucks and within ten minutes two five tonne forklifts appeared and Ron choreographed the transhipment. While the container was still in the air and Ian was reversing under it, positioning his trailer expertly I thought, Peter Stevens arrived with his two 20 foots. The first container was lowered onto the chassis within a couple of minutes and Ian raced round securing the twistlocks. Then it was my turn and Peter's rear container was lifted and Ron guided me back as I reversed my trailer underneath it and in between the two forklifts. This time I was not quite as precise as Ian had been and the chassis was slightly askew. However, as the container was lowered it managed to slide over two of the twistlocks and one of the forklifts was able to slew the container slightly so that it slammed down onto the other two. This whole operation with the four trucks involved took about 20 minutes of work after the couple of hours of argument and pacification we had endured. We were then instructed to drive our trucks through the factory over a weighbridge, where we checked in at about 16 tonnes, then to the despatch area where Ian jack-knifed his truck for loading. The ingots were placed at the rear of the containers and, heavy as they were, shoved further into the boxes by the next ingots as the forklifts powered them in with much diesel revving, wheel spinning and tyre burning. Ron then left for the weighbridge and the parking area while I jack-knifed my truck and the loading procedure was repeated. I couldn't help noticing the weight of the now-loaded rig as I shunted her over to the parking area. The steering was heavier and the engine markedly laboured when I tried to start her off in second with third split. Second with first split worked a treat however. My rig was then weighed again on the weighbridge so they could compute the exact weight of the load.

Ron and Peter were waiting for us in the office foyer. Peter, a slight man, under-dressed for this cold clime in cotton jacket and jeans replete with leather cowboy boots, was lean of face but sported an abundant crop of brown hair swept back to display his receding hairline.

"We're loading tomorrow," he told Ian.

Ron was on the phone to Salzburg checking in and notifying our imminent departure. He rejoined us and we were ushered into the canteen for another splendid lunch.

"You two should be away from here immediately after lunch," he informed us. "Gondrand have already completed the paperwork and the runner will be here shortly. Ian looking after you alright?" he asked.

I nodded, stuffing my face with the very tasty thick beef and potato stew which was the main item on today's menu.

"You should make Salzburg for the weekend," he asserted. "Strasbourg by Thursday night and then into Schwarzbach autobahn customs on Friday."

"Just in time for it to close," Ian commented. "You'll have to check in for your *laufzettls* and then see if there's anyone in the Pars office," Ron said. "If not, walk over to the Pension Fenninger for the night and do the customs on Saturday morning."

Straight after lunch the runner arrived on his velo bike and handed us the paperwork. We said our goodbyes to Ron and Peter, who were off to enjoy a night in Moutiers and, after examining our papers, we rejoined our Macks. As was always my habit, I walked around the truck hitting every tyre with my tyre lever to check for inflation, checked out that the rear lights were working and double-checked that the twistlocks were tight and that the trailer leg pinions were locked in place. Then it was up into the driving seat to place my paperwork securely in my document case. Once the motor was started and warmed for a few minutes, I followed Ian out of the parking area and turned right onto the slushy but gritted Albertville road. The difference in handling was quite amazing. We were grossing at around 38 tonnes and skip-changing was now out of the question. I started her off in second with first split and from then on every split had to be used unless you were going downhill in which case you could experiment a little bit. First or crawler was only really necessary, I found, when starting off uphill or as I was later to discover if you were one of the aficionados who made it a point of honour never to engage the clutch! Anyway, there we were, fully loaded on the open road and I was onto the next stage of my continental adventure.

19

The Doubs Valley

SNOW hung heavily on the pinewoods through which the Albertville road wended its way between the mountainsides. The branches were weighed down, the current lack of wind failing to relieve them of their burden. The road was clear and well gritted and the air had the freshness of the mountains upon it. Traffic was light as we passed through the myriad small villages lining the Alpine pass. Ian had instructed me simply to follow him without informing me about the route, though I was pretty sure we would be heading back the way we came once through Albertville as my map showed significant zigzag mountain passes on the most obvious route through Nantua. Sure enough, as we entered Albertville over the modern concrete bridge across the river which was swollen to torrent size, we struck out to the left, back towards Chambéry. The road was now a fast straight tree-lined Route Nationale and by 4 o'clock we were skirting Chambéry, but instead of retracing our steps towards Lyon, Ian appeared to be following the Aix les Bains signs and as dusk fell we were travelling along the bank of the Lac du Bourget on the D991. Once past the lake, we took a sharp left and immediately were on a bridge over the wide Rhone river and just outside Couloz, Ian pulled off the road into a shallow parking area, more of a layby really, at the far end of which I could see the welcoming lights of a low lying routier which rejoiced in the name of Relais de la Chat de Montverand. We entered, ordered coffees and sat at a table covered in bright red and orange plastic tablecloth.

"Nice run that," Ian said. "Next bit's up into the mountains but once the other side we're safe and sound. We're actually doing two sides of a triangle but that's because we're too high for the Tunnel du Chat. You know," Ian continued, once again rolling up, "we've got loads of time to get up to Salzburg. We'll be at Strasbourg tomorrow lunchtime at this rate which means we could hit Salzburg on Friday morning." Ian touched the side of his nose. "Never arrive in Salzburg before lunchtime on Friday."

"Why's that?" I asked innocently.

"Because they'll turn you straight round and you'll be back down the road, that's why," Ian confided, lighting up his incredibly thin cigarette. "What you want is a nice weekend in Salzburg at the Pension Fenninger, meet the other lads and then head out on Monday morning and if you're really lucky, offload, backload and return by Friday evening for another weekend at the company's expense."

The coffees arrived at our table and Ian settled comfortably into his chair enjoying his smoke. The snow had all but disappeared by now but Ian reckoned there would be some more at the top of the next mountain pass. I picked up a Menu Routier from the middle of the table and noted the set menu of crudités, Boeuf Bourgignone, Mousse au Chocolat and Fromages de Pays.

"Let's knock it on the head for the day," Ian announced. "We'll eat here and stay at that *chambres d'hotes* opposite, have an early start and hit Strasbourg tomorrow afternoon." As a new boy I wasn't going to argue. The Relais was cosy with a bright log fire burning in a huge stone fireplace, smoke intermittently billowing into the room as breaths of gathering wind blew across the chimney top.

"Weather's blowing up as well," Ian pointed out. "Sensible decision not going over the top in these conditions."

I looked out of the window at the rapidly darkening street with no sign of rain, sleet or snow but had to agree with my mentor who was more experienced than me and so we finished our coffees and I waited while Ian sauntered over the road to the pension. Luckily there were rooms, very basic rooms but clean and well aired. We were the only people staying there so the communal facilities were not a problem either. Back in the Relais we enjoyed the menu and the couple of bottles of free red plonk before retiring for the night. Breakfast of coffee, croissants and fresh bread with butter and jam was over by 8 o'clock and we roared out of the parking layby by 8:15 and onto the mountain pass. I was just starting to enjoy the ride, gear shifting had now become almost second nature, and the sight in my mirrors of the container sitting in front of the rear bogie with another length of skeletal trailer behind it, emphasised that I was in command of a real juggernaut. Then the snow started. Within a couple of kilometres past the village of Beon we were driving through a virtual whiteout. I wondered how Ian was coping. I had the benefit of being able to follow in his tracks. As far as I was aware there was no one in front of him so he was acting as trail finder. My headlights blazed into the storm and the strange thing was that as I looked up at the top of the screen, now sporting a layer of snow where the wipers didn't reach, I could see the reflected orange glow from the five running lights on top of the cab. We reached the summit fairly easily, there being no hairpins on this route and made the descent over the awe inspiring Gorges de l'Ain into Cheignieu-la-Balme in rapidly improving conditions. We turned right onto the D1504 and the snow was gone. We made rapid progress along this rural road with its large arable fields on either side and had reached Nantua by 10 o'clock. Heading west out of the city on the D979 we were once again up into Alp foothills, this time with hairpins but thankfully very little snow. North of Bourg-en-Bresse we were on the D1083, an ancient very straight highway reminiscent of the old Roman roads such as Watling Street in England. In fact, I thought the scenery was very rural English with successions of small villages and vast expanses of farmland broken up only by picturesque copses and the odd water tower. The weather was now dreary with the occasional shower but nothing to phase this newly accomplished Alpine trucker!

We stopped for diesel, a sandwich and a drink outside Lons le Saunier, with Ian once again insisting on settling the bill, touching his nose, then moving his finger forward and pointing at the sky saying. "We'll settle up in Salzburg." After this brief snack we took the N83 north east, a very similar road to the one we had been driving along all morning – a gently undulating straight road with regular narrowly compressed routes through villages which were in dire need of bypasses. I was becoming intrigued by the advertisements on many of the farm buildings, mainly for beverages such as Ricard and Suze. In particular, I was struck by the sheer number of posters advertising Vin Fou d'Henri Maire. With nothing better to do than explore my vivid imagination I got to wondering whether it was the product which was mad or were the drinkers of said product mad or, worse still, did the product drive the drinkers mad. Transiting

the picturesque small town of Arbois with its pant-
iles so similar to Tunbridge Wells, I actually saw a
large shop with "Henri Maire" emblazoned above the
windows. We were passing very slowly and I noted
that the whole town seemed to be a market place
for vintners, almost every establishment advertising
the merits of its vine based products. On subsequent
journeys I discovered that Vin Fou was in fact a fizz,
or a Methode Champenoise. The other thing that I
noticed, and I can't remember which village it was in,
was a University of the Dairy Industry. A University
would you believe? I was beginning to wonder if the
French were on the same planet. After this lush agricultural area we stayed on the N83 north eastwards
and bypassed the major conurbation at Besancon
whose major claim to fame according to the posters
appeared to be its Carrefour hypermarket. After
Besancon we now descended down into the valley of
the river Doubs, a good flat run alongside the river in
many places, and followed its many meanders. Here
the villages were very touristy with plenty of caravan
parks, especially at points where the river cascaded
over weirs bypassed by locks to accommodate the
barges which still plied up and down. The road left the
riverside after Isle sur le Doubs and we entered hilly
territory with the peaks of the snow covered Vosges
mountains visible to the left and the Swiss Alps to the
right. The road then took a sharp left turn and we
passed through the market town of Hericourt before
a clear run around the Belfort bypass and then onto
the Mulhouse to Colmar road still classed as N83. Just
after Colmar, Ian turned into the parking area of a
routiers. The time was now 3 o'clock and I was beginning to wonder if we would make it to the frontier
before it closed for the night.

"Only an hour from here," Ian reassured me.

"We'll clear ourselves out of France, then it's over the bridge into Kehl where we'll check in our papers and be cleared first thing in the morning."

The routiers was quite a modern building, flat roofed with large picture windows and a terrace which in the summer looked to be a good place to spend a rest period with its views across to Switzerland, the frontier of which was only about ten miles away. Our brief sojourn over, we drove out of the parking lot and by 4 o'clock had entered the parking area for Strasbourg customs.

This was a busy frontier and the size of the customs building and warehouse complex confirmed its importance as the main transit point between those old commercial allies, France and Germany. We passed the customs offices and entered the customs agent's building finding the offices of Gondrand Freres on the first floor, a smart bustling open plan office behind a glass partition through which we had to pass our paperwork. The clerk on the other side welcomed Ian as an old hand and I was once again introduced as a new boy learning the ropes.

"'E is good teach," the clerk smiled at me indicating Ian with his thumb as he turned away to complete the necessary paperwork. "Kom back one hour."

We returned to our trucks with nothing to do since, being Iranian registered, we had no log books to update or any formalities to complete ourselves.

"Got to be careful on the German side," Ian cautioned. "You've got things like the *tankshein* and *steurkarte* to contend with. The agent will do the necessary but it's your responsibility if there are problems at Salzburg."

The *tankshein*, Ian explained to me, was a certificate to prove how much diesel you had taken out of Germany on the previous trip. You could import the same amount on the next trip with no fees but any excess was subject to tax.

"This is your truck's first trip into Germany so you'll get taxed on whatever is in your tank," he explained. "I think they allow 50 litres but after that you, or rather Pars, will have to pay. We'll make reasonable declarations and they may not dip our tanks. We should have about 200 litres each. I've got a *tank-shein* for exactly that amount so I'm OK but you'll be paying for at least 150 litres." He then explained that the trick was to enter Germany with roughly the amount showing on your paperwork. The problem was that diesel was considerably more expensive in Germany than in France or the Benelux countries, so it made economic sense, logically, to see how much you could smuggle in. There was also a backhander system whereby you could by mistake interleave a 20 Deutschmark note into your paperwork when you handed it to the Tank control. If it was not there when the papers were returned, you were home and dry. There would be no dipping of the tank. If it was still there you would be for the high jump!

"Doesn't affect us really," Ian said as he reached the steps to his cab, "the company pay whatever invoices we present so it doesn't make any difference and anyway we make more money (here he felt his nose again) buying diesel in Germany than anywhere else."

On the other side of the truck parking lot from the customs house was a substantial railhead and I observed the shunting operations of the massive SNCF and DB engines as they detached from their respective trains and changed over for the run back into their own countries. The Germans appeared to be still using steam haulage on their freight trains while the French locos were all shiny green electrics. The shunters however on both sides were still steam.

At 5 o'clock we received our completed paperwork from Gondrand and crossed the steel trellised bridge across the River Rhine which separated France from Germany. Once over this bridge, the car and coach traffic went straight ahead to report to booths, rather like toll booths, strung out across the carriageways. Trucks took a right turn and then a bridge back over the main road and down into the freight customs. We parked up and, within minutes, a small Opel screamed across the tarmac and a not unattractive mousy-haired fraulein, rather tousled and a little unkempt, but dressed in a green leather jacket, knee length plaid patterned skirt and black nylons jumped out and started talking to Ian. He beckoned me over, making a sign which I took to mean "bring your paperwork", and I walked over to his truck.

"This is the lovely Helga from Transmaas, our agent," Ian said, as we shook hands. "She'll lodge the paperwork tonight. Customs closes at six but we'll be clear to roll in the morning, subject to *tankshein* control, of course." He smiled knowingly at Helga.

"How many litres each of you?" she asked in clipped English. As previously agreed, we declared 200 litres. She took all the papers and placed them in a red file. "I'll be back to take you to the hotel at six," she smiled at Ian, again I thought, a little too knowingly. We got our overnight things together and, sure enough, just after six, Helga returned. Ian placed himself in the front passenger seat of the Kadett and I scrambled into the rear and Helga took off at a ridiculous rate of knots to the gate at the far end of the parking lot. Here we had to show our passports to a uniformed ruddy-faced official who stamped them and handed them back. The gate lifted and Helga headed for the hotel which was situated on the outskirts of the town and seemed to be aimed at the more impecunious sort of commercial traveller. It was sparse, to say the least, but we did get our own rooms and I was amused to note the toilet arrangements with the inspection area before you flushed. There was a small restaurant on the ground floor.

"See you for dinner," I said cheerily to Ian as we parted at the top of the stairs to the second floor.

"Not tonight mate," he said. "I'm not feeling too good."

I shrugged, entered the room, stripped off and showered. While I was dressing I happened to look out of the window to the street below and there was Ian getting into an old and battered Opel Kadett!

20

Das Autobahn

I met Ian at breakfast time in the cheerless white-walled restaurant on the ground floor of the hotel. A reasonably decent buffet of cereals, muesli, cold meats, rolls and jams had been laid out next to a coffee machine and an urn dispensing hot water to add to the tea bags which sat listlessly on a saucer by its side. The linen underneath the buffet was white, the tablecloths were white – all unfortunately a rather dull in-need-of-a-wash white – and the view through the couple of windows which looked out to the main street was of a drizzly dull morning. It was a distinctly depressing start to what was to be the last day of my first continental journey.

"Enjoy yourself last night?" Ian asked.

"No, I just had a sandwich down here and then turned in. I was exhausted," I replied.

"Me too," Ian said.

I looked at him, thinking "I know what you were up to you lucky bastard." But I was far too polite to mention that I knew about his assignation with the little fraulein from the agents.

After breakfast we returned to our rooms and packed our meagre overnight things before meeting in what passed for the hotel reception area, an airless corridor with a desk, phone and chair behind which was a row of hooks for the room keys. We settled our bills just as Helga arrived and we were whisked off at the only speed Helga seemed to be able to master, which was breakneck, through the streets back to the frontier. She took us straight to the Transmaas office which was situated in an ancient warehouse complex built originally to tranship cargoes from rail to road it appeared, as there were train tracks and an offloading platform down the entire side of it. We climbed the steps onto this platform and at the back were the offices. Helga led us through the driver's area with its reception windows rendered useless by sheets of brown paper which had been stuck on the inside to prevent curious drivers from discovering how hard the incumbents were working or, more likely, not working. Here paperwork would be handled back and forth through the slots provided. Then we passed through a door and into the main office which housed six desks complete with their typewriters, and at the right side a Siemens telex machine and a Xerox photocopier. Her desk was right at the back and we were both invited to sit down although Ian, I was convinced, was being more warmly invited than me! Every time she looked at him it was with "come to bed" eyes and I was feeling increasingly envious.

"So sorry," she said. "Last night I had no time to present your papers into customs." I bet you didn't, I thought. "So," she continued, "I will do that now but let's just check to make sure all is in order." She laid our papers out on her desk, mine on the left in front of me and Ian's on the right.

"OK," she said. "Arthur you have from Gondrand, CMR note for 22 tonnes of steel ingots, Invoice from Carbone de Savoie, Certificate of Origin, German road permit and Tryptychs. Ian," here she flashed him what could only be described as an intimate smile, "you have CMR, Invoice, Certificate of Origin,

183

Tryptychs permit and *tankshein*. Do you have your *laufzettls*?"

Ian looked at her a little sheepishly.

"You were supposed to collect them from the gate when you arrived," she said with a slight hint of exasperation in her voice.

"Sorry," was all Ian could muster.

"I'll fix it," she said. "Are you paying for both the *steurkartes* Ian, or you each pay?"

"We'll each pay," Ian said.

"OK, come back in one hour and all should be ready and you can get your passports stamped and then go," she said a little wistfully and smiled up at Ian.

We returned to our trucks to find the parking area filling up fast as trucks came across from the French border post which also opened at 8 o'clock. I stowed my small case between the two seats, and walked over to Ian's truck.

"Coffee while we wait?" he asked. We locked the trucks and Ian guided me over to a driver's canteen situated in the middle of the vast customs complex in what had probably originally been an engine repair shop. We sat down and Ian collected the steaming cups from the counter. The small cafe was well patronised and there was a veritable babel of conversation in several tongues.

"I'd better explain those documents to you," Ian said, rolling-up yet again. He licked the edge of the Rizla and continued. "The CMR is basically the contract between the shipper and the transport company. It's not technically a customs document but they all want to see it and now most of them take a photocopy. The shipper keeps the top copy which is signed by us as proof of taking over the goods. We take the rest and at destination the consignee signs for the goods and keeps the bottom copy. The rest comes back to us as our proof that we've delivered. The invoice is self-explanatory. The Certificate of Origin is a legalised document raised by the shipper to prove that the goods were manufactured in a particular country, in our case, France."

"What about the *laufzettl* and the *steurkarte*?"

"I'm coming to that," Ian said, taking a long drag from his cigarette and blowing the smoke out in my direction. What with Gauloises, Gitanes, Marlboros and roll-ups my poor old lungs were starting to take a right bashing and I coughed.

"Sorry to interrupt," I said.

"Right," Ian continued, clearing his throat. "The *laufzettl* card is proof that you've gone through all the correct procedures. So you're supposed to collect one on entering the compound. It's then stamped by customs once they've cleared you, and by passport control and by the *tankshein* control. Then when you hand it in at the gate, they'll let you through. At frontiers where you have both customs posts in the same area, like Schwarzbach Autobahn for instance, you have to get all the stamps from the German and the Austrian controls on the same card. The *steurkarte* is proof that you've paid road tax. It's based on the number of kilos gross weight of cargo and truck, times the number of kilometres you'll be travelling. I've already explained the *tankshein* so now you know everything," he smiled.

I was starting to believe that actually driving a truck was a minor part of being a continental driver. It seemed you needed to be a bit of a secretary and an accountant as well! After coffee we both checked our trucks' engine coolant and oil levels, all the running lights and the tyres before reporting back to Helga. Everything was ready.

"You also have the German transit T1 paper," she explained. "And both trucks are now sealed."

Ian examined both sets of paperwork before she again flashed a naughty intimate smile at her lover of the previous night as we left the office. We had already paid Helga for our road tax. Luckily Iran had a special arrangement with Germany so our rate was substantially lower than British trucks would pay and I had parted with 49 Deutschmarks.

Our next stop was the passport control and we handed our *laufzettls* and passports through a tiny window space, where a faceless bureaucrat took them. We waited a couple of minutes and back they came both complete with Kehl am Rhein entry stamps. Back in our cabs, the diesels roared into life and we snaked our way through the parked Unics, Saviems, MANs, Mercedes and Magiruses to the exit gate. Ian handed over his *laufzettl* and was waved through. I took his place and handed over my *lauzettl*. "Plombe gut?" the guard asked me. I shrugged and raised both hands palm-up in a gesture of incomprehension. The guard beckoned me to dismount and I followed him to the back of the container. He looked at me accusingly.

"Plombe! Plombe! Wo ist die Plombe?" he barked.

Intuitively, I guessed he was looking for the doors which of course were at the front of the container so it was now my turn to beckon and I led him back and pointed to the doors. Then I realised that what he was looking for was the customs seal. He jumped up onto the tractor chassis and examined the door fasteners which sure enough now had a metal wire laced through them with a lead seal attached. He returned to the ground.

"Alles gut," he said. "Gehen, gehen!"

I needed no further encouragement and leapt back

up into my cab and drove through the raised red and white pole which descended again the moment I was out of the compound. Ian was waiting for me and together we took the national B36 road towards Rheinau, travelling on the right bank of the river Rhine which acted as the frontier at this point. The route was flat, bordered by tall poplar-like trees which were remarkable in that they abounded in huge clumps of mistletoe. At Rheinau we turned right towards Achern where at last we joined the autobahn system and turned north onto the A5 towards Karlsruhe. To the left were the flatlands bordering the mighty Rhine and to the right could be made out the hills and lushly wooded slopes of the Black Forest. We passed signs for Baden Baden and soon came upon the huge autobahn interchange at Karlsruhe. I could see that you had to be darn careful to select the correct lane of the six or more on offer at one point but Ian knew the route well and I followed faithfully in his tyre steps. You had the choice of Darmstadt/Frankfurt am Main, Landau/Kaiserslautern or Pforzheim/Stuttgart. We were very obviously following the Stuttgart lanes and soon we swung off to the right onto the E52 and immediately onto a steep uphill tract of road taking us up over the fringes of the Black Forest itself. Passing Rastatte Pforzheim on the edge of a deep valley we swept down and over it on a magnificent stressed concrete bridge. The road now descended but was still hilly as we passed Stuttgart and later its airport with a few tourist hotels clustered around it. At Kirchheim, just the other side of Stuttgart, Ian took the feeder lane into the services and parked next to a light green Bussing wagon and drag.

"Spot of lunch," he yelled up to me as I parked in the nearest available bay three trucks away next to a U.S. army wagon with its white star insignia on the door. I walked back to the Bussing which was between me and the restaurant and found Ian having a chat with its driver.

"Nice cab," Ian said. "Have a look inside."

The German driver smiled and opened the door for me. There was a perfectly flat floor and enough space to swing as many cats around as you could imagine. I looked questioningly at Ian.

"Where's the engine?"

"Under the chassis, just like a bus," he answered motioning me to look, and sure enough there behind the cab was slung very neatly under the chassis girders the engine and gearbox.

"If only!" I remarked, but the German driver was even more intrigued by our Macks and before we could access our lunches Ian showed him round his cramped accommodation.

"Schon, sehr schon," the driver beamed at us as we said our goodbyes.

"Very schon," Ian remarked. "If you don't have to live with it. I know what I'd prefer to be driving out of here!"

We ate lunch in the main restaurant, very civilised and clean, schnitzels, crushed roast potatoes and vegetable salad with mayonnaise, lubricated by strong black coffees, all for 15 Deutschmarks each. How very different to my previous life dining at Bert's on the A1 with its witty "Please don't ask for credit as a punch in the mouth sometimes offends" sign on its aged paint flaked walls. Drivers on the continent were definitely much higher up the pecking order here and were treated with a lot more respect. After lunch we dieselled up and checked our levels before joining the autobahn for the afternoon's thrash through to our destination. We were still in hilly country with one or two magnificent valleys down which we hurtled onto sweeping bridges across rivers before labouring up to the next hilltop, our smokestacks belching the black stuff. Snow was prevalent in the surrounding forests but the road was absolutely clear, there not having been a recent fall. After Ulm the road left the hilly region and by Augsburg we were cruising along a flat road with vast agricultural terrain on either side. As we approached Munich, industrialisation was rearing its ugly but highly profitable head and the factories and warehouses took over the views on either side. I was faithfully following Ian but he had already told me that if I lost him I was to follow the signs for the Mittlerer ring and eventually I would come to the exit for the E45 to Salzburg. Luckily I did not lose sight of him, managing to keep within a couple of car lengths the whole way around the city which was quite difficult as the ring was extremely busy and German drivers did not seem to live in fear of juggernauts, cutting us up at every opportunity.

Once on the E45, things calmed down and we were again travelling a fairly flat route through pine forests on either side. These had received a dusting of snow but nothing to particularly worry about. After the autobahn junction for Innsbruck and Kufstein, the road again rose up into Alpine foothills and snow became increasingly prevalent. Passing Rosenheim we descended into a long valley and soon were running alongside Lake Chiemsee which, amusingly I thought, housed an American Forces Rest and Relaxation centre.

"You can't afford to relax," I shouted to no one within hearing distance. "You're supposed to be out there on guard protecting us from the communist hordes!"

After a brief stop at Chiemsee services for a quick coffee we continued up into the mountains past Bad

Reichenhall and then we had arrived at Schwarzbach Autobahn frontier. We parked in the truck parking area on the right side before the customs gate which was situated next to a structure spanning the autobahn which looked exactly like something you would expect to see on a British motorway service area. Underneath this were a series of toll booths where the car traffic paused momentarily to show their passports before either continuing unhindered into Austria or being pulled over by the customs for a random search.

"Lock the truck up and bring your paperwork and overnight case," Ian shouted to me.

I noticed that it was 5:45.

"Just crossing over to the office," Ian said. "They should be there until 6 at least."

We mounted the steps to the bridge that traversed the autobahn and I looked back down the valley towards Bad Reichenhall backed by its mountain range. On the left was the arrival parking area and on the right the Austrian and German customs area for German bound trucks. The frontier appeared to be on a ridge between two valleys so that when you looked from the other side of the bridge, the road again was declining towards Salzburg which was a speck at this distance. All around was pine forest and once we had descended the steps from the bridge we could see ahead on the left, amongst the trees, a row of what looked like shops in a modern two storey retail precinct but was in fact an office block with the Pars office at the far end on the right. Ian approached the door, pushed it open and we both entered. Immediately in front of us, running the length of the office, was a wooden counter with a flap at one end. Behind this counter there was an opaque glass door leading into what I assumed to be a manager's office. Behind the desk was an Iranian.

"Ah, Mr Rahimi," Ian said. "How are you?"

The Iranian was dunking a tea bag into a tea glass. As he withdrew it he carefully wound the string of the tag around the bag and pressed it against his spoon in order to squeeze every last drop into the glass. He looked up and smiled, flashing his gold teeth.

"Mr Ian," he replied. "Welcome back! And this, I guess, is Mr Arthur?" Ian was about to answer when the office door opened and a slimly built man dressed in a sports jacket with dark beige trousers entered. His hair was blonde and his face still had the flush of youth though I guessed him to be at first glance in the region of 30 years old.

"Ian, you old son of a gun, you made it," he enthused. "Arthur, welcome to Salzburg." He extended his hand which we both shook in turn and then ushered us into the back office past a couple of desks which I supposed were used by the clerks as they each had their quota of typewriters, trays of forms and carbon papers.

"Sorry," Ian said. "I didn't introduce you. This is Gerhardt, our boss here in Austria. What he says goes. Remember that and you'll be OK"

"You're too much, Ian," Gerhardt laughed. "I'm just the office manager. I also have to do what I'm told although translating what I get from Tehran and London can often be tricky." His accent was perfect American, either he had spent time over there or learned English at an American language school. He called to Mr Rahimi to fetch us some tea and when it arrived asked us to give him all our paperwork. "Which side are you parked?" he asked.

"German side, it's easier to access," Ian said and Gerhardt nodded in agreement.

He turned his bright blue eyes to me and said, "Our basic problem is that we have three owners:

Mr Achemian in London who is more of an English gentleman than an English gentleman and also knows how to run this business. Then we have one partner in Tehran who, frankly, is an asshole and one who spends most of his time in Germany acting the playboy, draining our petty cash and worse still appearing here out of the blue insisting on screwing everything up. Other than that it's a pretty slick operation." Obviously he had a good sense of humour, someone you warmed to immediately and, I thought, a good guy to be working for.

"Can't get you back on the road before Monday," he sighed and winked. "Ian you'll be back out to Europoort and Arthur, there should be a container coming in. He passed Spielfeld border this morning, loaded for Bremerhaven, pickled goatskins, perfectly OK till you open the doors," he grimaced. "Anyway, we're finished for the day so I'll run you both over to the Pension Fenninger and then I'm off to Munich for the weekend. Janice will be here in the morning. She'll sort out your clearances and you can offload at the depot and then you're out on the town!"

Outside the snow was trickling down as we made our way to the parking lot behind the offices. Gerhardt's dark blue Mercedes with the company logo on the doors was soon trundling us on a track through the woods to the back road from Salzburg to Bad Reichenhall, which was more a country lane than a road and onto which we turned right and within half a kilometre we had reached the pension on the left side after some farm buildings, one of which had been converted into a restaurant. The hotel itself stood back from the road and was a fairly new construction but a typical Alpine chalet design, three stories high, with a huge steeply pitched roof. We said our goodbyes.

"See you guys on Monday," Gerhardt called as he waved through his open window and took off back the way we had come.

We entered the reception area, a light and airy lobby with wide stairs leading up to the rooms behind the desk. A middle-aged man with a receding hairline, slight build and hospitable demeanour welcomed us.

"Herr Jacob, how are you," Ian said, embracing our host. "This is Herr Arthur. He's new so we have to be nice to him."

Jacob shook my hand and handed us the keys to our rooms.

"You will eat in the restaurant tonight?" he asked. "Also we have Herr Bob here and Herr Mick. They are reserved at 8 o'clock so you could join them." Jacob enunciated his words very carefully as though he was constantly practising his English. He pulled Ian to one side. "Herr Bob is drinking too much," he confided and with a most concerned voice. "You should do something or he will end up very sick."

"Thanks, Herr Jacob," Ian said. "We'll see what we can do." We made our way up to our rooms which were on the second floor.

"There's a wonderful smell of fresh pine and chlorine," I observed.

"That's from the swimming pool and the sauna in the basement," Ian explained. "The girls from Lagermax come over at the weekend to swim, great fun," he asserted once more with that familiar touch to the side of his nose. My room was light and spacious with three beds all pristinely made up with white cotton duvets. My view was of the Untersberg Mountain, but darkness had already fallen so I didn't really appreciate it until the morning. I did note, however, that snow was building up on the ledges of the balcony outside. Stripping off, I entered the shower and enjoyed the flow of hot water splashing all around me. Next would be dinner with Ian, Bob (the alleged inebriate), and some of the other drivers. Tomorrow I would be tipping my container in Salzburg with a free weekend ahead and the delightful prospect of the Lagermax girls in the pool. On Monday I could be heading for Bremerhaven. What was there not to like about this new life?

21

Pension Fenninger

MONDAY morning saw me inching up the queue of trucks which were proceeding at a snail's pace towards the Austrian/German border. During the previous night it had been blizzarding and a substantial amount of snow had fallen. This morning however, was bright and clear with the sun shining down from its position over the Untersberg which dominated the border crossing compound. The queue had started from the point at which the Salzburg to Vienna autobahn joined the route coming up from Graz. I quickly learnt that this meant about two kilometres to the border post and right now it looked as though it was going to take all day to get there. On my left were thickly snow-coated farmer's fields behind which there were dense pine forests cowering beneath the weight of the previous night's snowfall. Above the tree line the mass of craggy granite which formed the Untersberg Mountain itself loomed up to its summit, the ridge of which crossed over the frontier into Germany. On my right was another vista of flat farmer's fields across which could be seen several agricultural chalets, the last of which just before the Forest, was the Pension Fenninger. The forest itself stretched right down to the autobahn about one kilometre before the border.

The weekend spent at the company's base had indeed been a memorable one, starting with dinner at the Pension Rohrwirt next door to our hotel. Ian had met me in the lobby and, there being no sign of the other drivers, we made our way over to the old farm building in which the restaurant was housed. This was another alpine chalet but of a much older design than the hotel. It fronted directly onto the original Salzburg to Bad Reichenhall road which still had a frontier post about two kilometres further on in the forest. The road end of the building was originally the farmer's accommodation, while the other half of the building had been designed for, and still housed, cattle during the winter months. The second and third stories housed bedrooms which were used as an over-flow from the Pension Fenninger and above the byre those two stories accommodated a hay barn. Both buildings, the Fenninger and the Rohrwirt, backed onto extensive pasture land. It was indeed a very rural setting. Inside everything was pine – the low ceilings with their exposed rafters, the highly polished floors, the tables and chairs and the partitions which divided up the room into cosy segments. The overall impression was one of timeless solidity. The smells emanating from the kitchen area were redolent of garlic and paprika and another I couldn't place but learnt later was from the local Stroh rum, a smooth sugary alcoholic scent which wafted delightfully through the room every time a door from the service area was opened.

"This was the original farmhouse," Ian explained. "Next door, as you probably realise, is only a couple of years old. What happened was that when they built Salzburg airport the farmers who lost land made a lot of money. The canny ones like Herr Fenninger used the money to build pensions for the tourist trade which was increasing by leaps and bounds partly because of the *Sound of Music* and then again because of the development of the airport."

A waitress dressed in the Bavarian serving-wench style of ample green skirts embroidered with red and yellow flower designs and a neat pinafore with a white lacy bodice, in this case amply filled with her charms, finished off the ensemble.

"Bourgey, how are you?" Ian exclaimed and almost swept her off her feet with his embrace. She was a very attractive woman in her late thirties, brunette with swept back hair gathered together by a dark red bow. Her face was lean and her ruddy complexion suggested that she spent as much time in the fields and the byres as in the restaurant. She was well built, but by no means fat, and her dress emphasised her mature feminine curves. Her legs also looked good and she wore, as did many Austrian women, neat white socks and soft shoes with open heels. After a minute of this close encounter, Ian introduced me and asked if Bob and Mick had arrived.

"Yes, they are here," she smiled winningly and led us round the corner of the next partition where our colleagues were already comfortably seated with steins of lager. Introductions took place and I learned that Bob was an Iranian Indian who had spent many years in England and working with British companies in the Gulf. I was just thinking that, for a driver, he was a little overdressed in a smart blue blazer, blue striped open necked shirt sporting a dark blue cravat, and light grey slacks, when Ian explained that he was in fact the yard manager in charge of transhipping the containers at the Pars terminal in town. Late middle-aged and silvery haired, he had a face that must have been very handsome when young and he had the air of being something of a playboy but without the lavish riches to back the lifestyle. He spoke perfect English and I could tell from the way that Bourgey looked at him as we sat down that he still possessed a charm that attracted the ladies.

"Bourgey," he asked, "please bring a couple of beers for the boys."

She hurried off and Bob turned his attention to me. He half stood and extended his hand.

"Welcome to Salzburg" he enthused. "It's nice to see another Englishman on the company." A frown passed over his face. "We have trouble at the moment keeping drivers. London send us so many who just are not up to it. A couple of weeks ago three flew in and even before they had turned a wheel, two of them disappeared. I think they have difficulty adjusting to the demands of the job," he finished.

"Demands?" I asked.

"Well," Bob explained. "They come out here never having left the United Kingdom before and they expect everyone to adapt to them, not the other way round. For example, very few of us speak German but at least we try to use as many words as possible. Some of these guys refuse to do that and end up rudely shouting at the waitresses in the Guter Halle, the restaurant we all use every day next to the transhipment terminal. It's embarrassing, and I tell Gerhardt to send them home. They're no good to the company. For me, I speak Farsi and English but now I've been here six months and every time I get the opportunity I try to communicate in German. The Austrians appreciate that. Personally I don't want anyone to know I'm stupid but these idiots wear it like a badge of honour. It's this abominable 'We won the war' cockiness but what they forget is they didn't win it. It was their fathers and you don't get far in life by living forever off the exploits of your parents. That's history." He settled back against the upholstered back of the bench and rested his arm on the sill of the window, like in most Austrian chalets, a very deep sill with secondary glazing fitted to keep out the cold. Bourgey returned with the beers and bending over the table to distribute them revealed a delightful amount of cleavage to the evident delight of Bob and, to be honest, myself.

"Could we have some menus please, Bourgey?" Bob asked, unable to take his eyes off her chest. Bourgey smiled, knowing the effect she was having on us sex-starved reprobates.

"More beer for you and Herr Mick?" she enquired. Bob nodded assent and Bourgey hurried back through the room picking up empty steins from other tables before disappearing through the kitchen doorway.

Bob smiled. "I can see you're a natural truck driver," he looked at me in a kind of confidential way.

"Why's that?" I asked.

"Your eyes didn't leave her backside until she vanished through the door," he laughed. I was beginning to notice that Mick was not taking any great part in our conversation and so far hadn't even been introduced. Ian had also noticed.

"So you're another new boy," he said.

"Came up by train. I picked him up from Salzburg station this morning," Bob interposed. "Never driven a Mack, so you boys can teach him over the weekend."

We extended our hands and I felt his slightly clammy one weakly take mine and then quickly withdraw. I could sense that the man was scared and out of his depth.

"First time on the continent?" I asked. "I'm on my first trip too. Just come up from France with Ian. You'll like the trucks. Great to drive. Very precise gearboxes. What have you been on so far?"

"I were working on Mandators for Nichol Stevens up Barnsley way," he replied a little sheepishly. "Night trunking in the main. Glasgow, London, Bristol that sort of thing."

He shuffled a little nervously on his bench sitting opposite Bob and took out a pack of ten Player's. He extracted one from the pack and lit up holding the cigarette between his thumb and forefinger as if he was about to eject it from his grasp like a dart at any second.

"No duty frees?" Ian asked.

"Didn't think," Mick answered.

"So," Bob said, "you've not driven in Europe?"

"Nope," Mick admitted dejectedly. "I told 'em that in't office but they reckoned I'd be alright anyways."

"No offence to you," Bob said, "but they must be getting desperate. We don't take on Austrians here because most of them haven't been outside their own villages. We need people with experience of Europe or what's the point? It's just like I was saying a moment back." He lifted his eyes ceilingwards and gave Ian a look which spoke of his incomprehension at the folly of the boys in the office. By this time I was beginning to feel a little guilty having blagged my way through my own interview with Mr Achemian and here was poor Mick who had apparently told the truth and still got the job.

"Don't worry," I tried to re-assure him. "You'll get used to the trucks and I'm sure they'll send you off with someone else on your first trip."

Ian nodded agreement as Bourgey once again leaned over the table with the two beers and handed out the menus while her accoutrements brushed the table in the most engaging way. We perused the German menus and Ian and Bob helped with translations and I had the chance to study Mick even closer as he was sitting opposite Bob and myself by the window. The menu obviously did not convey very much to him and he had already despairingly laid it onto the table next to his beer. His face was thin and sallow with sunken cheeks and a rather distinctive hook nose. The eyes were a pale blue and they darted about the room failing to focus on anything in particular and appearing to have an inability to engage with whoever he might be talking to. His hair was jet black and combed in an outdated teddy-boy fashion with a DA at the neck. He was dressed in a black leather jacket with open necked black shirt and the almost universal pair of jeans which in his case were badly creased, a probable result of having spent an uncomfortable night attempting to sleep upright in a rattler as it weaved its way through the European night across flat Belgium and the river valleys and mountain tunnels of Germany. I hoped that a good night's sleep might set him back on the right road.

Eventually we ordered Gulaschsuppes to start and Wiener Schnitzels with Rostkartofelln and salad to follow. Bob told us that the first loads from Carbone de Savoie had arrived the previous day and that Joe and Steve were staying in town at the Guter Halle hotel next to the transhipment terminal. More beers followed and even Mick seemed to cheer up a little, joining in the conversation with a couple of tales of dodgy overnighters and a frozen unexpected night out on Shap fell. After an excellent meal we had all returned to the hotel and turned in for the night. Next day would see me clearing customs into Austria, driving down to the terminal to discharge my container and then possibly some fun training up Mick on the two stick Mack.

22

Tanksheins

I awoke on Saturday morning feeling slightly the worse for wear after the previous night's beers in the Rohrwirt. A shower and shave soon had me feeling as right as rain and I opened the curtains to peer out across my balcony at the distant Untersberg. It was snowing steadily, not a blizzard, because there was no wind, but a steady soft snowfall drifting gently down to top out that already settled on the ground. There was a good foot of snow piled on the balcony rail overnight. I lumbered off down the stairway to the breakfast room, another heavily pined affair with bright red and green chequered table cloths laid out neatly down the right side as you entered. This was at the front of the hotel, offering once again unrestricted views of the magnificent mountains. A young girl, no more than 16 years old, I guessed, rustled over to my window table just as Ian entered the room.

"Morning," he greeted me. "And morning to you, young Teresa. We call her Terry for short," he confided to me.

"Good morning," Terry smiled a beaming welcoming natural smile. "What you would like for *fruhstuck*?"

"Two boiled eggs – Zwo geckoken Eiern," Ian replied. "And bread rolls with butter and jam – brotchen mit butter und Marmelade und tee mit milch."

"I'll have the same," I interposed.

"You can say, 'Auch fur mir' or 'Zwei mal bitte,'" Ian advised.

Terry laughed. "No, I speak good English," she said as she left us for the kitchen area. She might well have been 16 but she was another voluptuous Austrian serving wench as far as I was concerned, with the most delicious bosoms making full use of the space inside her lacy bodice.

"Bob and Mick have already gone down to the yard," Ian said. "We've got to trail up through the wood to the frontier and clear the trucks out of Germany and into Austria. The Pars office opens at 9 on Saturday so we're in good time." Teresa placed our eggs and rolls and butter and jam on our table together with a pot of tea and a small jug of cold milk.

Once we had finished, we picked up our document cases, pulled on our reefer jackets and set off through the snow keeping to the tyre tracks as we mounted the hill towards the customs post. Halfway up, Ian veered off to the left and we followed a trackway which wound through the middle of the pine forest until we eventually came out behind the frontier cafe which we skirted around and continued towards the office block, shuffling through the snow into the Pars bureau. Mr Rahimi was behind the counter, squeezing the last drops out of his latest tea bag. He flashed us a welcoming smile.

"Ah, Mr Arthur and Mr Ian, Mrs Janice is not here today, she phoned that she is sick but your papers are ready," he said and he handed each of us a small sheaf of thin, almost airmail-quality papers which Ian explained to me were the import and transit documents for Austria. We then completed our German *tankshein* declarations, each claiming that 350 litres were still in our tanks.

"Should be OK," Ian said. "We rarely get dipped by the Germans but the Austrians tend to be a little more meticulous. Anyway we'll see."

We then completed the similar Austrian *tanksheins* showing 200 litres each, for which Ian already had an exit *tankshein* from his previous journey which would mean him paying no tax.

"Luckily," Ian paused as he rolled another cigarette, "the Germans and Austrians don't compare documents so as long as we don't get dipped we'll be alright."

Mr Rahimi shook his finger at Ian. "You teach him bad ways," he said accusingly.

"It's saving the company money, not me," Ian riposted. Mr Rahimi shrugged and we left the office having inserted the new paperwork into our document cases. Once over the bridge and into the parking area, we fired up our diesels which warmed while we cleared the snow from our windscreens.

"Follow me," Ian shouted. "We stop at the gate by the bridge and collect our *laufzettls*, then find a parking space and we'll see what level of chaos there is in the customs house this morning." Smoke billowed from our stacks as we escaped from the snow and ice which had formed round our wheels during the night, and the tyres made a crisp crackling noise as they punctured the frozen surfaces until we were back on the gritted section of the parking lot. Ian stopped at the gate and collected his *laufzettl* before moving into the large customs parking on the far side. I followed and stuck my hand out of the window to receive the yellow card segmented to receive stamps from the various customs and immigration officers. I was able to park a couple of trucks away from Ian on the right side of the large customs sheds and, gripping my document case under my arm, I jumped down and joined him and we marched across to the office building which was situated between the parking area and the autobahn. It was a frontier building typical of its type, constructed between the wars, three stories high with regular windows set back inside concrete surrounds which jutted out from the walls and the whole had been thoughtfully finished in dark foreboding grey cement paint probably last redecorated in the thirties. It had a pitched roof which was currently supporting several feet of snow and managed to look quite picturesque even in this industrial setting. We walked round the left side of the offices and entered on the opposite side next to the autobahn. We were then in a long corridor which ran the length of the building with a door about halfway along which separated the German offices from the Austrian. On our right were a series of windows through which paperwork was being vigorously thrust and received back by a throng of drivers.

"Don't worry," Ian laughed. "We don't have to visit every one. We're technically in transit through Germany and again through Austria. Several of the queues are for what they call domestic German Austrian traffic." The first queue we joined was German exit passport control where we quickly moved through a line of five drivers and presented our *laufzettls* and passports. The functionary on the other side of the window wanted to see our ugly faces and immediately stamped the passports and *laufzettls* and passed them back. The next window was for exit German transit customs and here, after a wait of about ten minutes in a line of seven other drivers, we showed our manifests, invoices, certificates of origin, carnets de passages, *steurkartes* and German permits. The opaque window had opened to receive them, a surly "Nachste bitte" had been shouted through by a faceless officer, Ian's sheaf of papers had then been thrust through, "Alles in ordnung" had been shouted back by the faceless one and then the window had slammed shut. Within a couple of minutes it clicked open again and I followed the same procedure.

"Now we wait while they process them," Ian explained.

"How long?" I asked.

"Could be ten minutes, could be half an hour or if there's a tea break or shift change, could be an hour or more. Don't worry, no hurry," he finished.

We stepped back from the small windows, each with its queue of drivers resigned to their fate, waiting at the behest of officialdom while their expensive machinery stood idle in the parking lot. I now had time to take in the scene in the corridor. Right along the opposite side of the corridor were situated a row of old tables, some with rickety chairs, where drivers could assemble their paperwork or complete various forms which several were now in the process of doing. Indeed a veritable United Nations of drivers was milling about; Bulgarians in their state-issued black leather jackets, lanky Dutchmen in their jeans and clogs, Germans in their denim bibs and braces and Turks, often short wiry thickset moustachioed characters, continually attempting to muscle in on queues only to be repulsed by the westerners determined to see fair play.

"If you're lucky you'll see a fight but whatever you do, don't join in," Ian advised. There was no chance of me doing that. I was quite happy to stand back, lean against the large window sill and observe this throng of oppressed workers being seemingly needlessly harassed by plodding European bureaucracy. Every now and then the window next to the one where we had deposited our papers would open and another disembodied voice would call through a company name – "Schenker", "Ulusoy", "Vos", "Weiss" – and a driver would scurry over to retrieve his papers. Eventually we heard "Pars" called and we collected the papers almost thrown through the window at us.

"No respect," Ian observed, picking several of his up from the floor. "Check every one to make sure they're complete and also that they've all been stamped." Luckily they all were correct and we moved over to one of the desks to sort out our *tankshein* declarations and joined the queue at the last but one window. Soon we had deposited them and returned to lean against the window opposite while we waited.

"Either they'll stamp them and hand them back or we'll be dipped and checked," Ian helpfully informed me. "And if we're dipped we've a good chance of being fined. It's possible we've both got more than four hundred litres but we'll see." Five minutes later our names were called through the last window and we answered the call and were relieved when our stamped declarations and *laufzettls* were returned to us. We then walked through the door into the Austrian side, which was almost identical except for the uniforms which were a light grey instead of the dark green of the Germans.

We sorted out our paperwork on the first unoccupied table we could find and then went through the same procedures as for the German side, except that at the last window we were shockingly informed that our tanks would be dipped.

"Please to bring your trucks for Kontrol," the voice instructed us.

"But we have only declared two hundred litres," I protested.

"Don't worry," Ian said. "We should be OK." I looked a little mystified as we returned to our trucks.

Ian touched his nose and smiled. I followed his truck around to the far side of the office building wondering if we might be incarcerated for falsifying our paperwork. I pulled up behind him and jumped down to see what was going to happen. A rotund Austrian customs official appeared with what looked like a steel metre measure.

"Ah," he said. "Pars" with a tone which could either have been interpreted as delight at seeing us or pleasure at the thought that he was about to bring to an end our little game of subterfuge. Our attempt to defraud the Austrian nation was about to end in ignominy, I thought, but I noticed that Ian was still smiling and that had to be a good omen. The official dipped both of Ian's tanks and wrote down his depth reading.

He was about to measure them when Ian piped up, "Standard Pars Macks," and thrust a couple of packs of Rothmans into the hands of the grateful minor flunkey. He pointed at me.

"Colleague, same same."

"Ah, ja, ja. Keine problem," said our erstwhile antagonist as he disappeared into his wooden shack. Within a minute he re-appeared and beamingly handed all our paperwork over including the vital, fully stamped *laufzettls*. We checked them thoroughly and the official coughed and pointed to my truck.

"Ah sorry," Ian replied and handed him another couple of packs of Rothmans. Then it was down to the gate, the *laufzettls* handed in and examined by a bored border guard, the gate lifted and we were through onto the Austrian autobahn.

It was downhill from the customs post and we were soon spinning along in sixth main and fourth split. At the bottom of the hill we followed the signs for Wien and curved off to the left while the other road signed for Graz carried on straight through the Salzburg valley. We passed the signs for Salzburg Mitte and then Ian swung right for Salzburg Nord and we found ourselves on the old main road from Vienna to Salzburg heading back into the city. The roads here were not as well gritted as the autobahn and we sidled downhill over a level crossing and swung to the right into a busy street with low rise housing. On our right I could see a sign for the Pension Guter Halle, yet another Alpine chalet, which was where the others were staying and Ian stopped next to it putting his emergency flashers on. I also ground to a halt and did the same and I joined him at the front of his truck.

"There it is," he said proudly but with a wonderful sense of irony. "The Pars International container terminal."

Underwhelming was the first epithet that came to mind as my jaw dropped. Between the pension and the terminal was a lane leading down to what looked like an animal market with thatched barns and stockyards which lay behind the hotel. Next to this road was what appeared at first glance to be, and in fact was, a large derelict building site which lay a good ten feet below the roadway and was accessed down a steep slope. At the back of the site, containers were stacked and in front of them was situated a venerable crane mounted on a low loader trailer chassis which turned out to be the only means of transhipment in the yard. Parked in the middle was a new Mercedes car in the colours of PIC and with the Iranian map on the front doors. Bob emerged from the interior and proffered his hand.

"Congratulations, you made it," he said. "Welcome to my empire." He gestured around the scene of third world technology plonked in the middle of Austria's sophisticated capital of culture. "You'll have to reverse in," Bob announced. "There's no room to turn inside at the moment!"

We returned to the trucks.

"Ian," I said. "How did we get away with the *tanksheins*."

"Aha," he smiled. "Our new Macks have much larger tanks, almost double the size of the old ones on the fleet, but the Austrians only have the measurements for the old ones. So far they haven't twigged but it can only be a matter of time."

23

Vogelweiderstrasse

REVERSING into the Pars International Container Terminal was the most fun I'd had so far. First of all it was a blind reverse as I was on the left and the terminal was on the right. Second, Bob had decided in his wisdom that my container had to be transhipped first so I didn't have the benefit of watching Ian carry out the manoeuvre. Third, Vogelweiderstrasse was one of the busiest thoroughfares from the north into the city and all the traffic had to be halted in both directions. Actually stopping the passing vehicles was a performance in itself as none of them wanted to obey the hand signals from the Iranian terminal workers and I watched for a few minutes as cars dodged around them quite dangerously. I decided that the typical Austrian driver had no regard for the safety of pedestrians and his only concern seemed to be to keep moving at all costs. So there was only one way to resolve the issue. I edged out into the traffic until my truck was straddling the road. Even at this point a crazy individual mounted the pavement opposite. I gave him the benefit of the doubt, deciding that he was probably a doctor on a mission to save a patient with a heart condition, and commenced to reverse very slowly, throwing the steering wheel hard left to skew the trailer round to the right. The traffic on my left had stopped so close that I had no room to manoeuvre so I stopped, jumped down from the cab and walked over to the first car which would quite clearly have to come out of line and drive to the other side of the road as there was no chance of him reversing.

"Sprechen sie English?" I asked innocently enough. The window opened and a corpulent face thrust itself through the gap.

"You goddam Iranians. Get off my road," he blustered at me.

"Ich bin Englander," I smiled at him. His blood pressure was much higher than mine, I could tell from the veins standing out on his temples.

"I don't mind who are you," he bellowed. "I will see the polizei and you are in trouble." Much more of this and we would need that doctor who'd escaped over the pavement I thought.

Ian now arrived on the scene. He looked at the Austrian and said, "You want to go quickly?"

"I want to go now. Get from my way," was the considered reply.

"The only way you will move anywhere is when this truck goes back into the yard. Your stupid parking so close means he cannot do anything else!" Ian turned to me. "Jump back into the cab. I'll sort this out," he advised. As I was climbing back up the steps I could see Bob joining in the affray.

Within a couple of minutes the Austrian's light blue Beetle shunted onto the far side of the road and came to a halt a few feet to the left of my cab. Ian appeared.

"Just do as I say and we'll get you in there quickly," he instructed. "Reverse and first split. Take it dead easy because when you go over the top of the pavement you've got a steep drop of ten feet into the yard." Either my good judgement or luck or Ian's gesticulating meant I had positioned the trailer into the terminal entrance in one shunt but I was skewed round too far to give me a straight reverse onto the crane. I had already noticed that the second my tractor was halfway across the road the traffic had started on that side and the light blue Beetle in an instant had performed a brilliant outflanking action which saw it spin round the front of my bonnet, narrowly avoiding a minibus as he regained his correct side of the road and sped off, no doubt to report my transgressions to the relevant authorities. Now I had no option but to shunt forward and straighten up the rig. So started a cat and mouse battle as I crawled forward to the point at which no car could technically pass but then one would mount the pavement and I was blocked from reversing with right hand down as I needed. Ian manfully strode out to the right of my bonnet and eventually a woman stopped far enough back to enable me to turn the tractor. Ian's advice about the gears was good because crawler reverse held us back as 38 tonnes of trailer, container and steel cargo took over, attempting to pull me down the steep incline. As it was, in the icy conditions I managed to slide down part of the ramp but luckily was able to reverse straight under the crane jib. As I jumped down from the cab a small group of Iranian drivers looked up from where they were boiling cay inside one of the empty 20 foot containers. They beckoned me over and Ian, Bob and myself joined them, sitting on a threadbare carpet inside the container.

"Tea break," Bob explained. "Nothing's going to happen until they're finished so we might as well join them." Each of us was handed a small glass of the strong heavily sugared brew and I sipped it warily. Bob looked at me. "What do you think?" he smiled. "Better than Typhoo?"

"It's different," I said, wincing as the thick liquid scalded its way down my delicate throat.

"Take it easy," Bob laughed and the Iranians laughed with him.

"A bunch of jolly fellows," I thought.

"This is Hassan," Bob said as Hassan extended a greasy hand towards mine. "He's the crane operator and yard foreman and this is his assistant, Abbas." Abbas's proffered hand was even more greasy, if that were possible, than Hassan's but I shook it all the same and he smiled, which was, I thought, a good sign. Abbas was a young lad, no more than 18, about five foot four, thickset but probably with muscle rather than fat. He had a jolly round face surmounted by an unruly clump of black curly hair and was clad in a red wool jumper under a filthy anorak and a pair of cheap brown trousers over what looked like plimsolls of an indeterminate colour. Hassan, on the other hand, was in his early twenties, thin as a rake, taller than Abbas by a good four inches with a thin, almost emaciated face, prominent thinly-bridged curved nose and a fine set of gold teeth. His preferred mode of dress was a greasy open-necked shirt with jeans and plimsolls which had had a fair coating of grease and muck liberally applied. His hair was again unkempt and black and his eyes were an interesting shade of green, unlike Abbass's which were dark brown. He had an almost permanent air of busyness which was never borne out by the amount of work he actually achieved. I discovered later that both of them lived, ate and slept in one of the containers, which accounted for their unkempt appearance.

Tea finished, Hassan made his way over to the crane and started the motor, a Volvo, which instantly purred into life. Abbas jumped onto my tractor chassis and inched his way up onto the top of the snow covered container while I undid the twistlocks which needed a sledgehammer to move them as they were frozen and caked in dirty ice kicked up from the road. I stood back to watch the majesty of the operation. The crane jib lifted and four wires dangled from its hook, each ending in a U bolt. Hassan expertly swung the hook round. Abbas caught the four wires and attached them to the four corners of the top of the container and twisted in the retaining bolts. Then Hassan revved the crane motor, the wires tautened and the container, with Abbas still on top, desperately clutching one of the wires to retain his balance, lifted off my skeletal trailer, releasing the pressure on the vehicle's springs, and swung up into the air. Hassan now gunned the motor as he effected the lift and turn at the same time depositing my container on top of a stack of three. Hassan now undid the bolts and, just as I was wondering how on earth he was going to get down from a four high stack of containers, he placed his foot into the crane hook clutching all four wires and Hassan lifted the hook and he soared up a good six feet before swinging him down to the ground. It was almost like watching a circus act. I couldn't help but applaud and Hassan flashed me a toothy grin.

Bob sauntered over. "Got your paperwork?" he asked and I dived into the cab and retrieved it. "I've got two 20 foot containers for you loaded with pickled goatskins," he continued. "They're actually destined for the U.S. but we tranship them from the containers in Bremerhaven into Hapag Lloyd containers for the onward journey. You'll keep the empties and get further instructions from Gerhardt once you're tipped."

"Where's Mick?" I asked.

"He's gone up the road with Joe to learn the ropes," Bob replied. "But I have my doubts. There's something wrong there. He seems scared stiff." Bob wandered over to his car which doubled as an office, sat inside and shuffled papers about before summoning Hassan and Abbas. He then instructed them in fluent Farsi which containers to load onto my trailer and the three of us – Bob, Ian and myself – settled into the warm comfort of the Mercedes and watched the performance as, once again, Abbas jumped about from container to container and was flown on the crane hook for all the world like a trapeze artist.

"He hasn't fallen yet," Bob observed when I raised my concerns for his welfare. "If he does he'll get flown back to Iran."

"Why's that?" I asked.

"Doesn't have a work permit," Bob admitted. "That's the way these boys work. I don't approve of it but neither Abbas or Hassan is legally here although Hassan has a short term permit as an interpreter for the Iranian drivers but he's not supposed to do any actual work. Abbas technically came into Austria as a co-driver and unless anyone raises the issue he'll stay for three months, take a trip down to Yugoslavia and come back in on the next truck." I must have looked a little apprehensive at this news of the way the Iranian's treated their own countrymen because Bob pointed out that the European drivers were all on legal contracts. "We couldn't operate in Europe in the same way," he asserted. "The unions would tear us apart and we'd get blacklisted in no time."

Once my containers had been loaded, I locked all eight twistlocks, shunted the rig to a corner of the yard and Ian reversed in to carry out the same procedure. He was loading a 40 foot container for Europoort destined for England with bales of mohair. When he had finished and had parked his truck alongside mine, Bob suggested we have lunch in the Guter Halle, so we walked over to a side entrance near the cattle market which led to the restaurant which was in the basement, as the land fell away on this site in the same way that it did in our terminal. This was another heavily pine timbered Alpine room bustling with farmers, stockmen and auctioneers from the market, some dressed in lederhosen and some in the bibs and tuckers of typical German workers. Steve was in the far corner at a large table which he was obviously saving for us.

"No Joe or Mick?" he asked.

"Not back yet," Bob explained.

"I'll take a bet with you," Steve said with an air of confidence. "Mick'll be on the train out this afternoon."

"Give the poor boy a chance," Bob admonished. "He seemed to be driving reasonably well as he left the terminal. Anyway, work's over so let's get the beers in!"

A rather raddled old dame, looking every inch mutton-dressed-as-lamb in her dark green dress with another revealing bodice, came over to take our orders and she swiftly returned with four foaming steins. It turned out that Steve was also loaded for Bremerhaven so we'd be running together. Joe was loaded for Bordeaux with sports equipment which had come overland from Pakistan and been transhipped in Tehran. After we'd polished off a couple of rounds, Joe appeared with Mick and inquisitive eyes turned on the couple.

"He'll do," Joe announced and Mick actually smiled, perhaps a little wanly but I thought he did look quite pleased with himself. Bob flashed an "I told you so" look at Steve who shook his head in return. Time would tell, I thought, but we had to give Mick the benefit of the doubt.

24

Dirty Work

OUR aged waitress returned to the table with her notepad ready to take our orders. She was a kindly enough lady but her over-rouged face and the veined legs which showed above the white socks and sandal-like footwear so beloved of Austrian serving wenches painted a picture which reminded me of the absinthe-sotted barflies beloved of the French turn-of-the-century painters. One had to feel a little empathy however, for a lady of her age having to do this kind of work amongst the ribald farming and hairy-arsed cattle market community who thronged the place. Wiener schnitzels, Bratwursts mit kraut and Jagershnitzels mit kartofelsalats were the main feature of the orders plus another round of beers, some opting for Stiegls and some for Augustiners. We settled back, our work of the day over, to enjoy some camaraderie. Bob kicked the merriment off by turning to Joe.

"What was that story you were telling us about Vince Black?" he asked.

Joe smiled and slowly looked around the table. "Any of you met Vince?" he asked in the sort of tone of voice you would use if you were enquiring into the whereabouts of an axe murderer. It appeared that, of those assembled, only Bob had experienced the privilege. "A bloody disgrace," Joe asserted. "The type what gets the rest of us a bad name." Ian was rolling another slimline cigarette. Steve turned to Bob with an "Oh no, not another of Joe's tall stories" look. Mick had his face stuck into a stein, and Bob sighed the sigh of a worldly wise traveller through life who had seen it all but could still not get used to the crass stupidities manifested by the driving fraternity into whose company he had been thrust.

"Made out he's a professional with more experience than the rest of us put together," Joe continued as Ian took the first puff from his rollup. "I can tell you, this is his first job, sorry was his first job (here Joe slurred the emphasis on the word "was"). I met him on the Lyon ring road. Well, 'met' was not entirely correct. He cut me up at a junction, flying down the outside of a queue he was. Lights changed and I was just taking off when I saw the orange top cab lights hurtling past. I was lucky he didn't smack the trailer into me as he hung a right on the far side of the junction where the road narrowed. 'You selfish bastard,' I shouted but all I got was his number plate and when I checked in with Gerhardt he told me who the driver was."

"Is that it?" Ian asked a little incredulously. "Is that why they sacked him?"

"No way," Joe replied. "There's a bit more." He cleared his throat, took a long swig of his stein of Stiegl and continued. "I dropped my load of cotton at a mill down near Pont Eveque and then ran up to Paris for a load on the Friday out of Gondrand at Quai d'Ivry. All went well until they told me the clearance was at Le Bourget TIR so I was weekended." At this point the food arrived and our serving wench made much of laying out the knives and forks and forgetting who had ordered what so it was a few minutes before Joe supped another swig and took up the tale again.

"Monday morning I cleared at Le Bourget and

phoned Gerhardt. 'Thank God you've called,' he said. 'Mr Black has turned his truck over in the market square in Wasselonne that's just before you get to Strasbourg.' He told me he needed someone there as soon as possible as the truck was loaded with extremely expensive chocolates which were highly pilferable. Well, I left Le Bourget by 9 o'clock, then it was back round the Périphérique to Quai d'Ivry and the N4 the rest of the way. Reached Wasselonne round about 4 o'clock virtually non-stop and there in the Place du Generale Leclerc is Vince's truck turned over on a straight piece of road. Luckily the traffic was able to weave its way round but here's the capper. Your Vince is sitting next to it, calm as can be, flogging the chocolates! The soft top had burst open and the damn things were strewn all over the place. He smiled at me as I approached with a 'Look how clever I am' expression on his stupid face. I went absolutely ape shit I can tell you. Stopped his little game and started to clear up as much of it as I could back into the top of the container. Just as I was about to point out to him that he was driving a customs sealed wagon the *douaniers* arrived. I speak a little French so I explained the situation without mentioning the sales aspect. However, they told me that the local gendarmes had already warned him to stop selling them before they had informed the customs men. Luckily I was able to prove my innocence with my date-stamped paperwork from Le Bourget. Vince was handcuffed and marched off to the local slammer and I was left to clear up but within an hour Theo from Gondrand at Strasbourg showed up with a recovery crane. Took them a couple of hours to right it and pour the chocolates back into the top. The damage to the truck was mainly cosmetic and I was able to drive the rig into the customs at the goods yard. We emptied all Vince's things from the cab and Theo took them down to the police station. Asked me if I wanted to come along to make sure Vince was OK but I told him I really couldn't have cared less. Afterwards, Theo jumped in the cab and I gave him a lift back to the border as the recovery team had already legged it."

"What about Vince?" Ian asked.

"Here's the bit you're not goin' to believe," Joe smiled and leaned forward onto the table almost beckoning us to close in to hear some monstrous secret. "He escaped from the gendarmerie and hasn't been heard of since." He sat back in his chair and took a deep drink from his stein.

"Just the sort of ambassador we all need," Bob said. "Thank God people like him are the exception rather than the rule. I thought he was a strange character. He claimed to have been a mercenary in Africa but couldn't tell me a thing about any European driving experience. I've told London to look into the driver's references much more carefully." I blanched slightly at this. My references wouldn't have stood up to further investigation either!

"The load was a complete write-off," Bob further explained. "Our insurance had to pay its value plus common market sugar subsidies and a hefty fine from the customs. That won't help our next insurance premium one bit! To be honest, the standard of a lot of the drivers they're sending over is just ridiculous." I looked over to Mick who by now had finished his beer. He was once again looking a bit ashen and withdrawn.

"Why don't you let the Iranian drivers deliver the loads direct," I asked.

"You must be joking," Bob laughed. "If you think we've got problems with the British drivers, you should have been here when we were rescuing

Iranians from police stations and prisons all across Europe."

"Why was that?" I interjected.

"Culture shock," Bob sipped some more of his Augustiner and continued. "Most of these boys have never been outside Iran before. They don't understand European culture. In Iran, outside northern Tehran that is, all the women are dressed head to foot in Muslim robes. These lads get the idea that all the girls they see in miniskirts and low tops are prostitutes so they see no harm in propositioning them and feel free to touch them. We've got two in jail in Denmark right now and they won't be coming out for a few months. It's not worth the hassle. A few of the drivers have got used to Europe and those we do let deliver, in fact we've got four running out on Monday morning with you guys. Steve is convoying them down to France."

After lunch, Bob gave Ian, Mick and myself a lift back up to the Pension Fenninger and I had one of my customary late afternoon snoozes before we met up with a couple of beers by the swimming pool in the basement. I'd never had a sauna before and when Ian switched the thing on I was all for giving it a go. The two of us had a couple of sessions of ten minutes each in the dry and then steamy heat when Ian threw some water on the stones on top of the heater. A swim in the pool and a shower and we were ready for dinner at the Rohrwirt. I noticed that Mick had slipped back into his shell and didn't join in much with the conversation although he did sink a few beers.

"You know what you were saying about it being difficult to recruit experienced drivers?" I said to Bob. "Well the money's OK but not fantastic. I would think the only people who would go for it would be single young men like me out for a bit of adventure."

"Oh," said Bob a little surprised. "I thought the basic plus what you make on expenses would be pretty good." I must have arched my eyes and looked a little quizzical as Ian interposed. "Haven't got round to fully explaining things to him yet," he said, turning to me. "Fact is they can only pay us about the same as the Iranian drivers otherwise they'd have another set of problems so it's understood that we make it up with slightly dodgy expense claims. So long as you stay within limits it's no problem. I've already got three fuel invoices for you which I'll go through in the morning," he winked and turned back to finish off his beef goulash.

Next morning found Ian and myself at breakfast listening to David Frost on BBC World Service as we munched our way through the crisp rolls, butter and jam. Jacob the hotel manager came in with a look of concern on his face.

"Did you know Herr Mick has gone?" he asked.

"No way," said Ian.

"Well he took a taxi from here about half an hour ago," Jacob insisted. "I thought it funny on a Sunday and he took all his things with him."

"Did he have any bills?" Ian asked.

"Ja," Jacob confirmed. "He has the dinners from the Rohrwirt and some beers from here."

"Let me know and I'll make sure Bob settles with you," Ian assured him. Jacob bustled out to the reception and Ian delved into his document case and came out with the invoices we had been discussing the previous day. "Now," he said. "What I do is top up each invoice by about 25% which is what all the others do so it looks OK in the accounts department. You don't get that full 25% because you have to give some to the attendant at the filling station. Usually, on a 60 Deutschmark invoice, for example, you'd give him ten and keep 15 for yourself. Similarly, you can get all the hotels and taxis and whatever else to give you inflated invoices and that's the way you ..."

Just at that moment Jacob strode into the room with fury writ large across his countenance. "Herr Ian, please to come with me now," he said in a most sharp and strident tone. Ian jumped up and I could hear them climbing the stairs. Something obviously was amiss. Perhaps Mick had broken some hotel property or stolen some money or maybe something unconnected with Mick's disappearance had occurred. I finished off my rolls and poured another cup of hot chocolate from the pewter pot on the table. I could hear Ian and Jacob returning down the stairs, Jacob clearly outraged and Ian uttering words of abject apology.

"We must clear it up," I heard Jacob stress and Ian entered the room, sat down and so did Jacob.

"I am so sorry Herr Jacob," Ian said. "We will clear things up I promise you."

"Herr Fenninger will stop the drivers staying here," Jacob said wringing his hands. "It is very embarrassing for me. I am responsible for taking the contract with Pars so it is my fault." He did look careworn and like a man worried for his future.

"I'll go up and clear the room," Ian said decisively. "Mr Fenninger need not know what has happened. Please let me have some washing powder and we'll do the rest." Jacob slowly got to his feet, nodded and with a grateful look in Ian's direction took off for the kitchen to retrieve the washing powder.

"What's happened?" I asked.

"Friend Mick has crapped his bed and left it in a hell of a mess," Ian replied, turning up his nose. "You stay here and I'll go and attend to it. I can't leave it to poor old Jacob and if old man Fenninger finds out we could well be out of here." So it was that Ian and myself, I couldn't leave it to him alone, spent a couple of hours flushing excrement down the toilet and washing sheets in the shower in a mountain of soap bubbles. Luckily the bed itself was not stained and after it had been stripped and sprayed with a Dettol-like substance it smelled as fresh as an Alpine maiden's cleavage. Jacob was beside himself with thanks and the three of us finished the morning with refreshing coffees in the lounge. Bob showed his face at about 12 o'clock.

"What have you boys been up to?" he asked.

"You really and honestly don't want to know," Ian said. "Let's get the beers in!"

25

The Girl from Lagermax

BOB was outraged when we told him the sorry tale. Jacob appeared with our beers and insisted on shaking our hands vigorously.

"I cannot tell you how thankful I am," he said. "Herr Fenninger would have been so cross and I am to blame."

Bob put his finger to his mouth. "Please, Jacob, no one should say any more about this," he emphasised. "It's our fault for bringing such people here and I will make sure it does not happen again." He turned to us. "You boys are in for some fun tomorrow." His eyes twinkled as he explained, "Italian customs have just gone on strike."

"How's that going to affect us?" I asked.

"Means all the traffic which would normally go through Italy will have to divert up here to get into Europe," he explained. "I spoke to our Spielfeld office this morning to find out how many Iranians are down there and they told me the border is inundated with traffic waiting to flood into Austria at midnight tonight."

"Last time that happened," Ian observed, "took us three days to get through!"

"Well there's eight of you going up to the border tomorrow morning," Bob pointed out. "So if you stick together you can probably help each other out in the queue. Make sure no one pushes in."

Bob drove us into Salzburg for lunch at a little bistro he knew, located on a cobbled side street which he took great delight in informing me led up to the brothel. The Piccolo Trieste was a little drinking den situated in the basement of an old tenement building and we descended the steps, opened the glass door and Bob embraced the not unattractive proprietress.

"Maria, I didn't see you at the Guter Halle on Thursday," he said somewhat accusingly as if a rendezvous had been broken.

"So sorry," Maria replied. "Helga didn't show and I have no-one to run the bar." She smiled a welcome to us, made ever so slightly less attractive by the fact that she was missing a front tooth! We settled down and lunched on sandwiches containing cold schnitzels with side salads and frothing Augustiners. Then, to finish, Maria brought out a bottle of Stroh Auslander rum and some small shot glasses.

"These for you from me," she unfortunately smiled again. "To welcome you to Austria." It was the custom apparently to down these in one, a custom I then and there decided not to repeat as the high octane fluid coursed down my throat. "To keep you warm in the snow," Maria laughed as she saw my contorted face. I have to admit that it was a lovely rum, full of aromatic spicy taste and if its purpose was to warm up my insides it certainly hit the mark.

"Now we have to go swimming," Bob announced as we wrapped our coats around us against the cold outside. We left the warmth of the little bistro where I was to find a good deal of friendship and conviviality in the months to come.

I had quite forgotten what Ian had told me about the girls from Lagermax coming up to the Pension Fenninger for a swim, but nothing prepared me for what actually happened. Bob, Ian and I were comfortably ensconced in the sauna where, of course, it is extremely bad form to wear anything. After six minutes, we all had a bracing cold shower and returned for another session. Voices outside disturbed our tranquillity and soon the doors opened and three local men entered with their girlfriends, all as naked as we were!

"Gruss Gott!" Bob and Ian welcomed them in and they returned the "Grusses".

"These are our friends from Lagermax," Ian said, introducing them all, at which I had to shake hands with them and couldn't help but notice that the girls were as well-endowed as a sex-starved truck driver could normally only dream about. However, I was somewhat miffed that they had brought their boyfriends along. Our time in the sauna ended all too soon and we showered and made our way into the swimming pool which had a bland white-tiled wall at one end and a large picture window looking up an embankment towards the Untersberg at the other. The three of us, now clad in swimsuits, had swum a few lengths and were holding onto the side of the pool at the deep end when the girls came in still completely naked and decided to stand right above us affording us, as Gerard Hoffnung would have remarked, "delightful prospects"!

"Are you coming in?" I shouted and almost as one they plunged in over the top of us. The boys then arrived and lounged around on the sunbeds in front of the picture windows drinking beers until the girls enticed two of them into the pool and initiated some strange game involving the girls straddling the boys' shoulders and passing a ball back and forth, rather like our piggy-in-the-middle. As the third girl's boyfriend did not want to join in I was asked by her if I would do the honours and ended up with the long legs of this alpine blonde entwined around my neck while I staggered around desperately trying to keep upright as she lunged to intercept the ball. Afterwards, we sat around for a few beers and Gitte's smiles and continual eye contact told me that we had definitely bonded, much to the chagrin of her boyfriend. However, after another sauna session the boys insisted they had to return to Salzburg and my hopes of enticing Gitte up to my room were dashed. As she left she pressed a card into my hand and whispered, "See you next weekend," before she vanished up the stairs towards reception. The card was a Lagermax business card with her name, Birgitte Weiss, emblazoned on it and, of course, the all-important phone number. On the other blank side she had hurriedly scribbled three kisses. My neck ached for several hours afterwards but, believe me, it was a small price to pay!

I was having ample time to reminisce about the weekend because the queue to the frontier was proceeding at a speed close to the aforementioned slow snail. The queue I was in had still not integrated with the queue from the Graz road and I was second in our group of eight trucks, Ian being the leader. By lunchtime we had arrived at the junction of the two roads and Ian had walked back to let us know about his plan to keep us all together. As we approached the merger he would swing over to the right blocking the route for the Graz trucks until we had all passed at which point he would take up position at the rear of the group.

"Slightly risky strategy," he said. "Might get one or two disgruntled Yugos but we've done it before. If we're lucky we'll get a surge as they re-open the customs gate at 2 o'clock and we can all go through at once. If we're not lucky, three or four of you will get through and I'll have some explaining to do."

As it turned out he was right. At about 2:15 there was what Chairman Mao would have described as a "great leap forward" and Ian swung out to the right blocking a lane of cars as he merged into the Graz trucks and came to a halt while the seven of us sailed through, ignoring the blaring horns, and almost like clockwork Ian took up the rear. Once we came to a halt a few hundred yards further on, we all made our way back to Ian's truck just in case there might be some trouble. Behind his truck was a brand new green and white Austrian, new generation, Mercedes 2224 of Gebruder Weiss, the driver of which, having dismounted from his cab, was showing signs of terminal agitation. However, one look at the eight desperate men who assembled at the rear of Ian's truck was sufficient to persuade him to remount although the look of simmering resentment in his eyes did not bode well.

"Anyone feel like lunch?" Ian asked. The Iranians had side boxes on their trailers and were already assembling cookers and pots and kettles but we had none of these luxuries and, although they invited us to join them, Ian organised for the four of us Brits to leave our keys with them so that they could shuffle the trucks along the queue while we walked the kilometre up to the border cafe.

"They're in safe hands," Ian assured me. "Absolute salt of the earth the Iranians. Do anything for you and they don't take kindly to trouble," he winked at me guessing that I was about to mention our friend from Gebruder Weiss. For lunch I had some Schinken mit Spiegeleir (ham and eggs) and a pot of hot chocolate and after lunch we sat on the verandah and watched the relentlessly slow progress of the truck line towards the customs gate. After about an hour we sauntered back down the hill to the trucks only to discover that our Austrian friend had seized the opportunity to barge his way into our convoy during a truck move and was now in front of two of our trucks glowering at the Iranian drivers who quite clearly were ready to have a go at him, a course of action which Ian and Steve were able to convince them would only lead to further trouble as we were, after all, guests in his country. The four of us then took over the keys of the Iranian trucks and kept up the good work during the afternoon while the Iranian drivers relaxed. However, during one move, when the queue had progressed quite a way, we suddenly realised that the Austrian was once again making a move to bypass as many of our trucks as he could. This time he managed to pass another couple of trucks before we were able to block his progress so he was now positioned only two trucks behind mine. At about 4 o'clock we were within sight of the border cafe and we decided to leave Steve and Joe in charge to shunt the trucks as the Iranians had returned. So Ian and I walked over to the cafe and sat on the verandah with a couple of beers watching progress. Suddenly we realised that the trucks were on the move again and we watched in awe as Herr Austrian calmly pulled into the car lanes and drew level with my truck, now driven by Steve. He was making every effort to jam the nose of his truck in front of Steve but that gentleman would have none of it and was able to shunt forward and prevent this from happening. From our vantage point we could see that the front bumper of the Mercedes was about a couple of feet in front of the Mack. We also noticed Steve make a small move with the truck and then climb down from his tractor. Ian looked at me and touched his nose.

"This should be fun," he said. "Wait and watch."

Sure enough, as the next move took place, Steve

did not even start his motor but sat there and watched as the Austrian, thinking he had caught Steve on the hop, lurched forward and we heard a terrible rending of steel followed by a loud bang as a front tyre burst. Steve gunned my engine into life and shuffled his way up towards the customs gate as though nothing had happened.

"Come on," Ian shouted, "we'd better get down there."

We raced down to the scene of the accident to find an incandescent Austrian surveying the damage to his brand new truck caused by himself. As we arrived he was furiously descending on Steve who had now jumped down and was making his way back to the truck behind. Suddenly his look of anger changed to one of fear as, ashen faced, he dropped the tyre lever he was brandishing and took off back to his truck. We looked to see what the problem was and there was a small phalanx of Iranian drivers led by Joe who was brandishing a bowie knife with which he was now nonchalantly cleaning out his finger nails. Suddenly, we realised that another great leap forward was taking place and we all raced back to our trucks and within a few minutes were all safely parked inside the customs area just as it closed for the night. There was no chance of our Austrian friend joining us. He was left to change his front wheel, organise a wrecker and to explain to his boss how he had managed to rip out the entire lower valance of his cab on his truck's first trip. My Mack had sustained scratching to the front bumper and along the side of the fuel tank and I made Steve well aware of how upset I was as we merrily sunk some more beers later that evening back at the Pension Fenninger.

26

God Save the Queen!

NEXT morning Bob gave us a lift up to the border in his company Mercedes and the four of us English drivers were all in the office by 8 o'clock. Curiously, on the way into Austria, we had had to execute our own customs clearances, whereas on the way out, the office did it all for us. Mr Rahimi vanished customs-wards with a briefcase full of our documents and we were about to repair to the border cafe for sustenance when ...

"Well, son of a gun!" A beaming Gerhardt appeared from the inner office. "Arthur and Ian, I've still got your expenses to finish before you leave." He remonstrated with us somewhat balefully, as though we had deliberately been avoiding settling up, whereas in fact we had arrived too late on Friday evening to complete our trip paperwork. Bob handed Gerhardt receipts from the *tankstelle* on Vogelweiderstrasse where we had all filled up on leaving the terminal the previous morning. I was down for 260 litres and Ian had consumed a couple of hundred which meant that both of us had saved the company some tax on our Austrian *tankshein* declarations. It was standard practice I learnt for all the Pars trucks to enter Germany from Austria with full tanks whether or not fees had to be paid.

"We'll finish our expenses forms over some coffee if that's OK?" Ian suggested. "I paid for all our diesel en route so I'll be claiming for Arthur as well."

"You wanna make it real easy?" Gerhardt asked. "Just put all your expenses on one claim and settle up between yourselves."

Steve and Joe had already finalised their expenses before the weekend so we all sauntered over to the cafe where Ian bent over his running sheets scribbling furiously after I had handed over my meagre expenses for the trip which were mainly in the form of hotel receipts. Ian then disappeared back to the office while we passed a pleasant hour over a couple of coffees' watching the huge and seemingly interminable queue inching its way inexorably towards the customs gate. We had already noticed that the Gerbruder Weiss trailer had been parked on our side of the road a little to our right. Of the tractor unit, there was no sign.

"Don't worry about your expenses, Art," Steve said between mouthfuls of croissant. "I show you the ropes on way up to Bremerhaven. Basically," he confided, "you get to know which *tankstelles* give you best deal. You know what I mean? All them do deals but better off the autobahns." I nodded, hoping that Bob's counsel concerning the official blind eye to these practises was indeed a wise one.

"Should we go back to our trucks?" I asked.

"No, no, no," Steve answered. "They come for us when ready. Better we wait here, more warm." As he said this he lit up a Marlboro and signed to the waiter, a very slim aristocratic looking gentleman with a crisply cut moustache, to refill our cups.

"Don't worry," Joe was looking at me quizzically. I must have been exhibiting signs of nervousness.

"Steve already said that," I said.

"No, I mean we all know ropes so to speak," Joe continued. "Only problem we get is someone don't work the system, in which case ..." He fell ominously silent and crossed his fingers across his throat in a gesture, I thought, probably typical of the Maltese mafia who were currently rumoured to be running all the illicit operations in Soho. I blanched and Joe laughed and so did Steve.

"You be alright," Steve drawled in his Hungarian English. At that moment Ian returned and sat next to me on the green moquette bench.

"Here's your expenses," he said, carefully placing a pile of Austrian Schillings in front of me. "And here," he winked, "are your extras." The extras came to the equivalent of 60 pounds which I carefully folded into my wallet. "One thing you gonna remember," Steve intervened. "Don't be stupid. We show you what you do but if you too clever also …" Once again he finished the sentence by drawing his fingers across his throat. This time Ian laughed.

"He's talking about Will, the wild colonial boy," he explained as the waiter placed our refilled cups on the table. "Great guy, filthy rich, only did the job for fun but Joe psyched him up so much because at first he didn't want to, shall we say, increase his dividends. That last time back in U.K. he got himself a John Bull printing outfit to make his own invoices! They rumbled him on his first trip. Do you know what he did?" He paused and looked at me as though I must have heard the story somewhere on the road. I shook my head and he continued.

"Took his autobahn *tankstelle* receipts, they have wide gap between station details at top and date and amounts at the bottom, cut them in half and using the outfit printed in his own amounts on top half and station details on bottom." Ian, Joe and Steve were now convulsed. "Might have got away with it," Ian said, having gathered himself together. "But he forgot that he was presenting two invoices from the same *tankstelle* on the same day."

"But wouldn't the printing from the John Bull outfit have been different from the *tankstelle's* receipt?" I asked.

"Yup, that as well," Ian guffawed. "Nothing they could do, especially as Achemian was in the office at the time. Paid off, lift to the station and that was that. He even had to pay for his own transport back to Blighty!"

"Yeah, but what they don't know," Steve said, "is when Bob left, he took a taxi to the airport and flew back."

The door opened and an icy blast swept through the cosiness of the cafe as Mr Rahimi entered and made his way over to our table with sheafs of paper-work held apart by his fingers. These he carefully distributed to us.

"Mr Arthur and Mr Steve are clear to go but you must check with Mr Gerhardt for expenses," he instructed us in his halting English, then he beamed at Joe and Ian. "You two are for Grosse Kontrol." Still smiling, he hastened back out with an air of someone on an important mission who was continually late for every appointment.

"What's the Grosse Kontrol?" I asked, pronounc-ing the words a little haltingly.

"It's when they strip out your load and give it a thorough examination including a going over by the sniffer dogs," Ian explained. "As our loads have come up from the Middle East they always suspect we're smuggling drugs or worse."

"Same every bloody time," Joe remarked. "They never open pickled goatskins. Stink place out they do. If I was goin' to smuggle something that's the load I'd put it in. Even hashhunds can't handle them."

Ian was loaded with mohair for somewhere in Yorkshire and Joe's load of sports equipment didn't, on the face of it, seem a cargo I'd have targeted if I'd been a customs official but there was no way of telling. The Kontrols were supposedly random but given that they chose not to be opening up our smelly cargo, I suspected a degree of selection was going on in the customs office. I made a mental note to let the drug barons know about this the very next time I was drinking with them, for a substantial fee of course!

Steve and I made our way to the office, and Joe and Ian to the customs area as they had to be present when the searches would be made.

"You guys ready to roll?" Gerhardt rhetorically greeted us as we entered the office. We nodded and were ushered into the back room to receive our running money which was worked out on the basis of what we hadn't spent on the previous trip plus the balance to bring us up to speed on our next designated journey. "Arthur, you've got to go down to Van Hove in Brussels for your first service once you're tipped and Steve," he paused and shuffled through some paperwork which must have been the loading plans for the following week. "Steve, you son of a gun, you'll like this one. Skoda works near Prague for you so we'll make your money up for the round trip. Arthur, you'll pick up more from whichever agent we backload you with but at the moment it looks like Kuehne & Nagel in Mannheim. We'll let you know when you reach Van Hove." He then counted out two crispy bundles of Deustchmarks and we each received typewritten instructions, in my case with our offloading address in Bremerhaven and the address of the Van Hove garage in Brussels. "One small thing," he smiled up at us from his position behind his desk. "You can't leave just yet. I need to check with Hapag Lloyd in Bremerhaven that they've got the U.S.

bound containers ready plus I need confirmation that they'll steam clean your boxes once they're empty." He grinned again. "Nobody's gonna load a smelly container. So come back in an hour and hopefully all will be ready."

At that moment a beaming Ian entered.

"Great news, Gerhardt," he announced. "They broke my seal, opened the doors, let the dog in, no problem. Closed the doors, re-sealed and I'm ready to rock."

"What about Steve?" Gerhardt asked.

"No, he's on a complete turn out," Ian shook his head as he replied. "Just got to the end of a batch of tennis rackets when I came off the bank."

"OK," Gerhardt said. "Everything's ready. You're taking this one through to England. Our brand new Guy shunter's broken down and won't be through the service pool for at least a week."

Ian decided he wanted to leave then and there so he would have a good chance to catch the evening ferry from Europoort on Tuesday night. We said our goodbyes and I thanked him for all his help. "Think nothing of it," he said. "But if you bump into Katya again tell her I'll be back soon."

"If you bump into Annatje," I replied with an ironic laugh, "keep your hands off her."

With that, Steve and I repaired to the cafe to while away the time until Gerhardt had received the confirmation he required.

"Doesn't matter 'ow much we do or 'ow fast we drive," Steve observed as we took our places once again at a table near the bar, "they always finding excuse to stop us. Know what I mean?"

I nodded, I was learning fast. Steve ordered a coffee cognac for himself and a jug of hot chocolate for me. By lunchtime we had heard nothing and I was about to suggest that we remove ourselves back to the office when Mr Rahimi came in, looked at us, shook his head and took a seat on a bar stool.

"Might as well have lunch," Steve muttered and so it was that we spent four hours waiting for confirmation that everything was in place for our arrival in Bremerhaven. Eventually Gerhardt himself arrived and I timed his appearance at 3:15 with the good news that we were clear to go.

"You guys look after yourselves and take care," were his parting words as he exited through the curtained doorway. "It's blizzarding out there but the road's clear."

Steve and I picked up our overnight cases and our document cases and made our way out past the footbridge towards the customs gate through which the endless file of trucks, now with their wipers fighting to clear their screens, were still ceaselessly crawling. I shook the snow out of my hair as we passed the gate. On the left were the customs offices and butting onto them the covered grey loading bays where inspections took place. I noted that Joe's truck seemed to have gone. We sloshed through the snow and slush to our trucks which were parked at the far end where everyone was waiting to hear their fate – either all clear or the dreaded Grosse Kontrol. Back in the cab I turned the key and the engine spluttered into glorious life and I left her running while I placed my overnight case between the seats and sorted out my cargo documents. Everything was correctly stamped, the invoices, the certificates of origin, the sanitary certificate for the goatskins, the *tanksheins*, the road tax and lastly the all-important *laufzettl*. Only one thing was missing, which I already knew would be the case, and that was the passport control stamp out of Austria and into Germany. So we both plodded back up the parking lot passing the Iranian's and Joe's trucks as we went, and into the customs building.

"Should have done this on the way in," Steve complained.

"What, with our overnight cases and all?" I protested. He grumpily agreed and we entered the building and the mêlée which was its permanent feature during opening hours. Luckily we did not have to queue at the customs windows, and the passport ones were virtually free. So we received our stamps within minutes. Turning to leave the building, we bumped into Joe with an entourage of Iranian drivers who insisted on shaking hands all round.

"Bloody Grosse Kontrol," Joe fumed. "I've spent six hours watch them offload and inspect everything. Hashhund all over my truck and cab. Split down most of my cartons, spill out rackets, shoes, shorts, t-shirts, tennis balls all over ramp and then they get to last consignment. Footballs! 'Ah,' says Obersturmfuhrer. 'At last we have them!' I thought they'd been tipped off and I was off to the slammer. But cool as anything he picks up five balls and walks off. That's all he wanted, the son of a bitch. They come back with my papers and instruct the Yugo workers to reload me. Damn ridiculous it is!"

We said our farewells and left Joe still fuming and returned to our trucks. My engine was humming away nicely and the hot air hitting the screen had already melted the internal ice which had built up the previous night. I checked round the truck. All the lights were good, the rear number plate was still in place, the twistlocks were all secure, the legs were firmly locked and the susies were all connected. As I jumped back up into the cab, Steve was already pulling away. I selected second main and third split and followed him down the decline towards the exit gate onto the autobahn. He sped through, the gate came down in front of me and I opened my window handing my fully stamped *laufzettl* to the guard.

"You are Eenglish?" he asked.

I nodded.

"Sehr Gut," he barked, as he pressed the gate button. Then he made a mock salute and shouted, "God shave the Queen!!" as I gunned the engine and rolled out onto the open autobahn.

27

A Small Accident

I was still chuckling at the chain of thought triggered by the German guard's "God shave the Queen" joke as I caught up with Steve trunking along in a cloud of blown snow for all the world looking like a ferryboat nosing through a channel storm, snow spraying out from each side of his truck like the bow waves of a ship. We descended the short hill past the Bad Reichenhall exit, then the Aral *tankstelle* and after that a slow ascent back up into the mountains. The snow was falling thicker and faster the higher we climbed and by the time we reached the peak of this pass, near the fascinatingly named village of Anger, the wipers were having difficulty clearing the screens. The road was now covered in rutted ice and the going was slippery to say the least. I was beginning to worry about such things as jackknifing, with one hand resting on the trailer brake ready for instant correction if needed, when we passed the turn for Neukirchen and it became evident that the gritters had been through this section as the surface became slushy and I was able to relax a little. There was nothing to see on either side as a light fog had descended but I knew that this route ran through thick pine forests until we approached the long descent onto the Chiemsee plateau. In front of me Steve's right indicator was flashing and I followed him into a long parking area which ran for at least a kilometre along the side of the autobahn. I drew to a halt behind him and switched off the engine. Jumping down from the cab, I walked around the nose of my Mack and realised that, on the other side of the parking, the waters of the Chiemsee itself were lapping against the shoreline. I thought, somewhat ironically considering the mist and the snow flurries and the cold, that this must be an idyllic spot in which to park up during the summer months.

Steve was trudging his way along the snow covered pavement, his breath steaming in front of him.

"There's good *gasthof* about half hour more drive," he said. "We stop there for the night. If you miss me look for Ausfahrt Frasdorf and middle of village, Pension Kampenwand."

I watched as he shuffled through the new lain snow back to his truck, stepped back up into my cab, restarted my engine and followed him back out onto the autobahn. My window was open so I could hear my front tyres cutting a crisp trace through the ice which had been formed by previous vehicles compacting the snow but soon I was back on the gritted road following Steve's tail lights which glowed a reassuring bright red through the murk of windblown snow and slush kicked up by his wheels. The going really was bad and I could feel the trailer wheels tramping from left to right as they were caught in the ice tracks. As it was we were motoring along at a safe 30 or so miles an hour and my watch was showing 8:45 by the time Steve's indicators sprung to life and we took the exit slip down to the intersection under the autobahn which indicated Rosenheim to the right and Frasdorf to the left. Here the road had not been gritted and we were ploughing virgin snow as we executed the left turn under the motorway bridge. The road then swung to the right and we were travelling parallel to the autobahn as the village houses with their warm, gaily lit windows standing out through the gloom welcomed us to what we hoped would be the safety of a snug hotel room for the night. About half a kilometre further on, Steve came to a halt alongside the Pension Kampenwand which was set back slightly from the road. I watched him as he disappeared into the building, only to re-appear several minutes later. I could tell all was not well from his somewhat dejected gait as he retraced his steps and I jumped down to meet him by the back of his trailer.

"No luck," he shook his head. "Everywhere is full. They say conference in Munich. Hotel Mack tonight for us. They say we can use their bathroom and then we park on other side of village. Never mind," he smiled. "Save money for beer in Bremerhaven!"

Clutching our wash bags we trudged through the snow-laden garden at the front of the hotel and into the warm bright lights of the typically Bavarian reception area, all heavily pine timbered, glossily varnished and low ceilinged with a door to the left into a restaurant area, one to the right into a heavily populated bar and two straight ahead. The one on the right led into a rear vestibule where the toilets and the stairs to the bedrooms were situated. The one on the left was behind a low reception desk with rows of empty hooks on the wall demonstrating that every room was indeed taken. I guessed that the left hand door led into the kitchen area from the clatter of pans and raised voices emanating from that direction. The clammy warmth contrasted sharply with the crisp icy atmosphere outside and gave the pension an air of hospitable welcome which unfortunately we would only be able to enjoy as itinerant visitors. A mature, full-bosomed serving wench dressed in Alpine costume emerged from the kitchens, laden with hot sausages for the bar.

"Ah, Herr Steve," she smiled en passant. "Gruss Gott." And she beamed at him as she bustled into the heaving throng.

The toilet area was, as expected, squeaky clean with ample washbasins in front of a huge mirror. The *pissoires* were at the far end and on the right were a couple of cubicles plus, joy of joys, a shower room. I needed a good sit down after the trip along the snow covered autobahn and was amused as ever at the German, load inspection toilet where you had the chance to examine everything before flushing it away! After a glorious shower with loads of soap and shampoo I emerged back into reception to find Steve engrossed in conversation in German with one of the smartly dressed waiters.

"Fancy quick beer?" he suggested and, not waiting for my answer, he deposited his kit behind the reception area, motioning for me to do the same, and led me into the bar. The throng turned out to be, in the main, German businessmen enjoying their downtime after their conference in Munich and everything was very jolly and convivial. Once Steve had informed them that we were truckers and that he was from Hungary and I was British we became focal points for their interest and were plied with beer and sausages in exchange for tales of the road which Steve seemed happy to deliver with considerable embellishment. It was his good luck that, with the warm atmosphere and the considerable influx of alcoholic refreshment which these salesmen had imbibed, that none of them called any of his far-fetched reminiscences into question!

Eventually we said our goodbyes, retrieved our washbags from the reception desk and braced ourselves for the short journey through the front garden to our trucks.

"We drive out of village back up onto autobahn," Steve explained. "Don't want to keep these good folk up all night with our engines running. Besides, there's parking area only five kilos away."

Braced we needed to be! Outside the cold was dry and cutting after the moist warmth of the bar. A bleak wind was blowing from some high Alpine peak right down across the village and into our faces as we determinedly set our feet into the blizzard which greeted us. Back inside the relative calm of the cab I was relieved that the motor started immediately, though I knew it would be some time before any warmth emanated from the heater flaps. Steve's lights came on, his indicators flashed and he was away through the centre of the village with me following. Within a couple of kilometres we were back on the autobahn and ten minutes later were thankfully pulling into a rest area set in the middle of a forest, so shielded from the blizzard conditions howling all around. I set my motor to a fast idle and arranged my overnight case between the seats before unfolding my sleeping bag across the undulating base which was to be my bed for the night. I undressed and slid between the layers of nylon and foam which would shield me from the elements if my engine decided to pack it in for some reason during the night. At 5 feet 6 inches, I could just about stretch out but my feet coming up against the icy driver's window soon put a stop to that and I curled up in a semi foetal position which was the only way possible in that ridiculous cabin. Luckily it was pitch black outside so there was no street lighting to disturb my sleep and I did indeed sleep like the proverbial log.

I awoke to the sound of tapping on my window and I blearily looked out to see Steve shouting up at me.

"We need to go if we avoid traffic in Munich," he said, "stop for breakfast after." And he was gone.

I just had time to struggle out of my sleeping bag and into my t-shirt and jeans before Steve's truck vanished out of the rest area and I was left to play catch-up. Luckily I knew the route we would be taking having gone through it on my map with Steve in Salzburg. It would be a straight run down to the Munich suburbs, then a skirt around Munich on the Mittlerer ring and onto the A9 autobahn in the direction of Nuremberg. However, I was still a rookie and wanted to hang on to Steve's coat tails. Out on the open road the blizzard had blown itself away during the night and all was calm as dawn became grey and then as white as the snow-burdened forests and mountains. The road was in reasonable shape. It had been gritted but needed more traffic across it to entirely dissipate the night's snowfall. Within a couple of kilometres I had caught up with Steve. First I saw the bare outline of his container and then, as I closed, could see his lights amid the cloud of disturbed snow he was kicking up. The journey into Munich, especially after the Innsbruck junction, was uneventful. We were traversing the plains south west of Munich and the road was flat and ran through thick forest laid back several hundred metres from the autobahn on either side as if it was intended to widen the road eventually. The early morning progressed. The autobahn was still quite lightly trafficked and it was not until we left it and entered the suburbs of the city that there was anything like a rush hour build-up. Steve's right hand indicators flashed at the next set of traffic lights and we turned onto the Mittlerer ring, a dual carriageway with two lanes on each side which circled the city, joining all the major routes together. At each major intersection there were traffic lights, almost all of which appeared to have been specially set to red that morning just to give us practice on the quadruplex gearboxes.

This road was nowhere near as busy as the arterial carrying commuter traffic which we had just left but there were still impatient German car drivers and the odd slow truck to be dealt with. After one junction where we had not been forced to halt but had slowed anyway as a precaution, Steve had picked up speed faster than I had and was a good half kilometre ahead when I saw him pull out into the fast lane to overtake a slow moving, green Bulgarian truck. I checked my mirrors and noted that the lights at the previous junction had just turned green again and a car was entering our section. As he was a good half kilometre back I switched on my indicators and started to pull out to overtake the Bulgarian. Immediately the car started flashing its headlights but it was so far back that I took no notice and continued pulling out. As was my wont, I constantly checked the mirror and watched with some fascination and then growing alarm as the car, which I could now identify as a black Mercedes seemed to be intent on overtaking me and I judged that his speed, far from lessening to allow him to take his place behind me where he belonged, was worryingly increasing and the headlights were irritatingly continuing to flash. I was well into the outside lane by this time, at least two thirds of the way over and he was still charging towards me, now, I guessed, within a couple of hundred yards of my trailer. The nose of the Mack was now level with the rear of the Bulgarian's trailer and there was no evasive action I could take so I continued and watched in morbid fascination as the Mercedes driver, realising at the last second that there was no room to overtake, jammed on his brakes, spun on the slippery road surface out of my view and then hurtled back into it as he smashed into the Armco and bits and pieces became distributed across the road through the cloud of dust. Discretion being the better part of valour I kept going. There were plenty of cars behind him to help with the mess. My worry now was that someone would inform the polizei who would haul me in and, innocent as I was, as a foreigner I would probably be incarcerated and accused of dangerous driving or some such trumped up charge. It was therefore with a high degree of trepidation that I pulled up behind Steve at the next lights. They turned to green and we traversed the junction. Once again glancing in my mirror, I saw that there was no traffic behind me whatsoever so I guessed that the accident would have closed off the road. However, I was well aware that the polizei had radios!

28

A Friend from the Bundesbahn

I spent the rest of that journey around the Mittlerer ring with my heart in my mouth, panic stricken that at any moment a blue light would flash in my mirrors or at the next junction a police ambush would be lying in wait but my fears were unfounded and within a quarter of an hour we were turning north onto the A9. On the left, immediately as we entered the motorway, were the headquarters of BMW with their massive silver office buildings in the shape of four attached-in-the-middle engine cylinders. Half an hour later, having passed the suburban sprawl of Munich city, we were entering into the service area at Furholzen Ost. This was one of the older *rastattes*. As you entered there was a filling station with snack facilities and toilets. Cars were filtered to the right of this and lorries to the left. Once past this, assuming you had filled with fuel and didn't want to stop, you carried straight on back to the autobahn. Otherwise you swung right immediately after the fuel station and then hung a left to run parallel with the other road but at the rear of the truck parking area. You could then saunter back to the station for a snack or use the facilities of the restaurant which was set back on the right side of the area behind the car parking lot and up some steps. We did not need fuelling so swung round to the truck parking area, passing sundry Schenkers, Kuehne & Nagel and Kube & Kubenz tankers until we found two vacant slots. As we parked, a Deutsche Bundesbahn Bussing unterflur wagon and drag pulled up alongside. I had just climbed down from my cab when I was accosted by its driver.

"Hey buddy, you Iranian?" he enquired in what I took to be a good impression of a New Jersey accent. I turned round to find the inquisitor to be a dapper fellow, all of five foot five and dressed in the standard German dark blue bib and tucker supplied by DB who had stamped their logo in black on the bib. He had attempted to brighten up the overall effect by wearing a red and blue check shirt underneath which appeared to be straight out of the Wild West. If he had burst into *Carolina Moon* at that point it would not have been out of place. His hair was close cropped with a flat top, and he sported a small tightly clipped moustache on his otherwise clean shaven visage.

"Hi," I replied a little incredulously. "You German?"

He laughed. "Name's Heinz, but I'm a Yank, and you?"

"British," I replied laconically.

"Hey, I didn't think youse guys were goddam Iranians," he maintained, pronouncing the word 'Iranian' with a hard 'i'. "I seen your trucks round and about and all the drivers look European but your plates is Iranian."

"We've about 30 trucks based in Salzburg with mainly Brits driving them," I explained.

"That so?" he asked, somewhat rhetorically, scratching his chin. "You guys eatin' here?" he asked.

"Sure thing," I said lapsing accidentally into a mid-Atlantic drawl. "You wanna join us for a late breakfast?"

"That'd be real cool," he agreed and the three of us walked over to the restaurant.

Once seated on one of the leatherette banquettes, pairs of which with a table in between were arranged down the window side of the restaurant facing the car park, Heinz made my blood run cold.

"Say, was it youse guys I was following round the goddam Mittlerer ring?" he asked.

Panic struck deep within me and I weighed up the chances that this seemingly friendly fellow trucker might just be about to blow my cover and phone the polizei. I looked at him straight into his Aryan blue eyes and decided he looked to be friend rather than foe and I decided to own up and then told the sorry tale from my viewpoint which, of course, Steve was now hearing for the first time. Halfway through my tale the waitress arrived and we ordered coffees and all plumped for Ruhreirs mit Schinken. Once I'd finished, Steve denied all knowledge of the incident. Understandably, being in front of me he hadn't seen a thing.

"Say, Buddy," Heinz drawled, "I was right behind youse at those goddam lights but had to stop 'cos they turned red as you went through them. This dude in the black Mercedes came up alongside of me and was revving his engine like some kind of 'Speedy Gonzales'. I thought he'd spin his wheels once the lights changed. Anyways on the G of green he was away like goddam Roadrunner and his wheels was smokin'. I could see you pulling out and watched him closing on you. Crazy guy didn't hit his goddam brakes till the last second and then he was all over the goddam place." Here he paused, stroking his chin and looking thoughtful before continuing. "Several cars had already passed me so those guys was out on the road dragging him out of what remained of his car right against the Armco in the slow lane, and seeing the only bit of clear road was over to the left in the fast lane I crawled along it till I had to stop to avoid a piece of fender which was strewn across the lane. Whiles they was picking it up, some guy comes over and wants me to be a witness but I told him I seen nuttin'. Lookin' over I see them dragging this guy from the goddam car and he collapses on the road." Once again he paused as the coffees were served by our crisply green and white dressed fraulein.

"Oh, my God!" I said. "Was he dead?"

Visions of manslaughter raps were now circling my fevered imagination.

"He was dead alright," Heinz paused and gave me a lengthy stare. "Dead drunk, least that's what this dude tells me whiles I'm explainin' why I'm no witness material on this case. ''Sides,' I said to him, 'I've got a tight schedule to maintain. Drivin' for Deutsche Bundesbahn technically I'm a train.' Luckily they let me go but this goddam guy behind me must have fancied himself in the box 'cos he parks up and blocks off the fast lane as I take off."

My sigh of relief would have felled a few trees as the stress I'd been under dissipated.

"Close call, eh Buddy?" was Heinz's comment. "If I was you I'd say nuttin', anyone asks." Here he adopted an advisory tone. "Tell them you didn't see a thing. Otherwise it's yo' ass for the witness box and you'll sit here for days whiles they sort it out."

The ham and eggs arrived together with some thin slices of grainy brown bread and conversation stopped while we tucked in. After our coffee cups were refilled Heinz told us how he'd come over to Germany as a conscript in the military stationed at Kaiserslautern where they'd taught him to drive trucks.

"Jimmy Astros was what we had. Trunking between depots, nights mostly. Mainly with PX supplies. That was me, Heinz goddam Schmidt from Noo Joisy after

three months training down in Alabama as an infan-
tryman. There I am delivering goddam diapers and
such week in, week out." On demob he had found
that his German antecedents allowed him a German
work permit, albeit as a *gastarbeiter*, but armed with
his LKW licence and his fluent command of the language, which he had learned at his mother's feet, he
had easily won recruitment into the new DB intercity
fleet. "Seems these guys in Bonn decide to boost the
railroad. They're gonna make certain classes of freight
travel in boxcars," he explained. "No way can those
boys handle these cargoes. So overnight DB becomes
the biggest road truck operator in the country. First
they're using contractors. Turn out to be same guys
who was truckin' the stuff in the first place, charging
even more as now it's classed as railroad freight. Same
time they're buying their own trucks but where they
gonna get the drivers? So as well as our guests from
Turkey there's quite a few Yanks 'cos they came onto
the bases and almost begged us to help out. That's
what your goddam socialists are all about. You'd
think they'd learn their lessons from the East but
no ways. Next thing, they're bankrupting the small
truckers who've lost the work and then they put 'help
wanted' ads in the papers and take on their drivers.
Crazy world, man!" He shook his head in disbelief at
the stupidity of the political classes.

Glancing over Heinz's shoulder I had a view of the
truck parking area on the far side of the car park. I
could also see that two green and white cars of the
polizei had stopped and their uniformed occupants
were wandering down the line of trucks. I gestured
over to the scene.

"Looks like I've been rumbled," I said visualising
the next scene where they would enter the restaurant
and ask who was driving the *Iranisch* trucks. Heinz

surveyed the mini-drama now playing out before our eyes.

"Don't worry about it, man," he advised. "I guess those guys are looking for signs of damage. They don't see any, there's nuttin' they can do. Stay cool man."

A few tense minutes passed as we watched expectantly. The police found our trucks and were giving their rear ends a close inspection but then they moved on and performed the same task behind a couple of Romanians.

"See," Heinz said. "They got nuttin'. You're OK, man. Anyways, I'll go and confuse the issue even more. Take care guys, and stay loose!"

Hopefully he wasn't referring to my bowels which I have to admit were feeling pretty agitated at that moment. We said our farewells and agreed to have another coffee while Heinz sauntered down to the parking lot. We had a good view of him wandering towards his truck and then being accosted by the police. He engaged them in conversation for several minutes and then we saw a cloud of smoke as he gunned his motor into life and sped out towards the autobahn. A few minutes later the police also left in the same direction so we assumed that Heinz had told them that he was behind the accident, saw nothing and was especially certain that those good ol' boys in the Macks were as innocent as the driven snow!

29

Diesel Deal

WE paid our bills and made our way out of the restaurant down the stairs and through the brightly lit shop.

"You got good German map?" Steve asked.

"Only the Europe atlas," I replied.

"Here," he said, guiding me to a stand full of maps and atlases and town plans. "Falk plan is what you want." He reached over and removed a package from the stand and proceeded to open it and fold it out. "See, each page is in three or more sections so you have main map and then you fold out right or left and you have whole of Germany in small booklet. You can fit easy in pocket" he explained. It was indeed a brilliantly conceived package and I thought good value for money at thirteen and a half Deutschmarks. So I bought one and later on it was to prove invaluable during my period with the company.

We descended the newly sanded and salted steps down to the car park and I crossed the car parking area and entered the truck park with some small degree of trepidation. I was still convinced that some lone policeman was waiting to pounce and that would be the end of what should have been a good day! However, nothing happened and I was able to remount my vehicle unhindered. The engine roared into life and once again I was out on the open autobahn following doggedly on Steve's heels.

The Mack driving position was surprisingly comfortable for such a basic truck. The seat was not sprung but the cushion was very supportive. You were seated quite high in the cab with a panoramic view through the front and side windows and an expansive rearwards vision via the oversize wing mirrors on the end of the long catenary-like stalks necessitated by the fact that the narrow cab was sitting in the middle of a full size truck chassis. The wheel was flat, rather like a commercial bus wheel and, although there was no power steering, it fed easily from hand to hand once you were moving. Manoeuvring in tight spaces was a completely different matter and required a fair degree of muscle. The overall effect, however, was a commanding one with the long bonnet stretching out beneath the driver's window with its Mack Bulldog in the vanguard leading the way. You really felt on top of the rig and the direct manual controls put you and the machine in delightfully close contact with the road, on this occasion however, somewhat unfortunately!

It became quickly evident that the A9 was one of the original Hitler autobahns and an important one at that, being the link between Berlin and Munich, the old capital tied to the Nazi power base. Unsurprisingly it did not appear to have been resurfaced since its concrete surface had been laid in the mid-thirties. In other words, the road surface was badly corrugated. With leaf springs, an unsprung cab and driving seat seemingly bolted direct to the chassis, the ride quality could have been better. Every jar and pitch was transmitted directly to the spine. Everything that was not tied down took on a life of its own and meandered about the cab in a most alarming fashion. A couple of miles of this would have been purgatory but this went on for a good 50 before resurfaced tarmac road was reached. You got to the point where, rather like with seasickness, death almost became an attractive option. A time came when the jarring became so predictable that you braced yourself against it, lifting your rear end off the seat just to gain some relief. This was a mistake because all you were doing was moving the agony to a different part of your body, arching yourself between the top of the rigid seat and the equally unyielding cab floor. Those with some horseriding experience did best because they had already learnt to cushion themselves against the movement of the horse's back during a canter by riding it out; judging the movement and physically pushing yourself up and down against it so minimising the impact and in the end this was the preferred option. However, this itself was physically demanding and, although you could claim this as exercise, that claim was about as valid as ticking off your bottle of Fanta as one of your five a day! In these conditions there was no way we could proceed at our service speed of just under 60 miles an hour. Steve had slowed to about 40 but even at this pace the joggling was almost unbearable and the rig was taking a lot of punishment. It was a great relief when the tarmac appeared, but even this had seen better days and was in need of urgent renewal. There were potholes, most of which were thankfully avoidable, and sections where the tarmac had almost disappeared and the concrete underpinning surfaced, which once again threw you off balance but the ride quality was so infinitely superior to the corrugated concrete that these were small irritations.

Back up to 60 miles an hour we made good time for a couple of hours before Steve left the autobahn at junction 56, signed for Neumarkt. At the roundabout he turned right and we entered the village of Meckenhaus and just after the village sign, swung right into an Aral *tankstelle*. This was a small village filling station with three pumps and a small white-washed concrete office at the back, signed with the blue diamond Aral logos. Steve drew to a halt and signalled to me to join him as he entered the office.

"Gruss Gott," was his greeting to the attendant. This was the standard Bavarian form of introduction I came to learn. You didn't use "Guten tag" in the south east of the country.

"You speak English?" he continued.

"Yah, ein bistchen," came the reply. The attendant was a late middle-aged gentleman, grey before his time I thought, with a gnarled ruddy face and red veined nose evidencing possibly an agricultural life, his body moulded by long exposure to the elements. His stomach however, had definitely been moulded by a lifetime's exposure to Bavarian beer and constant supplies of wurst! He was dressed in the normal workman's blue bib and tucker but this time in the company's light blue emblazoned with Aral logos back and front and this also applied to his forage hat which sat at a jaunty angle to his thick mop of curly hair. The office itself was spartan. A desk housing a simple cash register and a single chair were situated at the back, and on the right was an oil stove stuttering away, throwing out a good deal of welcome heat across the concrete floor. Behind the desk was a row of shelves containing a selection of oils, anti-freezes and wax polishes and that was it.

"We can fill tanks with diesel. Pay geld," Steve was explaining and showing a sheaf of Deutschmarks to the suddenly engaged functionary. "You give us rechnung plus ein hundert litre. We give you twenty Deutschmarks. My colleague," and here he pointed at me, "the same." I noticed that the man's blue eyes were now brightening under his straggly grey eyebrows and he was appreciably warming to Steve's suggestions. Unexpectedly he frowned.

"Same?" he asked. "Was ist?"

"Same ist Egale," Steve explained.

The man was still frowning. "Egale ist Gleich?" he suggested.

"Yes, yes," Steve agreed. "Egale is Gleich!"

The attendant visibly brightened, dawn rose across his workmanlike gruff visage and he beamed at both of us, the prospect of 40 Deutschmarks to spend in the *bierstube* at lunchtime obviously an attractive proposition on such a cold dreary winter's morning.

He shuffled out of the office and across the frost-rinded forecourt to Steve's truck muttering some incantation or other as he undid the filler cap, detached the nozzle from the pump and inserted it into the tank. He pressed the autofill lever on the nozzle and then turned to us.

"Hundred litres here, and hundred on other side," Steve requested, indicating the position of the two tanks.

"Ach so, keine problem," the attendant nodded, turning his attention back to the pump guage.

"I thought you spoke fluent German, Steve?" I said.

"Best not to," Steve replied. "They prefer to think they are dealing with foreigner. Big trouble for them when they get caught. Safer they make deal with *auslander.*"

While the tanks were filled, Steve pulled out his map and we pored over it on the desk in the office.

"Easy route up to Bremerhaven," he asserted. "Nurnberg – A3 to Wurzburg then north on A7 all way to Hannover. Stay on A7 towards Hamburg but take A27 to Bremen and then Bremerhaven. Piece of cake!" He traced out the route on the map as he talked and I followed it on my new Falk plan. The attendant shouted, indicating that he had filled both of Steve's tanks and he left the pump running while Steve moved forward and I took his place.

"Same," I said, then remembered the German. "Gleich, two tanks hundred litres each." He nodded and stuck the nozzle in my nearside tank and continued the fill, the steady pinging of the pump bell indicating each litre flowing through the pipe. It was now approaching midday and Steve reckoned if we drove virtually non-stop we could make Bremerhaven by the evening.

"We get some rolls from bakery over there," he suggested. "Cheese, ham OK?"

I agreed and he crossed the road and disappeared into the shop. The bell pinging stopped and the attendant replaced the nozzle into its pump before walking back towards the office.

"Look, look," he beckoned me out to inspect the pump and I agreed that he had pumped four hundred litres.

"Two receipts," I insisted.

"Rechnung?" he answered, scribbling in the air to represent filling in the paperwork. I held up two fingers.

"Zwei," I said.

"Ach, Zwo," he replied, and I nodded, assuming his pronunciation was at fault. It was only later that I discovered that "Zwo" was widely used in Bavaria and Austria instead of "Zwei". He hastily wrote down some figures on a piece of graph paper and showed them to me. Three hundred litres charged to each of us and then the figure for the actual 200 litres.

"Und fur mir, zwanzig Deutschmarks," he looked at me conspiratorially and we both laughed as Steve re-entered the office with two paper bags of rolls, one of which he handed to me together with a plastic litre

261

bottle of water. I showed him the figures, he nodded approval and the attendant pulled out a duplicate pad and laboriously filled in the columns showing our 300 litres alleged fill but skilfully managing to ensure that his duplicate showed only two hundred. We paid him and separately gave him the 20 Deutschmarks sweetener.

"Danke," we chorused as we left the office.

"Bitte," was his reply before we exchanged "auf weidersehens".

Back in the cab I positioned my bag so I could reach the rolls and wedged the bottle between the seat and door and then we both swung out of the fuel station and retraced our route back to the autobahn. Replete in both fuel tank and belly we were back on the open road!

30

A Close Shave

WHO was it who said, "A motorway is a motor-way is a motorway"? I would paraphrase those bon mots to read "A motorway is an autobahn is an autoroute is an autostrada is an autoput ad infinitum". They're the same the whole world over, and unless you have a few useful tools at your disposal, they can in short, be damned boring and extremely soporific. My truck being brand new did not have a radio fitted. At that time, very few cars came with them either. So I was forced to make my own entertainment. Log books were just coming into fashion but there were so many loopholes – running two logbooks, being economical with the truth or, as we did, claiming that Iran did not have a logbook system – and they all worked well. This meant that driving hours and statutory breaks were meaningless to us. I became a great believer in the maxim that every individual is an individual. Rigid rules are not necessarily safe rules. I found that sometimes I could wake from a good eight hours sleep, start driving and within an hour or so need to stop for another nap. On other days, I could drive for ten hours non-stop and still feel fresh. The safe rule was to stop when your eyes started to droop regardless of how long you'd been at the wheel. Once in the parking lot, either another nap or exercises around the truck or a cup of coffee would see you back fit to drive again. Once at the wheel, I tried to stay alert by following all the rules of the road, keeping to the nearside lane unless overtaking, always using my indicators even if there was no other traffic in sight, using my gears to slow me down and looking well ahead to assess the possible hazards. Most lone truckers will be familiar with the thoughts that race through your head while driving. Thoughts of home, wife, children – I had none since I had avoided going down the aisle so far! All sorts of thoughts were now occupying me, about women, the previous weekend in Salzburg, the possibilities of seeing Annatje again, how I might handle that meeting and to what it might lead. Many exciting outcomes involving once again handling that exquisitely slender body and travelling as far down the road to paradise as possible, flooded through my fevered brain as we circled the leafy out-skirts of Nuremberg and left the E9 to travel north-west on the E45. Not much of the city could be seen from the autobahn and it was not long before we were hurtling along in light afternoon traffic towards Wurzburg, light flurries of snow drifting across the windscreen intermittently but having no effect on the road surface which was virtually dry.

By the time we reached the Wurzburg conurbation, the weather had deteriorated. Steve's wheels were now throwing up a mist of filthy slush and I had to hang back to avoid it continually splattering across my screen. Just before the actual city, the E45 forked right and the Frankfurt autobahn exited and disappeared underneath us continuing its north west heading while we pursued a due northward course towards Schweinfurt and Fulda. Even though the light was now fading in the late winter's afternoon I could see that we were passing through deciduous forest and our route became hilly but without inclines steep enough to seriously slow us down. Thoughts tripping through my mind, triggered by the spelling of Schweinfurt now included Pschitt, the French soft drinks manufacturer whose adverts were plastered across most French city buses; Schweppes following naturally from that; Tate & Lyle sugar tankers; we'd been overtaken by several what I took to be empty tankers with Bussing units bearing the name of Kube & Kubenz; and then, of course, back to the lovely Annatje and how I might engineer a weekend in Rotterdam. Would she be there or would she have taken off with Katya on another wild weekend trip? I fumbled in my pocket for the piece of paper on which was written her address and phone number and my eyes moistened as I once again looked at those hastily scrawled kisses. The scent of her delicate skin once again wafted under my nostrils and the memory of those gentle lips brushing my cheek coloured my daydream. She was without doubt a very special lady and I was determined to treat her with a lot of respect. "Nice and easy does it", as Frank Sinatra would have advised.

There are two schools of thought on the subject of women, I casually observed to myself. On the one hand you could take advantage of every opportunity and seize the moment. On the other your enjoyment would be vastly increased by mutual understanding and shared pleasure. Lust versus love. Regrets resulting from the former would include the inevitable diseases and the visits to the "special" clinics, the constant possibility of paternity suits and having to live with a guilty conscience that you might have caused considerable problems and hardship for your consorts. From the latter the regrets would stem from wondering what would have happened if only you had been brave enough to push things just that little bit further. Did you misread the signs? Was she actually gagging for it when you thought she was hanging back?

I was just weighing things up when a flashing blue light passed me and the polizei waved Steve and myself onto the hard shoulder. We were about 50 kilometres short of Fulda and before I switched off the engine and dismounted I already knew that we were in some degree of trouble. While some of the meaning of life had been occupying my conscious thought I had noticed orange roadside signs featuring a black truck overlaid by a transverse red bar and the words "1400 ab 1700" underneath. I had originally assumed that this meant that trucks were not allowed on this section of road between those hours and this was backed up by a sudden complete absence of any other trucks on the road but, as Steve had soldiered on, I had shrugged my shoulders assuming that he knew best.

I walked past Steve's truck dodging the spray from passing vehicles to find him in deep discussion with two officers dressed in the dark green uniforms and smart peak caps of the autobahn police. Joining them I was pleased to find Steve conversing in English and not blazing away in German which would have put me at a considerable disadvantage.

"You are Englander?" the taller of the two enquired, his piercing blue eyes staring accusingly at me. I could hardly deny it so I nodded agreement. He paused moving his peak-capped head to one side as though to observe this specimen of the island race a little more closely.

"You haf identity?" he demanded. I reached inside my donkey jacket and produced my shiny new royal blue passport. He flicked through it as if searching for some incrimination which might lie within its almost virgin covers. He looked at me again comparing the photograph with the reality.

"Schein," he ordered, handing me back the passport. I looked somewhat vacant.

"Schein, schein," he snapped.

"He means your licence," Steve interjected. Once again I reached inside my jacket and this time produced the small black booklet with the gold Ministry of Transport crown emblazoned on the front which was almost snatched from my hand by the impatient official. He leafed through it and handed it back.

"Your driving forbidden now," he said curtly. He turned to Steve. "You pay 50 Deutschmarks," he ordered. And then to me, "You also pay 50 Deutschmarks." I looked at my watch and drew the policeman's attention to it.

"It's 4:50," I pointed out. "Only ten minutes until we can drive. We make mistake with time. Can we make a special deal for only ten minutes?" The officer threw me a look of absolute contempt. Steve turned away, utter despair seared across his countenance.

"Ah, so," exclaimed my adversary with a witheringly slow drawl, "you want to be funny? Maybe you come to our bureau and we can complete the papers."

"My friend, he crazy guy," Steve interposed touching his forehead with his fingertip and giving me a look which very clearly told me to button it and stay buttoned. "He's new. On first trip." He threw his hands in the air indicating his absolute contempt for his stupid colleague. He quickly thrust 50 Deutschmarks into the hands of the haughty functionary and gestured to me to do likewise. I needed no bidding. I had by this time realised that we were halfway round sense of humour bypass without a map! I had also noticed that the second policeman had hung back but I also noticed he had three pips on his jacket whereas my tormentor had none. Clearly this guy was the boss and despairingly I played a joker card.

I turned to him and said, "I'm sorry. We made mistake. We entered the autobahn too early, inspector." I had used this word to ingratiate myself judging that he might look a little more kindly on me if I were to refer to his senior rank. His previously disinterested demeanour disappeared and he took on a thoughtful air which I was interpreting as meaning he was mulling through the various charges he could pin on me over and above the serious matter of being on the autobahn during a forbidden period.

"How long on the autobahn you have been?" he asked, peering at me through rimless glasses, his crew cut greying hair betraying his advancing years. Standing with a military bearing, straight backed and immaculately dressed he was a markedly different character from his associate who was a tall beanpole of a young man, sporting tousled ginger blonde hair and wearing his junior rank with some degree of nervousness which had resulted in his clipped manner when dealing with us foreigners. The inspector, on the other hand, was of medium build showed signs through the greying of original dark hair and was ruddy of face.

"About five minutes," I lied, and watched Steve as his jaw dropped in disbelief and not a little horror.

"So," the inspector paused, either to emphasise a point or in the belief that he was about to trump my joker, "from where haf you come?" He smiled, and I noticed that his voice contained a slight but unmistakable lisp, a sure sign of menace from a cunning brain out to trap me. I gulped but remembered the last *ausfahrt* we had passed.

"We parked at Bruckerau," I asserted and saw that this time Steve had got the message and was nodding agreement even though his eyes had the look of a man who had lost all hope.

"Ah, so," the inspector looked me straight in the eye.

"Bad Bruckerau you are meaning?"

"Yes," I quickly agreed.

His eyes narrowed and he threw down his last card.

"And so where in Bad Bruckerau did you park?"

31

Congress at the Hanseat Hotel

THERE are times in life when the realisation suddenly dawns that you have wittingly or unwittingly blundered into a situation beyond your control. This sudden standoff between myself, the insouciant inspector looking increasingly confident that he had nailed me and an increasingly desperate Steve, almost jumping up and down with fury in the periphery of my vision, was one such. I turned to Steve and threw him a "calm down for goodness sake" look. I could judge from his demeanour that he was desperately looking for a way to extricate himself from his impending doom by piling all the blame onto me. I decided to press on as my old friend Pantin would have advised.

"We were parked next to the Aral station," I found the words gushing from my mouth before I could stop them. Was there an Aral station in Bad Bruckerau? There was in just about every town in Germany. They were the national fuel retailer rather like BP in the U.K. The good inspector was now looking at me somewhat quizzically, formulating his next bombshell question. I decided to throw caution completely to the wind and pulled my wallet from my inside pocket. Opening it, I pulled out the receipt from the Aral *tankstelle* where we had filled up at Meckenhaus.

"Look, here is our diesel receipt," I blurted out. By this time Steve had evidently decided that all hope was now lost for he also pulled out his wallet and brandished his Aral receipt. I have to confess at this point that this was not quite as suicidal as might be thought since most rural filling station receipts did not have the fuel station address printed on them. Normally that was rubber stamped at the time of sale and I had already noted that the cunning attendant had failed to do this. Steve had assured me that this was not a problem since many of the other drivers had John Bull printing outfits which could always be used to rubber stamp such receipts. The inspector smiled, a smile that said, "I know you bastards are lying but I like your English sense of humour."

"Ah," was all he said, then turning to his subordinate he gabbled away in German for several minutes and both of them laughed. "You boys are very lucky," the inspector continued. "Maybe yes, maybe no," he paused, looking us up and down and a feeling of relief washed across me and his face lightened as he handed back to Steve the 50 Deutschmarks. "This time you now go, before our minds are changed. Next time you at wrong time are driving, we have your number already so no excuses," and he turned on his heel and both policemen jumped into their green and white car and were gone!

"You ever do that again Arthur, I kill you!" were Steve's first words as he turned to me with a look of disbelief on his face.

"Saved you 50 Dmarks," I countered, spreading my hands in an explanatory fashion. "What were they gabbling away about?"

Steve looked at me as his face took on a thankfully amused look and continued. "The chief, he said to the other guy 'We can't prove anything but I know they lying' so the other guy says, 'Let's run them down to the station anyway' so the chief say, 'You want Heinz to bloody shoot us? These guys are not bloody stupid as they look. Special deal guy, he's crazy,' and that's when they laugh." I shrugged and turned to retrace my steps to my truck. "We still five hours at least to Bremerhaven," Steve asserted. "You want to drive or stop halfway? I can phone ahead and book hotel there we use."

"So long as we have a bed for the night," I said. "Let's keep going."

I noticed that it was just gone 5:15 as we motored back onto the autobahn, still quite lightly trafficked in the gloom as day became dark winter's evening. Our lights were already on, piercing through the odd snow flurry that threatened heavier falls ahead but luckily they did not arrive and by 6:30 we were leaving the autobahn at Kassel *rastatte* which was one of those services situated on the west side only, which meant we had to transit across the motorway to access them. The problem with most of these German auto-bahn restaurants was that, especially during the winter months, they offered an aura of such warm comfort within their mock timber-heavy decor and warm smells of coffee and hot food, that you had no desire to venture back out and continue your journey. We were soon sat down on deep banquettes supping our hot drinks while waiting for our Bratwursts, Kartoffel und Saurkraut and Steve sauntered over to the bar to use the phone. He returned with a broad smile.

"No problem," he announced as he sat down opposite me. "We're booked in to Hanseat just five minutes off autobahn and we park next to it." That was good news indeed and half an hour later, lights blazing through the dark night, we were northbound again and I was once again following Steve's tail lights through the murk of kicked up slush. We passed the *autobahndreick* for the route into Leipzieg and Eastern

Germany and then passed the city of Hannover before taking the A27 towards Bremen, which we again skirted, and by 10:30 we had arrived outside the hotel in Bremerhaven, the street lamps throwing an eerie light down through the gloom onto the pavements, highlighting the snowflakes which were now falling relentlessly as we parked in the public car park on the opposite side of the road. We had to wait for a slow moving, brightly lit tram to pass in front of us before crossing the road to the fifties concrete edifice which was to be our hostel for the night.

Frankly, anything would have been better than another night in the Mack cab – a tent in a forest, a bench on a railway station concourse where at least you would have the luxury of being able to stretch out, a sleeping bag laid across the load inside the container if only it were not sealed, a sofa in a friend's front room or even the deck of a storm-tossed ferry. These were all to become familiar places of rest but tonight we sought warmth, a hot shower, cotton sheets and a good night's sleep. In fact, we attained none of these things. We were greeted in the sparse and surprisingly chilly white lobby by a lugubrious gentleman of indeterminate but advanced years.

"I am so sorry England drivers," were his first words to us. "We no heizung, er heating haf. Our furnace is kaput. Maybe it will fix. I await the man now."

We looked at each other and both shrugged. There was no heat, so no hot shower but at this time of night we had no option but to accept the inevitable. Our host had the hangdog look of a man set adrift in an open boat by a mutinous and ungrateful crew, as far as he was concerned through no fault of his own. Everything was conspiring against him and the current situation was way out of his control. Thin of face, with concave cheeks and protruding cheekbones, his high forehead was surmounted by a seriously receded hairline followed by an unruly shock of greasy greying hair which he had a habit of continually sweeping back with his nicotined right hand as if it would overtake his field of vision at any moment. On the desk in front of him, his half-finished cigarette, its smoke purposelessly spiralling towards the yellowing ceiling, was burning in a white ashtray helpfully supplied for the purpose by the West tobacco company. He was dressed in a brown cardigan which had probably once been quite smart but now was fraying at the collar and cuffs, and a pair of shapeless grey trousers underneath which protruded a pair of beige slippers. All of this I took in while Steve completed the mandatory overnight *auslander* cards and we grudgingly paid the full amount of 20 Deutschmarks with no rebate for the lack of heating. He handed two keys to us and motioned us towards the stairs.

"First floor," was all he said as he shuffled off with the air of one who had come to the end of a long and trying day and was not prepared to take any more, thank you.

Once in the room, I looked in longingly at the now redundant shower, placed my overnight bag on a chair and lay on top of the bed. At once I realised the sheets were not the pristinely ironed white cotton ones I had been daydreaming about ever since we had passed Hannover but in fact were most tasteful pink nylon ones. As far as I was concerned, the only place for this man-made fabric was around the legs of a well-shaped woman and not crackling and raising sparks around me while I tossed and turned in its clammy folds. There was nothing for it but to sleep fully clothed on top of the blanket, borrowing a second blanket from the other bed which just about enabled me to warm up to sleeping temperature. So, two out of three had failed and as I dropped off, number three also kicked back at me. The walls of the establishment proved to be paper thin and the odd voice and snatches of radio music could be heard emanating from other rooms. These intermittent noises were not a great problem but as I was about to enter the land of dreams I became aware of a thudding noise overhead; a slow monotonous thud at first accompanied by creaking as though a stately galleon was proceeding out into a heavy sea. It then increased both in volume and regularity and then human sounds both male and female were laid over the thuds and the creaks and the reason for the noises became embarrassingly obvious. Eventually, like all good things, the furore ceased and there was sighing and then soft conversation and eventually I succumbed to slumber. How long I remained asleep I couldn't tell but it seemed I was immediately awakened by a repeat performance. Maybe they didn't get it quite right the first time, I thought, as I was forced to vicariously take part in these strange rites. Sleep was an impossibility while the rutting season was in full swing but eventually it was over and I nodded off, only to be awoken again by another repetition, and so it went on at least five times during the night and a sixth as I was brushing my teeth before breakfast! So, three out of three disappointments was not a bad record for my first night in Bremerhaven.

At breakfast in the charmless white-walled dining room I was at least hoping to meet the entertainment staff but sadly they did not bother to grace us with their presence.

"Very good night," Steve observed. "Slept good like log."

That cheered me up no end, but at least we had hot tea and the eggs and ham were not at all bad either.

32

Bremerhaven

STEVE was just about to launch in to what I knew would be an interminably convoluted tale about how he had put one over on a previous boss, when our aged host entered the room followed by a freckled slip of a youth clasping a wad of papers to his chest. The decrepit functionary motioned over to our table and muttered something that sounded like "Englander LKW fahrers," before immediately departing in a flurry of dandruff and flaking dry skin as though he had urgent business needing his instant attention. Perhaps at long last a plumber had been located to fix the hotel's boiler system. Perhaps he needed to organise medical attention for the nocturnal performers. Unfortunately, we were never to know! The ginger youth sidled over to our table and holding out his hand introduced himself as Wolfgang from Van Ommeren.

"I was seeing your trucks outside," he explained. "And we are organising your transhipment. If we can offload you this morning we can catch tomorrow's sailing for New York."

"What about steam cleaning?" Steve asked. I already knew that once you had carried pickled goatskins in a container you couldn't load anything else until it had been thoroughly sanitised of the awful smell which would leech its way into anything it came into contact with.

"Ja, we always are steam cleaning the P.I.C. containers," Wolfgang nodded. "By tea-time you can go."

He sat down with us and Steve ambled over to the buffet table to pour him a coffee. Wolfgang had an air of youthful keenness and efficiency about him. Of average height, he was dressed for the cold outside in a dark blue gabardine coat which had some kind of beige faux fur lining around the collar and cuffs. He proceeded to take this off and lay it across our vacant chair. Underneath he was clad in smart office casual – a blue blazer, red and brown checked shirt and brown chino-like slacks finished off with what looked to be black trainers. Fresh of countenance, blue of eye and with sharply defined facial features, his crowning glory was his ginger hair which was emphasised rather shockingly by the fact that he wore it a l'Africaine. In short I was to learn later that he was known as the fuzzy wuzzy. All our drivers knew him well as one of those characters who stood out from the mundane crowd. Sitting down, he turned to me and I could swear that although his head moved, the hair stood stock still.

"You are Herr Arthur?" he enquired.

"Ja, Herr Arthur," I replied. He extended his hand.

"Herr Stefan, I know him already," he explained, smiling as though there were some distant recollection of a shared joke or bizarre event colouring their relationship. "He can be crazy guy; some of the stevedores in the terminal get scared when he shouts at them." Here Wolfgang paused with a chuckle as Steve returned with the hot coffee and joined us.

"He says you're crazy," I asserted. Steve laughed.

"That's because I make the Yugos work when they offload containers. Can you imagine?" he continued. "First thing they do in morning is hit vending machine for beer, break time hit vending machine, lunchtime beer, afternoon, beer. Any time they not working they hit the beer. No wonder they work like no strength in them. Takes two to lift one bloody barrel. If you paid good wage you have good German workers," he wagged his fingers accusingly at poor Wolfgang.

"Not our workers," Wolfgang riposted apologetically. "They work for the Port Authority. Van Ommeren have no control on them." Steve shrugged.

"Yeah, but all time we have to sit on backsides and then we miss re-load and then we not make Salzburg for weekend. It's no bloody good." Wolfgang looked back at him with mocking sternness.

"You shout too much," he admonished. "They will not work at all. Then we haf big problem and they black your company. You must be careful Stefan." Steve shook his head with an air of experienced resignation.

"I know," he agreed. "You don't worry. I be good today!"

Wolfgang heaved a sigh of good humoured relief. "You haf your papers?" he asked, sipping his dark black coffee. Luckily we both had our document cases with us as we had already agreed to collate our paperwork during breakfast. We laid them out on the table, which was now in the process of being de-crumbed and cleared by a laconic lady of indeterminate years, her dark skin indicating that she hailed from a warmer climate. Steve selected out the invoices, packing lists, sanitary certificates, permits, carnets de passage, *steurkartes*, CMR notes, passports and fuel declarations.

"They want everything as if we boarding bloody boat ourselves," Steve commented with the resignation of someone who had been through it all before, complained and got nothing but grief in return.

Wolfgang swept them all up and taking a final swig from his coffee cup, stood up, donned his coat, said he would see us in the terminal office in half-an-hour and left through the reception doorway. "Good guy," Steve gestured towards the disappearing figure. "Anyone else, they leave us here and when we arrive in terminal say we too late to lodge papers and make us wait a day. With luck we on road before teatime." With that we both returned to our rooms, packed our things and, having already paid the night before for our lodging, made our way across the now heavily trafficked main road to the parking lot.

The snow had now abated but a layer of a couple of inches was evident across the bonnet and cab and some fell onto me as I opened the driver's door. I took off my reefer jacket and shook it dry before taking my seat at the command centre. Cloudy grey exhaust spurted from Steve's stack and I immediately started my motor in case he should try for a quick getaway but he was content like me to let the engine idle while he sorted out and tidied up the cab. Five minutes later Steve revved his engine, made a wide 360 degree turn in a still almost empty car park and nosed into the exit lane. He had to nuzzle his way into the traffic before it got the message and stopped, a tram on either side of him as he crossed the carriageway and turned left. I stuck to his tail as if glued, knowing that if I had been courteous and allowed the traffic to intervene, Steve would have been long gone by the time I managed to infiltrate the rat race. The route to the container terminal followed the bank of the mouth of the river Weser and, within 15 minutes, we were at the terminal portals. As I flicked back the handbrake button, I could see that Steve was gesturing to me to remain in my cab while he conversed with the gateman. Then he turned, indicated a thumbs up and we were in the terminal itself. We weaved our way between stacks of containers and straddle carriers before entering a parking area outside a long modern three-storey office building finished in light coloured bricks with dark green window surrounds. The logo of the port authority was displayed on a neon sign across the top and on the right side of the building on the ground floor was a large Zollamt sign.

We left our trucks and entered the building through a door to the left of the customs sign next to which was a perspex board with the names in alphabetical order of all the agents and shipping lines who occupied the block, with their allocated floor and room number inscribed next to each one. Van Ommeren was on the second floor in room 205 flanked by the offices of the Hapag Lloyd line on one side and the DSR Line on the other. The building was spotless, with white brick interior walls and white flooring speckled with brown and white. I surmised that this was probably to differentiate the floor from the walls for the benefit of the inebriated stevedores. The office was a standard freight agent layout with a long desk separating the itinerants (us) from the incumbents (the staff). There were about ten desks arranged in a regimental fashion, two abreast down the length of the room which had windows on the right side and an opaque glazed partition on the corridor side. Behind the far end of the reception desk stood a cream and brown Siemens telex machine and a red and cream Xerox copier. As we entered, Wolfgang was feeding punched paper tape into the reading slot of the telex. He closed the small flap onto the top of the tape, pressed a button which resulted in a short electric hum and then the clatter of telex typewriter keys as the machine both sent the message to a distant address and also typed it out on a paper roll for record purposes.

"That's your message of arrival to Gerhardt," he explained as we leaned over the counter to watch the wonder machine at work. "Now you come with me to offload."

We followed Wolfgang down the stairs and out into the parking area where he leapt up into the passenger seat of Steve's truck and off we went further into the terminal to the next building, almost identical to the first except that it appeared to have offices only on the third floor. The bottom two floors were warehouses, indicated by the massive dark green double doors which flanked the hundred metre run of the structure. I followed Steve to the far end of this parking lot at which I could see three trailers standing, one loaded with a 40 foot container and the other two having a 20 foot each. All three were a silver grey colour with the words Hapag Lloyd emblazoned on each side in black. Steve's hazard indicators started flashing so I pulled to a stop and watched as he expertly turned the wagon round to face me, jumped down, opened his container's doors and fastened them back along the sides and then reversed on to the empty 40 foot container, stopping about four feet away from it. Several blue-clad workmen clambered up into the empty container, a steel plate was passed up to them to bridge the gap and transhipping commenced.

Steve walked over to my truck and shouted up to me, "Only one bloody gang. They'll have to finish mine before starting yours. Should take them a couple of hours handballing it all."

Wolfgang was deep in animated conversation with the gangmaster and we sauntered over to discover what was happening. A good amount of banging and scraping and incoherent shouts were emanating from the transhipping operation as we passed. Wolfgang finished his discourse and turned to us.

"Second gang coming in half an hour," he said. "If you position your truck onto that chassis," here he pointed to the nearest of the two, "normally we empty the rear container first. Then we go back to my office for some coffee and maybe a telex from Gerhardt with your reloads."

Reversing onto the chassis was easy peasy.

"Wait 'till you have to jackknife the trailer round so they can empty front container," Steve said helpfully. "Then we see what you made of!" Steve wandered over to the back of his container and shouted something up to the work gang which I assumed to be words of warm encouragement or thanks for their hard work in the bitter windswept cold of the sea terminal, before rejoining us as we walked back to the office block. Wolfgang looked at him somewhat reproachfully.

"Stefan, what did you say to them?" Steve flashed him a guilty smile.

"I just said 'Put your bloody backs into it'," he confessed.

"Thank you so much," Wolfgang said. "You do not make my life any easier."

Once back in the office amid the cacophony of the telex and the massed clerks at their typewriters, Wolfgang ushered us into the quiet of the staff rest room at the back, took our drinks orders and started the omnipresent coffee machine which was soon gurgling away encouragingly as it emitted puffs of steam and the most evocative of smells. While the machine was percolating he strode out of the room and re-appeared a few minutes later with a telex message.

"From Gerhardt," he announced, handing it to Steve. Steve read the message and smiled.

"For me good news, I load in Prague at Skoda works, machinery for Tehran. For you, not so good.

Go to Van Hove in Brussels for first service on your truck. You not gonna make Salzburg for weekend."

"Not so good?" Was he crazy? My mind was already racing. Brussels was only an hour or so by rail from Rotterdam. Maybe just maybe I could engineer a meeting with the lovely Annatje. I allowed my face to fall as the coffee was poured out, the additives added and the cups presented to us.

"You don't look too pleased," Wolfgang said.

"Nothing I can do. The tractor has to be serviced," I replied, trying not to reveal my mounting excitement about a delicious little lady who also needed a service.

"You were hoping for an assignation?" Wolfgang enquired.

Yes, I thought, there was another possible assignation, sexy Gitte from Lagermax who had wrapped her naked legs around my neck in the pool. That would have to wait until the following weekend. Gitte or Annatje, Rotterdam or Salzburg, lust or love. Thrashing a transporter up and down the A1 or watching the exotic continent unfold through the front windows of an R600. The decisions one has to make in life become harder and harder, I thought.

33

On a Promise?

I must have overdone the crestfallen bit because Wolfgang adopted a concerned expression as he put his arm round my shoulders.

"You need to make a phone call?" he asked in a tone which suggested he understood that I had probably been on a promise and would need to repair some fences.

"That would be very kind," I replied. Steve gazed knowingly at me still convinced that I was looking forward to a weekend of unbridled lust with Gitte in Salzburg.

"If you want," Wolfgang continued, "Steve and me can sit at my desk while you phone."

"Thanks," I said, brightening up considerably, "I would really appreciate that." Steve touched his nose a-la-Ian and gave me a conspiratorial wink as he picked up his coffee mug and headed to the door.

"Austria code is 0053," Wolfgang helpfully advised over his shoulder. "Outside line you dial 9 but don't wait for tone after. It is automatische."

Once they were safely out of the room, I retrieved my now crumpled piece of paper complete with the treasured kisses, dialled 9 and then 0031 for Holland followed by the hallowed number. There was a considerable delay and some clicking on the line and I was about to replace the receiver when the Dutch ring tone came through. I waited in excited expectation.

Maybe Annatje was at work. Maybe she could be on holiday? Or worse still, maybe her boyfriend would answer, blowing away all my heated preconceptions. There was, I thought, an infinite wait, although it was probably only thirty seconds or so, and the receiver was picked up at the other end.

"Dag?" It was a female voice.

My excitement rose almost to fever pitch and I looked across through the glass screen to the desk at the far end near the reception area where Wolfgang and Steve were deep in conversation over their coffees. Satisfied that they could not hear me I replied. "Annatje? This is Arthur. Remember me?"

"Nee Ik ben moeder Annatje," came the disembodied voice through my receiver. I didn't speak Dutch but I rightly guessed that I was through to Annatje's mother.

"Do you speak English?" I asked.

"Ja, a little," came the reply. "I am mother Annatje."

"I am Arthur, English driver," I explained. "I met Annatje two weeks ago."

"Ah, Arthur, ja, she told me you take her to Paris. I think she want to see you. You are in Rotterdam?" she continued in her halting English.

"No, but I may be this weekend. When will she be home?" I asked even more excitedly since I had just been informed that she actually wanted to see me.

"She finish work at 2 so think she be home at 3," Annatje's mother affirmed. "You will call back? I think she be sad she miss you."

"Thank you," I said a touch breathlessly. "I will call back then."

"OK, please you do, goodbye," she finished.

I said goodbye and replaced the receiver already feeling as though I was walking on air. I saw Wolfgang and Steve on their way back so my feeling of imminent pleasure had to be contained. I was adjusting my facial expression to what I thought would look like a frown of disappointment as they walked in.

"Not in," I sighed. "But I spoke to her mother and she'll be back after 3 o'clock."

"We should have finished your steam cleaning by then," Wolfgang smiled. "If you wish you can phone again." He looked at his watch, waving my expressions of heartfelt thanks aside. "They should have started on your truck now," he continued. "Let's go over and check them out."

We made our way back towards the two trucks, dodging the stacks of pallets and bales of cotton and cases of machinery, strewn rather haphazardly for a German operation, I thought. In fact, this terminal was a major transhipment centre for trucks emanating from all over Europe, Eastern Europe, Turkey and Iran. They arrived largely in tilts or boxvans and their cargoes were transhipped into the containers which would take them across the Atlantic and into the American heartland. At that time, this type of port operation was blacklisted in the U.K. which was, however, leading to the creation of inland terminals. Here there were no such restrictions and business was obviously booming as a result. As we wove our way between the stacks of cargo, a crane was lifting a batch of cotton bales from a Turkish trailer pulled by a superannuated Fiat belonging to the Er-Sen company of Istanbul and dropping them into an open-top 40 foot container. Reaching our trucks, it was evident that work had already commenced on my rear container and when we investigated we found that Steve's was three quarters finished. The stench from the pickle barrels was indeed quite nauseating and we had to stand upwind of the operation, something the poor Yugoslav stevedores were unable to do. They were in the thick of it and no amount of rudimentary masks or kerchiefs tied round their faces could counter the nauseous odour. At 10 o'clock a klaxon sounded and all work halted. The Yugoslavs, sweating even in these snowy conditions, emerged from the bowels of the containers mopping their brows and disappeared across to a canteen where Steve assured me they would be assuaging their thirsts with draughts of the local Becks beer.

"Timed that nicely," I observed to Steve as we kicked our heels waiting for them to reappear, but 15 minutes later the klaxon sounded again and the straggle of workers emerged from the canteen and made their ways to the various work locations. Within half an hour Steve's container was finished and the doors thankfully closed.

"We have to drop trailer and let them take it off for steam cleaning," Steve explained. "We not allowed to move trailers in dock area."

I gave Steve a hand to drop the legs and detach the susies and after a wait of half an hour a superannuated Maggie Deutz hove to, picked up the trailer and disappeared to some far-flung outpost of the port where steam cleaning took place. Almost at the same time, my rear container was empty and I then had to reposition it so that the front 20 footer was flush with the Hapag Lloyd container. Steve told me how to do it and stood back to see how many times I would have to shunt to get it right. First I had to turn the rig around and then head straight for the recipient container. At the last minute I was to hang a right, stop and then jackknife reverse to bring me flush against it, remembering that I still had to leave a gap of a yard or so for the workers to squeeze through. One thing Steve didn't mention was that I was supposed to open my container doors before the operation. Luckily as

I hung the right I could see the stevedores opening the doors of the other container and it occurred to me that I really ought to do the same so I stopped, jumped down from the cab and back up onto the tractor chassis and opened said doors. In the background I could see a slightly crestfallen Steve who, I reckoned, had been hoping I would complete the operation and alight from my cab shouting "Ta-ra", only to be regaled with the laughter which would echo all around from my foolishness at positioning a closed container where it would be impossible to open the doors. Back in the cab I selected reverse and first split and gingerly jackknifed with a hard left on the steering and my eyes locked on the mirror to ensure I did not hit the other container. I had been a little worried that I had turned right slightly too early but in fact I was extremely lucky in that she came back perfectly almost as if I knew what I was doing and, with the susies stretched almost to their limit, the two containers became perfectly aligned. Both Wolfgang and Steve had the good grace to applaud as I exited the cab and bowed low to the assembled company.

"You a jammy bastard," Steve conceded. "I never see anyone do that first time." I grinned back full of unearned confidence and to tell the truth an air of slight conceit. The workers squeezed up into the Hapag Lloyd container and transhipment commenced. Wolfgang returned to his office and Steve and I idly passed the time chatting in his cab.

"Trouble with this job," Steve confided, "we never get home. Either we weekend Salzburg or we marooned in some goddamned back place in spin mill or customs yard."

"Where is home?" I asked.

"Now is Walsall," Steve sighed. "My family, we come over in revolution 1956, I was 15. We cross border in Austria with nothing. My Dad had been hunted by police so in middle of night we leave our village by Gyor in friend car, old Skoda," he laughed. "No room for nothing, just Mum, Dad, me and brother. We think we go on holiday but ten miles before Austria border car light flash us. We stop. He tell us police check ahead so then we get out and walk through fields and wood and more field and more woods all night. I don't remember too much. Suddenly I see we not alone and when we reach road again, many people also walking, some had carts, some also had horse. My dad ask them where they going. They say "Austria" so we join them, my dad thinking safety in numbers. When we get to border we talking to people my dad worried we have no document. Later he told me our papers sewn into my mum's clothes. But at border nobody stop us till Austrian side so we free. Then my Dad got choice, America or England. Funny, later he told me if he chose America we would come here for ship from Bremerhaven but he love England so we get Red Cross train from Vienna to Calais, then ferry to Dover and train to Birmingham. Funny world eh? Here we in Bremerhaven," he paused deep in thought and I noticed a tear in his eye. "We lucky guys eh? Many didn't make it out." At this moment the klaxon sounded and Steve started out from the reverie he was entering. "Lunchtime, Yugos drinking more beer. We go to office canteen eh?" he suggested.

The office workers' canteen was on the top floor of the office block itself and situated at the far end with a view over the container cranes up the river Weser towards the sea. We learned from a colleague of Wolfgang's that he was away into town to see a "friend" for lunch. This information was delivered with a knowing wink so we guessed that an assignation with a fraulein was the order of the day for our lucky friend. After a Zigeuner Schnitzel mit Rostkartoffel and a couple of beers we heard the outside klaxon signalling the end of the half hour lunch break and Steve and I strolled back to find the stevedores rolling the last of the barrels from my front container into the U.S. bound box. The foreman asked me to uncouple the rig so they could take it away for steam cleaning and this I did. Steve and I resumed our earlier conversation and I discovered that once they reached Birmingham they had been housed in an old army camp while permanent accommodation was found. The old Nissen huts had been spartan and cold that first winter but the fact that they were safe meant so much to them that there had been no complaining from any of the large group of refugees living there. Their main pre-occupation had been the need to learn English and almost daily lessons had been provided for them alongside schooling in Hungarian for the younger children. Eventually they had been moved into a prefab in Walsall and Steve's father had found training and employment as a bus driver with the Midland Red Company. Steve had picked up a good foundation of English but as he was by then 16 and with no education certificates he had also gone out to work and had ended up as a warehouseman where over the years he had talked with the lorry drivers and decided that that was the life for him. Many years driving in Britain had led to the, for him, inevitability of continental work and he had found, with his knowledge of German, a natural affinity for life on the European road. So far, however, he had not ventured back into Hungary!

The aged Magirus trundled alongside us and dropped Steve's trailer before collecting and disappearing with mine. I helped Steve link up and we kicked our heels again for another hour before my trailer was duly returned. We then parked up next to the office block and ascended the stairs to the Van Ommeren office. Wolfgang greeted us and I wondered if that was the flush of youth or the flush of an exciting lunch hour on his face. Whatever it was, he explained that our papers had not come out of customs yet and we would have to wait.

"You wish to make that phone call again?" he asked me.

"Thanks, that's very kind," was my reply and Wolfgang lifted the gate in the reception desk so that we could enter the sanctum of the office staff. Steve took a seat at his desk and Wolfgang motioned me to the rest room at the back. With quivering fingers I lifted the receiver and dialled the magic numbers. After an almost interminable pause I heard the ringing tone and then the receiver at the far end was lifted.

"Hallo" came the voice at the other end. Oh, my God, it definitely was Annatje this time!

34

Assignation

"HELLO, Arthur here. Is that Annatje?" I said, as nonchalantly as I could, hoping that she would not sense any trepidation in my voice or be able to hear the noise my heart was making.

"Ja, it is me," she laughed, with that carefree laugh that had entranced me as we headed south a couple of weekends ago. "I wondered if you would call back when you missed me. My mother said you sound very nice but what would she know?"

"She married your dad," I suggested, thinking that I couldn't keep this small talk going for too long, I had to know if she really wanted to see me again. I took a deep breath. "I'm in Bremerhaven at the moment but should be in Brussels later in the week. Maybe I could catch the train up to Rotterdam?" I ventured.

"Or I could come to Brussels?" she suggested. I relaxed a little. No mention of unavailability owing to hairdressing appointments or girlfriend evenings or family reunions or whatever.

"You sure you're not washing your hair?" I joked.

"What?" she replied a tad indignantly as I luxuriated in the mellow tone of her sexy Dutch accent. "I wash always every day!"

"It's a stupid English joke," I explained. "When a girl doesn't really want to see you, she makes up an excuse like she has to wash her hair so can't make the date."

"Oh! But I want to see you," she said with delightful openness.

"Oh, Annatje," I said. "You shouldn't say things like that. You're supposed to keep me guessing whether you like me or not."

"Oh, OK," she giggled. "Sorry I can't make it, my mother needs me to do the washing up. Is that better?" I looked up through the partition and could see Steve and Wolfgang rising from their chairs. Time was not on my side.

"I have to go," I said, "but I'll phone tomorrow when I get to Brussels."

"OK" was her reply. "I'm home at this time for the next couple of days. Don't forget," she finished with a flirtatious and suggestive lilt in her lovely voice and I could just visualise for a few seconds those yielding lips so far away.

"Bye for now," I said, replacing the phone just as Steve entered.

"Any luck?" he asked.

"Yeah, I got through OK. She was disappointed but I'll see her next time I think," I replied trying to conceal the sudden lightness and excitement that had taken over my whole body now that I was sure there would be another meeting with Annatje.

"Your papers are on the way," Wolfgang announced as I thanked him for the use of the phone. "Shall I telex Salzburg and tell them you're both on the way?" We both nodded assent and he returned to his desk, his fuzzy shock of hair slightly awry as he negotiated his way through the office desks. I asked Steve the best route down to Brussels.

"You make down to Bremen, then Osnabruck, Dusseldorf and Aachen border," he advised. "At Aachen you use Frans Maas agent on both sides but empty you have no problem. By the way," he continued, "you must to check the papers. Sometimes they don't sign something and then you having a problem get out of Germany." I eyed the Siemens cream phone with its plastic dial, standard issue from Deutsche Telekom, so different from our clunky black ones with the chrome metal diallers back home. How I would have loved to pick up the receiver and redial Annatje and perhaps take the relationship one stage further but it was not to be. At the far end of the office the entrance door swung open and a dock runner entered, signalled to Wolfgang and left a wodge of paperwork on the reception counter. I watched Wolfgang, or rather Wolfgang's hair, saunter over, collect up the papers and return to his desk.

"He's a rich man, you know," Steve ventured. "More money than you me put together. Or more exact his old man is rich. Editor of Hamburg newspaper. Sometime you go to Hamburg he have party at old man house. If you go there for offload, call him. He always like see you." Wolfgang rose from his desk, sauntered across the office and entered the lounge.

"Alles in ordnung," he announced, clicking his heels together in true Prussian fashion. He gave each of us our sheaf of papers to check our German permits.

"Make sure they don't stamp them," Steve muttered, *carnets de passage* still with the third *volet* intact and new *steurkartes*.

"They are for empty transit," Wolfgang explained. "You can't load in Germany on these." We then ensured that the CMR notes were properly signed and stamped by Hapag Lloyd and Wolfgang returned our passports and fuel sheets which were still not processed as they would be used for our declarations on finally leaving Germany. Once we had filed these documents into our briefcases, Wolfgang handed us our fully completed *laufzettls* to enable us to go through the dock exit gate.

"One thing," Wolfgang said, handing me a Van Ommeren business card. "If you ever come to Hamburg call me. My number is on the back." I pocketed it envisaging future parties and good times. "Of course, that depends if I am home. Auf wiedersehen, have a good trip," he finished.

We shook hands and bundled out through the reception flat, out of the office, down the stairs and out to the parking.

"You have no problems," Steve said as we shook hands. "I see you have good attitude. By the way," he continued, flashing me a serious smile, "follow me through to Bremen then take A1 direction Osnabruck and Essen. Follow Venlo signs then make sure you hit A44 direction Neuss and Aachen. Diesel cheaper in Belgium!" he finished, and with that he clambered up into his cab.

I regained my own command centre and, placing my briefcase on the passenger seat, just had time to start the engine to follow Steve out of the parking. The clock at the gate was showing 4.10pm. I handed my *laufzettl* to the guard and followed Steve through the streets of Bremerhaven back onto the A27 towards Bremen. The clouds were intermittent with just a tiny flurry or two of sleet necessitating the occasional use of the wipers to clear the screen and then, as we approached Bremen, the sky cleared and the wan evening sun struck its dying rays from the west across the pale blue sky dotted here and there with streaks of light cloud which blushed pinky-red indicating, I hoped, a fine tomorrow. Turning right onto the A1, I flashed a goodbye to Steve as he disappeared under the autobahn to head east towards Hamburg, East Germany and Czechoslovakia. Now the sun was right in front of me on the horizon and I had to screw up my eyes to see ahead as the visors were too high to cope. I made a mental note to buy sunglasses which, up until then, I hadn't envisaged needing until the summer months arrived. What made it worse was the surface water from the previous showers which now glistened and reflected the sun's rays up from the road. This situation only lasted for half an hour or so until the sun dropped below the horizon and dusk was quickly followed by nightfall and the road was delineated by the red rear lights on my side and the white piercing headlights of oncoming traffic on the left side.

Night driving could be boring, to put it mildly. Your mind wandered across many subjects, and thoughts could run riot. Here I was for the first time on my own. I had spent the previous two weeks slavishly following first Ian and then Steve across the high roads and the low roads traversing the European continent, not having to worry overmuch about routes, road numbering or crucial road junctions where a wrong turn could have resulted in serious delays. I had been completely dependent on my mentors who had made all the critical decisions. Left turns, right turns, route selection, fuel stops, night parkings, hotels, all had been chosen for me. Now the whole shebang was up to me. Here I was let loose with a plated 44 tonner, although current regulation only allowed 38 tonnes gross, my only aids; my map of Europe and the hastily gabbled route advice from Steve. Osnabruck, Essen, Venlo, Aachen were all racing through my mind. So far I knew I was set fair because Osnabruck was showing on the overhead signs at each exit, in German the delightfully named *ausfahrts*. This word alone was making me smile and leading to quite bizarre trains of thought. Was it a command? Was it a direction indicator to the nearest toilet complex? I knew that "aus" meant "out", so was it simply sound medical advice? Better out than in? And so on. It was amazing what one's mind could light upon. Several times I saw trucks approaching with similar top cab-light arrangements to mine, the outer ambers with three ambers in the middle which normally signalled American tractors. I already knew that most of these would be U.S. army trucks and several flashed me assuming that I also was of a military bent.

By 7 o'clock I was passing Osnabruck in light sleet and the old eyes were starting to droop. Moreover, the old stomach was reminding me that I hadn't eaten since the canteen lunch in Bremerhaven which had been filling but had also been seven hours ago. So when I saw the sign for the *raststätte*, Tecklenburger Lande West, I made an instant decision to stop for dinner and possibly for the night. As the *ausfahrt* approached I indicated right and gratefully swung the rig over into the deceleration lane, took my foot off the power pedal and started winding down through the gears, double-skipping as the trailer was empty. This was an old service area and had the classic layout of the fuel station block which also contained a shop at the filling station end, then toilets and a cafeteria at the far end. I kept to the autobahn side of the complex, passing the car parking and into the extensive HGV parking area where I was able to park alongside a Kube & Kubenz tanker and a French Bourgey, Montreuil tilt. At the back of the service area was what looked like a new three storey hotel facility which also advertised itself as a restaurant. I made another instant decision and, bearing in mind the cold and the now driving sleet, decided to see if I could book into the hotel. Taking a chance, I snatched my document case from the passenger seat and my overnighter from the footwell, locked up the cab and sloshed through the slush to the hotel. An aura of warmth greeted me as I opened the door. There was a hum and bustle indicating a busy restaurant and delightful cooking smells wafted through the foyer assaulting my taste buds and antagonising my hunger. A generously endowed Frau accosted me.

"Was wollen sie?" she kindly enquired.

"Ich bin Englander," I said in my halting German. "Haben sie ein fremdenzimmer bitte?"

"Ach, you are English," she smilingly replied. "Ja, we have a room only for 15 Deutschmarks. Breakfast is extra." I accepted the offer and she gave me a key in exchange for the three five Deutschmark notes I hastily extracted from my wallet.

"You would like some food?" she asked solicitously. "We serve for one hour more."

I made my way to the room on the second floor. The general décor was German minimalist, all walls were white-painted concrete and there were no carpets even in the bedroom but it was clean and warm and the beds had thick duvets, although it has to be said that the bolsters were rock hard. However, after a meal of Jagerschnitzel followed by a rum baba with loads of whipped cream plus a couple or three glasses of house red, I slept well, dreaming of what I hoped would be a weekend of excitedly getting to know Annatje a little better!

35

Interlude

THE motel bed was comfortable but that solid bolster did not help and, although I had slept like a log, I woke quite early and made my customary bathroom visit. On my way back I parted the curtains and looked down on the truck park. It was still dark but the massive overhead lighting picked out the truck shapes and, more importantly, showed me that there had been a heavy fall of snow. Everything was white apart from a couple of wheel tracks left either by early morning risers or perhaps ploughs on their way onto the autobahn. I had no snow chains so decided to go back to sleep, wake up, have a leisurely breakfast and hopefully, by the time I hit the road, it would have been largely cleared. One thing I did notice, however, was that alongside my truck, which I could easily make out owing to it being a bonneted tractor, unlike all the other cabovers, it looked as though the French 'Bourgey' had gone and its place had been taken by another bonneted truck. As I slipped back into slumber I wondered if that might be one of "ours"?

I must have fallen into a deep sleep because the next thing I knew was a loud banging on the door and a voice shouting.

"Come on. Get up you lazy bastard!" I instantly recognised the voice as Ron's, our venerable road boss.

"My God," I thought momentarily as I hurled myself out from under the white duvet and hastily pulled on my jeans. "These guys really are on my back! No slacking on P.I.C." I opened the door and there he was with his sardonic smile, dark brown leather jerkin, check shirt, faded blue jeans and winkle pickers just as I had left him back in Europoort.

"You staying here too?" I asked.

"No. Got here too late last night. Had to stop," he explained. "Autobahn closed in the blizzard so I cabbed it. Mind if I come in and use the facilities?"

"Feel free," I replied, closing the door behind him as he entered the sparsely decorated room, its only gesture to comfort, the large radiator under the window which thankfully was extremely efficient and had already warmed up the room more than adequately. Ron disappeared into the bathroom and I resumed my place on the bed listening to the hiss of the shower, the shush of the toothbrush and then the rasp of the razor. His ablutions finished, he walked back into the bedroom drying his face on a handtowel.

"Your turn," he remarked as he sat down on the end of the bed. "No pressure, no rush. The autobahn's still closed."

I'd gone into the shower room with a slight hangover but came out pretty refreshed and we decided to get some breakfast before returning to the trucks. The restaurant, although on the ground floor and closely connected, was not the same building as the motel. It was a much older structure, possibly pre-dating the war, so it had a comfortable and homely atmosphere about it with its wood panelling and beamed ceilings. The tables were arranged in alcoves throughout, each one capable of holding six people. The same Frau who had booked me in the night before showed us to a table close to some open refrigerated counters, one of which contained an array of cold meats and cheeses as well as a selection of mueslis, cereals and fruit. The restaurant was quite full, as could be expected with a thronging car and truck park and a closed autobahn. I ordered zwei Spiegeleier mit Schinken, and Ron ordered Ruhreier and we both ordered tea, ever hopeful that the bags would be dunked in the boiling water before their arrival at the table but, as usual, this was not to be. However, our smiling large bosomed Frau did bring us milk which, however, turned out once again to be depressingly hot! Ron told me that he had just offloaded a 20 foot container in Minden.

"They loaded it onto one of the Iranians and brought it to Europoort by mistake," he elaborated, lifting his eyes to the ceiling to indicate his disgust at the standard of expertise exhibited by the Salzburg office. "Gerhardt nearly had a fit. It was mohair for one of the Hugo Boss spinning mills and they had a deadline so I had no option but to drop everything and skidaddle back over here. I'd only just made it back from Salzburg so I was pretty knackered. That was yesterday morning. I was planning to get back to Rotterdam overnight, settle up things in Europoort and then have a weekend at Mrs Vermeiren's." He gave me a knowing wink and I knew that Mrs. Vermeiren would not be seeing very much of him once he'd checked in and departed for Vlaardingen! I told him I was heading for Van Hove's and my truck's first service. Then I asked him about the train service from Brussels to Rotterdam thinking he had probably utilised it for exactly the same reason that I was hoping to do.

"Every hour from Brussels central," he said, then paused for a few seconds with a slightly puzzled look on his face before it lit up as realisation dawned. "Ah, the Dutch girls you and Ian picked up." I nodded. "Well you don't want to go to Brussels for a start," he confided and I was suddenly stricken with a panic that he'd put the mockers on my planned weekend of passion. "Nah, come to Rotterdam with me," he continued, and I let out a sigh of relief. "Then get down to Brussels for Monday morning. The earliest you'd get there today, even if the autobahn opens now, would be after lunch and there's no way they'll start on your truck so late in the day." He smiled. "Ian said she was a bit of alright so once the road's open we'll pootle off down to Rotterdam. Settled?" he looked at me enquiring and naturally all I could do was agree, after all Ron was the road foreman wasn't he?

From our seats in the restaurant we had a good view across the parking lot and we noted the bright yellow ploughs attached to various MAN's and Mercedes Unimogs traversing both sides of the autobahn. After breakfasts were finished I strolled up to my room to recover my belongings and then rejoined Ron.

"Nothing moving yet," he confirmed. "Better go and check the trucks over, then make sure they start and run them up to warm so we'll be ready to get out on the road when it does open." Once outside, the bitter cold hit me, especially since the restaurant had been so well heated not only by the central heating but also by an extremely hot log burner which was a feature of the establishment. I buttoned up my reefer jacket and followed Ron across the truck park. The Kube & Kubenz tanker was still there and so was Ron's 40 foot skeletal with its single 20 foot container perched at the front, right over the tractor's tandem axles. The K&K driver was checking his rear lights as I arrived.

"Gut morgen," I laughed somewhat wryly.

"Scheisse morgen," was the riposte as he upturned his hands and gazed heavenwards. "Suppose to be Hamburg tonight. Have to offload Essen first. No bloody chance!"

I opened my passenger side door and shoved my overnight case up into the footwell and put my document case once again on the passenger seat. Then I jumped up myself and traversed over to the driver's seat, put my key in the ignition and started the engine which turned over a few times before spluttering into life. I set her to a fast idle, turned on all my lights and my hazards and jumped down to inspect everything. The heads and sides were all good, as were the front indicators and the amber top running lights. I checked that the tractor's rear lights were also working and then made my way round to the rear of the trailer where I had to brush ice and slush from the rear lights, all of which thankfully were ablaze. I cleared the muck away from the Long Vehicle sign which had been fitted by its manufacturers in England and which I knew would give me greater visibility to other road users and then returned to my cab, tapping all the tyres to ensure they were inflated. Once back in the cab the engine was just starting to warm and the gauge was showing a fraction above minimum. I turned on the heater blower but the air was still pretty cold so I very quickly turned it off again and sat behind the steering wheel with my hands to my mouth, blowing air onto them to try to revive some feeling. Luckily the snow had stopped falling and we were blessed with blue skies and bright sunshine made all the more bright by its reflection on the carpet of snow which enveloped absolutely everything. Luckily this reminded me about the sunglasses, and while we were waiting I took the opportunity to nip over to the Shell *tankstelle* where I was able to buy a reasonably cheap pair which, from a distance, could have been confused with genuine Ray Bans. By the time I had returned, Ron had already shut down his engine and was locking his cab.

"Coffee," he shouted. I leapt into my cab and was pleased to see that my motor was now showing about half its running temperature so I turned it off and followed Ron back to the *tankstelle* cafeteria.

As we reached the cafeteria, a snowplough drew up and disgorged a small band of autobahn workers all dressed in high visibility clothing, unheard of in Britain at the time. They looked for all the world like a bunch of gaily decorated elves with their orange hats and their furry earmuffs. They queued behind us at the automats and Ron soon elicited from them that they expected the road to reopen within half an hour. It appeared that there had been a couple of accidents during the night which had delayed their snow clearance operations. The apology for coffee that slipped out of the automat had only the fact that it was hot as a recommendation. Otherwise it was a tasteless mess and I made up my mind not to bother with such sludge again. One thing suddenly worried me.

"What about my permits?" I asked Ron as he almost spat out the rubbish he had just introduced to his refined taste buds.

"Benelux, Belgium, Holland and Luxembourg count as one unit so you've no problem there," he assured me. "Best we go back to the trucks and sidle out onto the slip road so we don't get left behind in the rush."

So that's what we did but Ron counselled that we let a few trucks out in front of us.

"To settle the road down," as he quaintly put it. "You OK for diesel?" he asked.

"I was planning to fill up in Belgium but I've got a couple of hundred litres at least," I replied.

"That's good," Ron confirmed Steve's advice. "It's cheaper outside Germany but you need a bit in your tanks when you exit for the *tankshein* paper. I'll point you in the direction of a good filling station once we get into Holland but I don't need any." He smiled and I got the message that he would not be around at that point to "cramp my style".

Back in the cab, I started the engine and followed Ron out onto the slip road where there was a layby for outsize loads. This we now occupied as we waited behind several other trucks, including my taciturn friend from Kube & Kubenz, for the chequered flag. Eventually another snowplough came through, this time with all its lights flashing and horn sounding and our convoy followed it out onto the freshly ploughed, salted and gritted autobahn. Progress was quite good and we were maintaining a steady 50 kilometres an hour until the whole convoy slowed down to pass flashing lights and a huge Kaelble recovery truck linked up to the rear of a trailer which appeared to have hurtled off the carriageway and down a steep bank into a clump of fir trees. As I passed I caught sight of the name on the rear of the tilt – Bourgey, Montreuil!

36

The Ruhr

MOMENTARILY, a chill ran down my spine at the sight of the wreck of the Bourgey. "So near and yet so far," and "There but for the grace of God." Some say that you make your own luck in this life. Some believe in predestination, or in other words "no matter what you do you're going to get what's coming to you". Others are fixated on various religions believing that so long as you pray or genuflect or count your beads or paint the evil eye on your truck, someone up there is going to look after you. Personally I'm agnostic about fate. Maybe there is a guardian angel and certainly I've been horribly close to disaster a number of times but I am convinced that at least I have a parking angel! Almost every time I hit town someone is just leaving a coveted parking spot so maybe I'd better start believing in something after all! I mentally wished the Bourgey driver well and immediately had to accelerate as Ron had taken it into his head to deviate into the middle lane and pass the line of trucks faithfully following the gritters. However, I soon realised that he was not so barmy after all when I saw that the autobahn surface was clearing dramatically and, in addition, the gritters were heading off the road at the *ausfahrt* for Munster. Soon we swung back into the right lane and within a few kilometres the overhead signs for the Autobahndreicke at Munster Zuid had Ron indicating right in the direction of

Dulmen, Bochum and Essen. Once onto the A43 the road had already become virtually dry although build ups of slush on either side indicated that the ploughs had done their work during the night.

By 11 o'clock we were switching routes again, this time onto the A2, another old two lane concrete Hitler autobahn which took us into the heart of the Ruhr industrial area. High walls claustrophobically skirted the road on either side for kilometres on end and I wondered idly if they were there to protect apartment block residents from the roar of the traffic or to protect us from the starkness of the industrial wasteland. The traffic was starting to impede our progress as we made our way between the vast steel mills and industrial complexes spouting smoke and ash which had given this area of the Ruhr valley the epithet of "Germany's black country". Everything appeared to be pre-war. Overhead, grimy black DB locomotives belching steam and smoke crossed frequent bridges hauling huge trains of coal and ore seemingly in opposite directions. The very concrete walls lining the autobahn were soot encrusted and crumbling from the constant chemical attack. The road surface itself had become corrugated from the relentless pounding of heavy trucks and the surface appeared to be disintegrating. Without a suspension seat my back was taking quite a pounding so I was more than happy when Ron hung another right onto the A40 towards Venlo and we entered a relatively newly tarmacked smooth road and my whole body was able to relax after having been stressed against the rigours of the jarring against my spine.

After the *autobahnkreuz* at Moers we left the urban sprawl of the Ruhr and indeed the autobahn system itself. The rest of the route to Venlo was for the most part standard dual carriageway which, from the amount of road works in evidence, gave every appearance that it was about to be upgraded to motorway status. The blizzard now overtook us and within 15 minutes the road surface became slushy and we slowed to a reasonably safe 30 kilometres an hour. We were lucky in that there were no hold-ups but it was 1:30 by the time we entered the truck parking at the Venlo border and cruised to a halt at the far end of the line of trucks awaiting customs clearance formalities. The main customs house was another low-rise brick and concrete block replicated on the other side of the dual carriageway where seemingly hundreds of snow blown trucks were waiting to be cleared into Germany. Ron knocked on my door and I opened the window and leaned out into the howling wind.

"Follow me," he yelled. "All docs. Frans Maas."

I closed the window, grabbed my document case, jumped down from the truck, locked the door and followed him across to the back of the parking area on the far side from the customs house where there was situated a row of Portakabin type buildings, each with the sign of the particular agent flapping away on top. Millitzer and Munch, Pakhoed, the ubiquitous Kuehne & Nagel, Wim Vos, and then Frans Maas. Opening the door to this office proved difficult as there was a throng of drivers assembled in front of the reception desk, all waving their papers trying to catch the attention of one of the clerks. The atmosphere was damp and clammy and it was patently obvious that we would lose a lot of time queueing, if that was how you could describe the melee of what appeared to be largely eastern European drivers all jostling and shouting and gesticulating. Ron took one look and hustled me straight out into the blizzard. We traipsed round to the back of the multi-Portakabin unit and entered a door marked "Eintrag Verboten" and underneath to emphasise the point "Prive – Geen Ingang".

Ron breezed through and we found ourselves in a staff room with a few easy chairs and some coffee making equipment burbling away, a scene of quiet domesticity seemingly divorced from the unwashed mob at the far end of the offices.

"Are we supposed to be here?" I asked innocently.

"Don't worry, make yourself a coffee," Ron advised as he poked his head round the door and called out. "Hey, Piet!" presumably to one of the clerks.

"Got those coffees poured?" he asked me on his return into the room. I hadn't even looked at the machine, still convinced as I was that we shouldn't really be there. "Come on, make yourself at home," he joked as he grabbed the glass coffee pot at the base of the machine and poured out a couple of cups to which he added sweeteners for himself and creamer for me. We both took off our wet coats and sat down for a well-earned drink after our long morning's trunk through the Ruhr. "What documents have you got?" Ron asked and I emptied my case onto a low table. "Just as I thought," Ron frowned. "You've got nothing to take you past Van Hove's so your deviation to Rotterdam is actually essential. Hudig and Pieters will have to doc you up for wherever you're going to load next." He shrugged and continued. "Only Salzburg, London and Europoort store our permits so you have to report to one of them to continue. I reckon they'd have sent you up by train from Brussels so you're actually saving them time by coming up to Rotterdam," he finished with a wry smile. Good old laid back Ron, I thought. You couldn't ask for a better road boss!

"Hi Ron," it was Piet who had now entered the oasis of tranquillity. No sign of any recrimination I noted as Piet poured himself a coffee and sat down with us. "Nightmare out there," he asserted as if we needed to be informed of the chaotic throng at the reception desk.

"We're both empty," Ron explained.

"You could clear yourself then," Piet asserted.

"Nah," Ron replied. "It's better we pay you guys to ensure no problems. You know what they can be like with Iranian trucks. Even when we've no cargo they can still insist on a Grosse Kontrole. We never get that when you handle things and we're pressed for time if we're going to make Europoort tonight."

"OK, no problem," Piet agreed. "Let me have all your papers and fill in your *tankshein* declarations and I'll handle it myself." We busied ourselves sorting everything out and handed it all to Piet. "Two hours," was his parting shot as he disappeared through the door.

"Come on," Ron said, rising from his comfortable chair with a creaking of joints. "Time for a quick ham and eggs before we hit the road."

We left through the rear of the building and as we passed around the front I noticed the throng was now actually outside the entrance door, still vociferously waving their transit papers. We were well out of that I thought as we crossed the car park to the end of the low customs house block where the driver's cafe was situated. We entered a damp warm smoky atmosphere in a sparsely decorated room with tables arranged in three regimented rows all with plastic cloths in various shades of green check. It was a self-service affair. We queued behind an assortment of Dutch, German and French drivers or so I had decided, sorting them out by their perceived languages. It was noticeable that there were no Eastern Europeans in the cafe.

"Can't afford it," Ron cheerily explained. "They

pay them nothing in their own currencies and the only western money they get is for their running expenses. Some of them make a bit on the side by buying cigarettes and jeans, that sort of thing, but then they run the gauntlet of their own customs boys who confiscate anything they find. I feel sorry for them but the danger for us is that one or two savvy European companies are starting to contract work out to them undercutting our rates. We've already lost a couple of Tehran customers to Willi Betz using Bulgarians. Thin end of the wedge if you ask me."

Clutching trays of coffee and Uitsmijters we found seats at a table by one of the large aluminium framed windows made opaque by the streams of condensed steam constantly trickling down them. The other occupants of the table were two large Dutchmen dressed in what I imagined to be country and western style, brightly coloured check shirts with denim jackets and trousers.

"Aha," one of them started.

"Ronnie von England."

"Wim Vos from Oss," Ron countered.

"Ha," replied the Dutchman jovially. "I wish it was me, I mean Wim. He's big man. I just small driver."

"This is Henk," Ron explained. "Never get close to his truck, chemical tanker. If it blows we're all finished."

"Nei, nei," Henk laughed. "I'm on plastics now. Just coming von Ludwigshafen, BASF powder granules to Philips in Eindhoven. Easy job. Home every two night. My wife don't know what hit her." Here he and his compatriot burst into uncontrollable laughter and I guessed there was something more to this story than immediately met the eye. Henk introduced us to his friend who turned out to be named Wim. He shook his head vigorously.

"Nei not Vos," he asserted. "He also small man like me."

He then fell into conversation with Ron, partly in Dutch, partly in English. They obviously knew each other very well and we passed a convivial half hour until Henk decided that his T forms would be ready and he must see if he could tip at Eindhoven during the afternoon.

"Tonight, I must my wife," here he rolled his eyes upward and looked doleful and the two Dutchmen were again convulsed in laughter as we left the cafe and headed back over through the lightly wind-driven sleet to the rear of the Frans Maas hut. Piet entered through the internal door, frowning as we entered.

"Small problem," he said. "Tankshein control German side." Immediately Ron reached into his coat and pulled out his wallet. He proffered a couple of largish Deutschmark notes to Piet who accepted them as if they were part of a normal transaction and then disappeared through the door. I must have had an amazed expression on my face because Ron looked at me in mock concern.

"That's why I always use the agent," he said. "If you or I want to, shall we say, influence the level on the dipstick, we don't know who to bribe or how much. These guys do it all the time." It might have been my first trip but I was picking up invaluable experience at the feet of a master in these dark arts.

"Do you think they'll mind if I use the phone?" I asked.

"If it's a Dutch internal just use it," Ron advised. You need nine for the outside line and dial immediately. "There's no tone on this system. Then you hear it beep beep beep as it transmits and then you get the ringtone."

"You staying at Doris's?" I enquired, referring to the residence of the welcoming Mrs. Vermeiren.

"I'll leave my case there but it's off to Vlaardingen for me," he smiled, knowing that I was in on his little peccadilloes. "What about you?"

"Yeah, I'll stay there," I replied. "But there's a chance of meeting that hitchhiker I took down to Paris a couple of weeks back. That's why I need to use the phone."

"Go ahead," Ron advised. "I won't listen!"

The phone rang for several minutes before that silky Dutch voice answered.

"Annatje?" I enquired.

"Ja, Arthur it is me," she answered. The way she pronounced Arthur sounded like "Ah the" but however it sounded, my pulses were now racing and I could feel my forehead moistening with the stress of wondering if I was about to get a "Dear John".

"Sorry I took some time but I am in the shower," she explained. "Now I only have towel around me." Oh my God, she's teasing me I thought, visions of that beautifully formed female body insufficiently clad flashing through my fevered imagination.

"Er, I'll be in Rotterdam tonight," I ventured.

"Oh," she replied in a rather disconsolate tone. "But I am on nights." The rose-tinted world suddenly became harsh, again lit by neon instead of softly focused fairy lights. "Where will you stay?" she asked.

"Maybe at Madame Vermeiren's again," I replied.

"You are not reserved there?" she asked, and I sensed a certain intimacy that changed the lighting once again back to fairyland.

"No, but she always keeps rooms for us," I countered.

"You can stay at my apartment and I will cook you breakfast," she said with a suggestive lilt in her voice.

I thought of Julie London's latest LP, *Nice girls don't stay to breakfast*, and fleetingly I wondered if that also applied to nice boys but anyway, I wasn't a nice boy, so why worry? I had to clear my throat in an effort to appear completely unconcerned while carrying on this conversation with a near naked nubile girl.

"You are still there?" she asked.

37

Vervulling!

MY imagination was rapidly taking over my senses and the fairy lights were starting to blink alarmingly. What I meant to say next was, "I was just hoping you might be able to swop shifts with a friend." Instead I managed to blurt out, "I was just hoping your towel was not slipping," and I immediately bit my lip realising that I might have gone just that little bit too far too early.

"Oh," she said in a little surprised voice. "You are a little naughty. Did you not see any girls since we left you in Paris?" Should I be honest and tell her all about the voluptuous Bourgey, or sexy Maria in the Salzburg bar or Gitte straddling my neck in the Pension Fenninger swimming pool? Luckily I may be daft but I'm anything but stupid so I diplomatically left out those small details.

"Since Paris we have been working too hard," I replied. "So," she continued. "Tonight I must work also but you could stay here. The key is with my friend on the next floor up. She will let you have it and you can let yourself in and make coffee or whatever. You have a pen and paper?"

"Sure have," I said, scrabbling around while indicating to Ron that I urgently needed a biro which he instantly produced.

"OK, my address is 77b, Lange Hilleweg. My father owns the house. I have the ground floor and my friend Helga is above. You must press her button on the door phone and she will answer. By the way, it is in Feijnoord, next to a canal on the south of the river. You can take a taxi or you could park your truck nearby."

"I think Ron will give me a lift into town from Europoort so hopefully he can drop me off at your place," I replied. "Shall I sleep on your couch?"

"Couch?" she emphasised the word. "What is couch?"

"Sofa?" I ventured.

"Nei, you can sleep in my bed as I am not there," she said and I detected a little suggestive laugh in her intonation. "But promise to take a shower before. So now I have something to look forward to while I work."

"You mean me or breakfast?" I asked. Just then Piet re-entered the staff room so I said my goodbyes and placed the receiver back on its cradle.

Piet looked at me enquiringly.

"Girl trouble," Ron helpfully interposed.

"A Dutch girl?" Piet asked. I nodded and feigned a pained expression.

"You be careful," Piet advised. "One minute they give you everything you want. Then they marry you. Then they make that you pay!"

"Personal experience?" I asked. Piet laughed.

"Better to pay up front," Ron muttered, the voice of bitter experience injecting some reality into the conversation. "The four F's!" and he touched his nose as though imparting a great secret.

"Everything is stamped," Piet interrupted. "So now you can visit your Dutch lady but don't say I did not warn you." He chuckled in a superior knowing sort of way as Ron sorted through all the paperwork and handed me mine together with the *laufzettl* now only requiring the one passport control stamp before we could exit the parking area into the Netherlands. "Don't forget next time you come," Piet was reminding Ron who took on a quizzical air and then realisation crept across his face.

"Ah yes, the cigarettes," he replied. "Direct from the Botlek. No questions asked."

Piet laughed. "When I worked at Europoort," he explained. "Every day I am getting them from the drivers. Now when I paying full price it is not so good."

We made our way back over to the customs building, glad that the sleet had now ceased to flurry across the parking lot and joined the queue at passport control, a small office situated at the far end of the complex, little more than a corridor in fact where eventually we posted our documents through the slot at the base of a window, this one transparent rather than the normal oppressive opaque as of course the smartly uniformed officer actually wanted to see our faces. The rest of the motley bureaucratic crew at frontiers throughout Europe couldn't have cared what we looked like. We were merely cattle herded in and out of their unwelcoming, poorly-maintained offices. That we were the only reason for their well-rewarded employment never seemed to occur to them. Their main mission in life appeared to be to organise the maximum inconvenience and delay to international transportation, procedures which must have added millions of pounds to overall cargo costs. I smiled at and thanked the Dutch officer as he handed me my passport back.

"God save the Queen," was his parting witticism! If I had known then just how many times I was to hear that over the next few years I might just have jacked the job in there and then! Ron looked at me and rolled his eyes heavenwards as we left the thronged

317

passageway reeking of the scent of the unwashed driverdom of so many nations. Once outside in the fresh cold air, Ron remarked on the absence of sleet in the air and hoped we'd make it through to Europoort without any hold ups.

"I'm running to De Beers direct once we've picked up diesel," he explained. "If I'm to get out to Vlaardingen tonight in time for the disco at Malle Baba."

"You won't see me there," I joked. "Why not?" Ron looked at me rather quizzically.

"Your girlfriend's on nights. You never know who you might end up with at Malle Baba."

"Or what," I countered. "Syph or gon or anything else unmentionable." No way was I going to risk what ought to be a perfect assignation for the distinctly distant possibility of an inebriated quickie! A cheap thrill which no doubt I could live to regret in oh so many ways.

Jumping in the Mack, I had just time to divest myself of my warm blue reefer while firing up the motor before Ron was already away as if on a mission, which I guess he always was when heading towards Rotterdam! We stopped briefly at the control post to hand in our completed *laufzettls* before guiding the motors back out onto the Dutch A67. Soon we were crossing the river Maas and the neatly laid out streets of Venlo with their tidy Dutch gabled houses and their large rarely-curtained windows flashing by on either side, annoyingly too fast to actually see any activity going on inside those lounges and bedrooms! We had to leave the main road and wander into the suburbs to find a fuel station where we tanked right up on cheap Dutch diesel, feeling elated that we had cheated the German *tankshein* system and could get back into the country with enough fuel to see us through to

Austria. The Tango fuel station was well known to Ron and he negotiated some kind of deal which netted us some much needed Guilders which I hurriedly stuffed into my wallet before a quick cup of free coffee gulped down too fast before we were on the road once more. The route took us past Eindhoven then up to 's-Hertogenbosch, over the Rhine and left towards Gorinchem and finally we were traversing the southern outskirts of the Rotterdam conurbation. Sleet recommenced as we crossed the canal bridges at Ridderkerk and by Spijkenisse snow was once again fighting the wipers for dominance of my windscreens. Shortly after Rozenburg, Ron turned left into the capacious car park of the De Beer Seaman's Mission and we parked next to the line of new Macks waiting for more drivers to arrive from England. Once inside the warmth of the lobby, Ron checked in with the concierge and by 8 o'clock we had detached his tractor from its Pitt skeletal and container and were on our way into town for the weekend.

"You sure you don't need a bed at Doris's?" Ron asked as he shifted up another gear, feeling the slight curbwards drift of the rear bogie as the clutch bit once again and the gears surged the power back through the propshaft.

"Well, I think I'll be OK," I ventured.

"If you need it," he continued, "just call round. She has at least one room booked for us every weekend whether it's empty or not." We reached the Botlek duty free complex after crossing several canal and dock bridges and Ron dropped me off with my overnight case. He handed me a piece of paper.

"Here's my phone number so we can organise your lift back on Monday morning," he explained. There were three taxis standing outside the Botlek stores and I was soon seated in the back of one of them, a Mercedes

220 which, after the privations of the Mack's unforgiving suspension, felt like it wafted me the rest of the way into Feijenoord. I was dropped right outside 77b Lange Hillweg and my heart was beating nine to the bar as I pressed Helga's bellpush. Would she be in or would this all turn out to be a dream. If she wasn't in, here was I in a residential area, snow now blizzarding against my reefer jacket and jeans, driven by a howling wind along the rippling canal and not another taxi in sight. As I waited for a response, I fervently wished that I had asked my Mercedes man to wait. Seconds that felt like minutes ticked by and then five minutes passed and I rang again. A few more minutes during which I was becoming increasingly aware of the cold and there was a crackle on the intercom.

"Ja?" came a husky female voice. I cleared my throat and shouted to be heard above the shriek of the gale.

"Hi, I am Arthur, Annatje told me to call you."

"Oh," the voice seemed a little hesitant. "So you are real! Wait, I come."

There was another agonising wait during which an inner excitement was being supressed by all the negative possibilities which sprung through my fertile imagination. I turned to face the door mainly to avoid the driving snow which was now attacking my unshaven face and running in rivulets down my neck. I pulled my recently bought Russian fur hat down on my forehead so that only my eyes and nose were visible but then thought better of it. I'd be presenting quite a frightening sight to Helga when she opened the door! Still she didn't arrive and I was wondering if I was going to be cast out into the bleak midwinter, a wandering soul, left to die of cold and hunger on the mean streets of the big city when the sound of the key turning in the lock saved me from even worse imaginings of my possible imminent demise!

The door opened and Helga peered out at me standing there in the gloom silhouetted by the street lights eerily glowing through the blizzard.

"Kom, kom," she clucked and then as I entered the hallway. "Mijn Gott. You are frozen!"

I had only been standing there for a few minutes but I must have given Helga the appearance of a walking snowman. I shook the remaining snow off my reefer and onto the mat and opened up the buttons taking off my hat at the same time.

"You must get warm!" Helga ordered as she unlocked the door to Annatje's apartment. In truth I was already shivering uncontrollably. "Leave your coat here," Helga commanded indicating the row of hooks in the passageway. We entered the flat and Helga hustled me into the warm kitchen area. "You have walked here?" she asked incredulously.

"No, I came by taxi," I explained.

"But it is very, very cold out there and the snow is unbelievable," she said.

I couldn't disguise the fact that my teeth were chattering and Helga stood me in front of a hot air fan while she organised some coffee.

"You know I also am a nurse," she said, and then added, "so I know a good way to warm you but you are not my boyfriend and Annatje would kill me." I laughed. "Anyway you need to get some clothes off. They are damp and not helping," she said and promptly started to pull at my sweater. "I'm a nurse," she emphasised as she stripped me right down to my Y-fronts. "I see these things all the time."

I hoped that she was not viewing items of my physique in a disparaging way but was feeling a little miffed that she had stopped at the Y-fronts. She vanished from the kitchenette and re-appeared with a large bath towel which she wrapped round me. I was now warming up and started to notice that Helga was quite an attractive girl. She was certainly not petite but by no means could have been described as plump. Her hair was black and hung in ringlets to shoulder height. Her eyes were dark brown and her face had a certain attractive swarthiness and sported a wicked little grin.

"Now take those off," she commanded, "and keep the towel round you." And then she completely unexpectedly flung her arms around me and planted her warm lips on my cold ones. It was a kiss to launch a thousand ships but, dear reader, you will be re-assured to know that I was able to regain my composure and join in wholeheartedly. Almost as suddenly as it had begun it stopped and Helga released her hold on me.

"So did my therapy work?" she asked. Reeling from the power of this delightful onslaught and somewhat dazed I nodded my head. "You say a word about this to Annatje and I will kill you. OK?" She looked at me menacingly and then poured the coffee and we both drank and chatted as if nothing had happened, me with a towel wrapped around my naked torso and Helga dressed, as I was now starting to appreciate, in nothing more than a towelling bathrobe which finished above her knees displaying a beautiful pair of naked legs. "Also," she continued putting paid to my increasing ardour, "if my fiancé was to hear something I would be in big trouble." Once the coffee was finished she gave me a peck on the cheek and departed saying "If it was not for Annatje and my fiancé I would have liked to stay."

I was now returned to normality and started to hang out my wet clothes over a wooden clothes dryer. Then I opened my case, pulled out my washing bag and, as Annatje had ordered, took a long hot shower. The flat was a large one. At the front there was a lounge area which also housed the kitchenette. Then the shower room which was windowless and at the back the bedroom which I guessed must have been two rooms knocked into one. Everything was Scandinavian design. The light-coloured wooden furniture, the brightly coloured curtains and cushions, and the simple pictures on the white walls. All gave an air of lightness and a degree of sophistication which was refreshing to the eye of a tired truck driver. The bed was a good double size and, throwing off my towel, I slid between the silky white sheets vaguely wondering if I actually could have handled a night with the bombshell from upstairs in my current fatigued state. Truly, trucking in Britain was nothing like this. Here I was at the end of my first continental trip, lying in a luxurious bed waiting to be joined by a woman who I was partly in love with already. I had travelled through five different countries in the two weeks since my departure from Rotterdam, had some wonderful experiences in many exquisitely beautiful locations, met interesting people and was working with a great bunch of colleagues. And this was just the beginning!

I awoke to find light creeping through the bedroom window and was immediately aware that someone else was present. Without stirring too much I turned and saw Annatje undressing and watched her softly walk naked out of the room to take a shower. I listened to the water caressing her voluptuous body and then heard the swishing sound of her towelling herself dry before she slipped in beside me and I felt the warmth of her breath, the exotic smell of her perfume and her soft smoothness as she snuggled close and the rest, as us historians say, is rock and roll!